# The Gettysburg
# Nobody Knows

## Gettysburg Civil War Institute Books

Published by Oxford University Press
Edited by Gabor S. Boritt

*Why the Confederacy Lost*

*Lincoln, the War President: The Gettysburg Lectures*

*Lincoln's Generals*

*War Comes Again: Comparative Vistas on the
Civil War and World War II*

*Why the Civil War Came*

*The Gettysburg Nobody Knows*

## Other books by Gabor S. Boritt

*Lincoln and the Economics of the American Dream*

*The Lincoln Image*
(with Harold Holzer and Mark E. Neely, Jr.)

*The Confederate Image*
(with Mark E. Neely, Jr., and Harold Holzer)

*The Historian's Lincoln*
(with Norman O. Forness)

*The Historian's Lincoln, Rebuttals:
What the University Press Would Not Print*

*Of the People, By the People, For the People
and Other Quotations from Abraham Lincoln*
(with Jakob B. Boritt, Deborah R. Huso, and Peter C. Vermilyea)

# *The Gettysburg Nobody Knows*

EDITED BY

## GABOR S. BORITT

*New York   Oxford*
OXFORD UNIVERSITY PRESS
1997

Oxford University Press

Oxford   New York
Athens   Auckland   Bangkok   Bogotá   Bombay
Buenos Aires   Calcutta   Cape Town   Dar es Salaam
Delhi   Florence   Hong Kong   Istanbul   Karachi
Kuala Lumpur   Madras   Madrid   Melbourne
Mexico City   Nairobi   Paris   Singapore
Taipei   Tokyo   Toronto   Warsaw

and associated companies in
Berlin   Ibadan

Published by Oxford University Press
198 Madison Avenue, New York, New York 10016

Oxford is a registered trademark of Oxford University Press

Library of Congress Cataloging-in-Publication Data
The Gettysburg nobody knows/edited by Gabor S. Boritt:
essays by Harry Pfanz . . . [et al.].
p.   cm.   "Gettysburg Civil War Institute books."
Includes bibliograhpical references.
Contents: The common soldier's Gettysburg campaign/
Joseph T. Glatthaar—Joshua Chamberlain and the American
dream/Glenn LaFantasie—"Old Jack" is not here/Harry W.
Pfanz—The chances of war/Kent Gramm—Eggs, Aldie,
Shepherdstown, and J. E. B. Stuart/Emory M. Thomas—I think
the Union Army had something to do with it/Carol
Reardon—Gettysburg's Gettysburg/J. Matthew Gallman
with Susan Baker—The Pennsylvania gambit and the Gettysburg splash/
Richard M. McMurray—From turning point to peace memorial/Amy J. Kinsel.
ISBN 0-19-510223-1
1. Gettysburg (Pa.), Battle of, 1863.
I.  Boritt, G. S.
II. Pfanz, Harry W. (Harry Willcox), 1921–   .
E475.53.G398   1997
973.7'349—dc21   96-52524

9 8 7 6 5 4 3 2

Printed in the United States of America
on acid-free paper

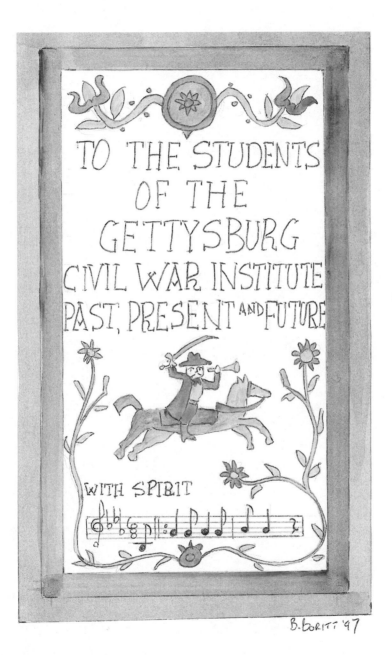

*By late June it is usually warm,*
*even hot in Gettysburg.*
*In the night at our farm,*
*the fireflies glow in the dark,*
*fleeting specks illuminating the woods and*
*turning Marsh Creek into a pageant.*
*In the daytime along the side of the road,*
*orange tiger lilies proclaim their eternal message.*
*My heart overflows;*
*it is time to see old friends again,*
*time to make new ones.*
*It is the time for the Gettysburg Civil War Institute.*

GABOR S. BORITT

*Confederate Prisoners.* One of the figures in the center of the group is an African American. Detail from *The Battle of Gettysburg.* Lithograph by Kurz and Allison, Chicago, 1884.

# Contents

# Introduction

Mʏsᴛᴇʀʏ shrouds Gettysburg for me. If I shut my eyes, I can see the crucial moment of its past with crystal clarity. The battle comes fearfully, totally alive. I can see a black farmer and veterinarian whose 1863 home is now my home. He takes his wife and children to safety and waits, waits, waits until at last the Confederates reach the town. Then, he, too, is on his way to be a refugee. I see woman after woman taking charge with so many men gone; for a brief time a new world. I can see cowardice in many places, or simply normal human weakness. I can see courage unending. I can see an artilleryman having his foot shot off. He stands up on his stump, and for a few moments, for eternity, he continues his deadly work. I can see two officers on horseback, talking, showing their broadsides to the enemy fire coming thickly around them. A shell explodes under the animals. Almost miraculously neither man nor beast is injured. Neither man flinches. Yet one looks down at the spot where the shell hit. Even decades after he will feel something close to shame for having possessed less composure than his comrade. Perhaps vanity to us; exemplary bravery to the soldiers of Gettysburg. I can see Lee and Longstreet together, deep in thought. Later I see the younger general unable to turn his face toward a subordinate as he gives the order for the Charge. I can see men going forward, some knowing with certainty this would be their last earthly act. I can see other men terrified at their coming yet holding their ground. I can see a sergeant abandoning safe cover to help men he barely knows and paying the final price. I can see death. Scene follows scene, scene follows scene, never ending.

But when I open my eyes again, the mists return and cover the battlefield. Its history grows dotted with question marks about what we think we do know and with questions about what we do not know. And because of the deep, personal meanings Gettysburg holds for me, I often wonder whether I can ever be a good historian of its past.

Yet I have the good fortune to direct the Civil War Institute (CWI) whose sessions in the summer are devoted to bringing together, at Gettysburg College, the literate public with some of the most learned scholars of the Civil War era. I have the good fortune of being able to lead others to grapple with important questions about the past. The CWI speakers address subjects of both public and scholarly interest and their task is to reach that public without slipping solid scholarly moorings. This they often do very well. And since Gettysburg remains for so many of us an object of both great love and mystery, it was imperative that it be made the focus of a CWI session.

I invited fine historians, most seasoned veterans but also some talented beginners, to come to Gettysburg, and posed problems for them that have long troubled students—in some cases since the Independence Day of 1863. In addition, I posed questions that have not been asked before or, when asked, have not been answered very well earlier. I asked that they look at problems in innovative ways. I held up to them as a model Richard Nelson Current's excellent book *The Lincoln Nobody Knows* (1958).[1] Quoting it, I asked that when appropriate they emphasize "the uncertain, the undecided, the unknown"; don't always shy away from the "might have beens"; and focus on the controversial and on the important. What generally accepted facts do we not really know the truth about? And what does each historian think we know?

The common soldier often looms large in this book even when looking at age-old controversies of command. In Chapter 1, one of the finest students of the common soldier's Civil War, Joseph T. Glatthaar, weighs the Gettysburg Campaign from the perspective of the fighting men. He sums up the campaign in a useful way for those not steeped in the subject—veteran students of the battle may wish to skim over this—and goes on to examine the soldier's role in the final outcome. Glatthaar starts with the assumption that a commander's ability to influence combat was limited. Thereafter he keeps his eyes on the subordinate officer's and the soldier's fight. He follows the Army of Northern Virginia and what he calls its "festive" air, heading into Pennsylvania; follows the Army of the Potomac as it catches up; and arrives at some surprisingly provocative conclusions.

In Chapter 2, Glenn LaFantasie faces the legend of Joshua Chamberlain. The professor–colonel from Maine is a folk hero today, the savior of Little Round Top, of the battle, and so perhaps the war and with it the United States. He is the hero of the most popular book of the battle, Michael Shaara's *The Killer Angels;* Ron Maxwell's film based on the novel, titled simply *Gettysburg;* the Gettysburg segment of Ken Burns' epic film, *The Civil War;* a plethora of popular art, histories, articles, and on and on. Yet forty-some years back, General Edward J. Stackpole's standard popular history of the battle did not so much as mention Chamberlain. Chapter 2 looks at how the hero of Little Round Top saw himself, how he held the horrors of combat at bay, how he measured himself against Joshua, the Old Testament warrior, and where that led him and us. Chamberlain and the American Dream.

In Chapter 3, Harry Pfanz, dean of Gettysburg scholars, surely our most knowledgeable student, examines one of the oldest controversies of the battle. How well did General Richard S. Ewell conduct his actions on Day One? With "Stonewall" Jackson dead at Chancellorsville, Ewell had unforgettable footsteps to follow. In the twentieth century Douglas Southall Freeman, one of the most fabled of Civil War historians, seemed to have driven the nails into Ewell's reputation. Yet students of more recent years have come at the problem from an opposite viewpoint. After examining the contrasting interpretations, Pfanz reaches his own, and many would say, most trustworthy conclusions.

In Chapter 4, Kent Gramm, the deeply provocative student of the moral questions surrounding Gettysburg, looks at Day Two and its two most persistent controversies. James Longstreet executed Robert E. Lee's orders slowly and, as so many add, sullenly. Simultaneously, on the Union side Daniel Sickles moved his Third Corps forward to an exposed position. George Gordon Meade and faithful thousands acted their parts. The troops clashed, the day was a draw, and students have fought over the day ever since. This has been a dispute about generals and command decisions, but Gramm goes at it through the experiences of the First Minnesota Volunteers, the common soldiers, and the "unpredictable outcomes of their violence."

Chapter 5 brings Emory Thomas, the biographer of "Jeb" Stuart—and Robert E. Lee—to search the role of the plumed cavalier's absence and presence at Gettysburg. From the moment the battle started, some Confederates have blamed their difficulties on Stuart's flamboyance, his fame seeking, that found his horsemen, the army's eyes, far from the crucial action. Yet here, too, the general who has inspired so much loyalty, and does to this day, can bask in the light of passionate defenders. Thomas examines the evidence and leads us to fresh conclusions that highlight the part played by "the fog of war."

Day Three and Pickett's Charge was, is, and will remain the most famous moment of the battle. Who can forget William Faulkner's words about the time it was "not yet two o'clock . . . the brigades are in position behind the rail fence, the guns are laid and ready in the woods and the furled flags are loosened to break out . . . all in the balance . . . it's going to begin . . . and that moment doesn't need even a fourteen-year-old boy to think *This time. Maybe this time.*" The charge of the brave may turn out differently.[2]

Carol Reardon, who is becoming this generation's premier expert on what we know as Pickett's Charge, notes in Chapter 6 how Northerners and Southerners fought each other, and among themselves, over the laurels of the day. She asks: What really happened on that July afternoon? "The uncertain, the undecided, the unknown" at times grows overpowering in her telling. She makes clear that history is not "bunk," as Henry Ford had exclaimed. But the road to the past takes very careful travel. In the end, what American imagination has come to call "the high water mark of the Confederacy" becomes an eloquent, sophisticated, and sometimes discouraging high water mark not merely for the Gettysburg nobody knows but one nobody can ever know fully.

The town of the battle was almost a city by the measures of the 1860s. With nearly 2,500 souls, three-quarters of the country's people lived in less populated places. What did the battle do to the borough? We have countless stories of varied trustworthiness on the theme. In Chapter 7, J. Matthew Gallman, helped by a young assistant, Susan Baker, brings—for the first time—the learning and the sensibilities of the highly trained social historian to the subject. "Any talk of historic 'turning points' is almost inherently misleading," Gallman maintains. "The past has few right angles." Was there one at Gettysburg? Even before General Meade declared the affirmative, Americans had started to move in that direction and have not stopped much since. Through an examination of newspapers, census data, and personal accounts, this chapter sketches the life of the borough before, during, and after the battle. It surveys class, gender, and race relations, and searches for the meanings of local and national identities. The chapter's conclusions are sure to set new fires among the Gettysburg controversies.

The same is true of Richard McMurry's Chapter 8 that lands him, appropriately, next to Gallman in this book, and in the historiography of the battle. McMurry searches for the military meanings of the Gettysburg battle. At the CWI session, before he had a chance to begin, a loud, mirthful voice from the audience called out to say that we were about to hear "Professor McMurry explain why Vicksburg was the most important battle and Gettysburg didn't matter." McMurry did not disappoint. Of course his approach is that of an acute student of military history. He brings his knowledge of the western theater of operations to bear on understanding Gettysburg. He evaluates the Confederate grand strategy that lay behind Lee's invasion, what it might have accomplished, and what it did accomplish. His carefully crafted and sharply stated views deserve a respectful hearing. Perhaps it is unnecessary to repeat that those views, too, will fuel the Gettysburg controversies.

And so to a concluding chapter: the cultural meanings of the battle, from an explosion of a birth in 1863 to the last reunion of Gettysburg's still living veterans in 1938. What has happened since many students of the Civil War may regard, perhaps snobbishly, as too fresh to permit more than ruminations about contemporary events. In Chapter 9, Amy Kinsel surveys historical arguments, artistic representations, commemorative activities, and battlefield reunions. She finds a national interpretation emerging in the decades after the war and holding sway long after. She focuses on the military meanings the culture gave to the battle, what came to be emphasized and what was sidestepped, and what the memory of Gettysburg has wrought for the nation. In the end, she glances, almost sadly, at what was and what might have been.

The contributions to *The Gettysburg Nobody Knows* have much in common—and much not. A little repetition in the bibliographical notes to the chapters is the price for highlighting what each historian considers significant. I take pleasure in the diversity of the authors' perspectives on history, Gettysburg, scholarly method, and style—down to the footnotes (uniform format notwithstanding). I hope that readers, too, will enjoy this marbling as they move from the broad brushstrokes of Chapter 1, to the detail of Chapter 2, and on to the end of the volume.

This book is done and, of course, plenty remains controversial about Gettysburg, plenty that nobody knows. The 1884 lithograph of the battle by Kurz & Allison on p. viii makes a fine illustration of this point. A searching look in the detail reproduced here will reveal a black man marching among the Confederate prisoners. The meaning of this detail needs to be carefully explored and when done will surely lead to sparks flying. For now we know next to nothing about African American participation in the battle. Blacks played a central part in the Civil War, but we have yet to uncover their full role in the war's most famous, perhaps most important, engagement. As time goes on, we will know more. Human ingenuity will conquer seemingly insurmountable obstacles. Hope springs eternal. With good reason.

In creating a book like this, the work of many people came together. I owe thanks to many.

Thanks to the Lehrman Institute for its generous support of my study of the Battle of Gettysburg. The Institute knows how to make a difference.

Thanks to Sheldon Meyer of Oxford University Press, one of the truly distinguished editors of the American world of publishing. It has been a privilege to work with him on six books. Thanks to Rosemary Wellner who provided fine copy editing for this volume. Thanks to Helen B. Mules who served as production editor.

Thanks to the talented historians who heeded my call to face the challenge of *The Gettysburg Nobody Knows*. Thanks to two scholars in particular, Harry Pfanz, and Scott Hartwig of the Gettysburg National Military Park, who discussed the contents with me. And thanks to Steven F. Miller of the University of Maryland and Robert H. Prosperi, former historian at the Gettysburg National Military Park, who helped in other ways.

Thanks to the staff of the Gettysburg Civil War Institute, "the girls," as they are affectionately known, who consistently perform beyond the call of duty: Tina Fair Grim, Linda Marshall, and Marti Shaw. At the risk of getting myself into trouble, I must single out Marti, who not only made sure that the chapters of this book would be delivered on time, got the book into the computer, and made fine editorial suggestions, but also rode herd on me.

Thanks to the students who served as cheerful assistants at the Civil War Institute session devoted to Gettysburg: Melissa Becker, Daniel Boritt, Jakob Boritt, Susan Fiedler, Michael Karpyn, Benjamin Knuth, Dana Ledger, Stephen Petrus, Tracy Schaal, and John Quinterno— fine young people, one and all. Thanks to the equally fine Civil War Institute interns who (in addition to the book's contributors and editor) read proofs: Paul Hutchinson, John Barnes, and Brent LaRosa.

Thanks to my family. To the two younger boys I listed with pleasure above. To Norse who created the primitive Pennsylvania Dutch design of the dedication page. And to Liz, who together with our sons, helps make life meaningful and books possible.

I reserve my final thanks, on this occasion, to the students who attend the sessions of the Civil War Institute each summer. They range from high schoolers, and other beginners in the study of the Civil War era, to learned scholars, winners of the Lincoln Prize and the Pulitzer Prize. Gettysburg works its magic on teenagers as much as on people pushing their nineties. The improbable and wonderful combination of individuals who are the students of the CWI make it a success year after year. To these friends, "the old and the young, the rich and the poor, the grave and the gay, of all sexes and tongues, and colors and conditions"—as Lincoln described Americans once, long ago[3]—to them, and to those, too, who come from abroad, this book is affectionately dedicated. We are a band of brothers and sisters.

*Spring 1997*                                            G. S. B.
*Farm by the Ford*
*Gettysburg*

# The Gettysburg
# Nobody Knows

# 1

## *The Common Soldier's Gettysburg Campaign*

JOSEPH T. GLATTHAAR

In one of the most misinterpreted statements in the Civil War, Confederate General Robert E. Lee once explained his command style to Prussian military observer Justus Schiebert. "I think and work with all my powers to bring my troops to the right place at the right time." Once he had completed that, Lee continued, "I leave the matter up to God and the subordinate officers," because to interfere "does more harm than good." Lee was not abdicating responsibility for the course of battle, as some scholars have suggested; rather, he was merely concurring with Union generals Ulysses S. Grant and William Tecumseh Sherman that a commander's ability to influence combat was finite. Success on the battlefield depended on subordinate officers' capacity to command, and soldiers' ability to fight. In short, Lee could bring his forces together at the proper location and the precise moment, but the army, its officers and its men, had to execute for victory.[1]

In historical examinations of the Battle of Gettysburg, the emphasis has been misplaced. Military leaders and subsequent scholars have devoted far too much attention to command decisions and paid far too little notice to the performance of "common soldiers." In the literature of Gettysburg, scholars have posed the proper central questions: "Why did the Union hold?" and "Why did the Confederate attack fail?" Unfortunately, they generally look for answers in the wrong areas. They wonder how George G. Meade contributed to the Federal victory; why Richard Ewell did not storm Cemetery Hill on the first day; what prompted James Longstreet to delay on the second day; whether Lee should have swung around Big and Little Round Top, instead of assailing the Union center; and what impact the absence of Stuart's cavalry had on the battle's outcome. Thus, issues of high command have dominated the debate.

Perhaps the answer to those fundamental questions of why the Union won and why the Confederacy lost at Gettysburg, though, lies with the common soldiers of the Union and Confederate armies. Over the course of a month-long campaign, and three of the most savage days of combat in the war, some 160,000 men endured the hardships, suffered the privations, thrilled to the exhilaration, bore the sorrow, and fought that battle. Their story is truly the Gettysburg nobody knows.

Since the Confederate victory at Fredericksburg in December 1862, when weather and road conditions deterred a follow-up offensive, Gen. Robert E. Lee's "desire" to raid enemy territory "haunted" him. Once before, that September, his Army of Northern Virginia had surged across the Mason–Dixon Line. Having driven the invaders from Confederate Virginia that summer, Lee intended on sustaining the initiative by campaigning in Maryland and Pennsylvania throughout the fall, hoping to influence the Northern elections and enable Virginia farmers to harvest their crops unmolested. Unfortunately for the Confederates, a lost campaign order compelled him to contract operations prematurely, and straggling and heavy casualties at the Battle of Antietam brought the expedition to an early close.[2]

This time, Lee had the luxury of ample time to plan the raid carefully. In February 1863, he took the first step by asking Lt. Gen. Thomas Jonathan Jackson to order his expert map maker, Jedediah Hotchkiss, to sketch the road network of central Pennsylvania all the way to Philadelphia. Later that spring, Lee requested that authorities in Richmond repair the Virginia Central Railroad, to draw critical supplies for any advance into Maryland and beyond, and he commenced the tedious task of accumulating the necessary wagons to support his command.[3]

Lee had multiple objectives for launching the invasion. A campaign into the North could influence Confederate operations as far west as the Mississippi River by drawing Union troops eastward. It could also spare Southern farmers and ease commissary burdens by enabling the Confederate government to feed its largest army on Northern grain and livestock. And like everyone else in the Army of Northern Virginia, Lee sought an opportunity to defeat the Federal army far away from the works around Washington or the naval gunboats of the Atlantic fleet, where he could follow up his victory with repeated attacks and extinguish the Army of the Potomac.

Supply problems, however, postponed the implementation of his plans. Confederates had great difficulty obtaining long forage to strengthen their animals for a lengthy march, and the need to draw artillery ammunition from the Deep South taxed the railroads. In early February, an explosion and fire killed forty-three employees and closed the Richmond Arsenal for two months. The Army had a sufficient supply of shot and shells on hand to support a battle, but a lengthy campaign would require much more ammunition. Authorities had to redirect carload after carload of case shot and shells northward from Charleston and Augusta, to accumulate a stockpile. Meanwhile, the ammunition consumed valuable cargo space on trains, which could have hauled the necessary forage.

Despite the ensuing delays, Lee hoped to "assume the aggressive by the 1st of May," sweeping Federals from the Shenandoah Valley and turning the giant Union Army of the Potomac out of Virginia, to some position north of the Potomac River. Maj. Gen. Joseph Hooker, commander of the Army of the Potomac, refused to cooperate.[4]

In late April, Hooker's mammoth command rumbled forward, forcing its way across the Rappahannock and Rapidan Rivers and sandwiching Lee's Army between its two wings. Undermanned with a pair of Longstreet's divisions on detached service, two choices confronted Lee. He could select the safe option, fall back to a strong defensive position, and abandon hope of a raid northward until late summer or autumn. Or, Lee could stand and fight, defeat Hooker's command, and follow up his triumph by pressing on into Maryland and Pennsylvania. A gambler to the core, Lee chose to stand and fight.

The Battle of Chancellorsville was the single most costly engagement up to that point in the war. In driving Hooker's army back across the Rappahannock River, the Confederates inflicted 17,000 casualties on the Union, while suffering a staggering 13,000 themselves. Among the fallen was Lee's most able lieutenant, Stonewall Jackson. "I have heard such sounds, & seen such sights, as make my flesh almost crawl when I think of them," described a Confederate. After gazing at a train of wounded soldiers creaking rearward, a New Yorker recorded, "how little do the folks at home know the miseries of war. may they never witness its horrors, as I have." Several days after the battle, a North Carolinian still could not write properly from the prolonged stress. "I have Got the trimbles," he confessed to his wife. Descriptive words failed a Massachusetts man. He could only utter in dismay, "What a life we lead, and all for $13 a month."[5]

Confederates taunted Yankees, especially their failed commander. "'Fighting'—*fainting*—fleeing" Joe Hooker had an appealing ring among Rebel circles. Yet the heavy losses cut deeply into the ranks. And Jackson was irreplaceable. "General Lee is a far greater General than 'Old Stonewall,'" conceded a Georgian, "but he can never excite the enthusiasm which this old war horse did with his old faded coat and cap and his sun burnt cheek,— '*Requiescat in Pace.*'"[6]

With Jackson gone, Lee restructured the army by creating three corps instead of two. Ewell and A. P. Hill now joined Longstreet as corps commanders. Once Longstreet and his two divisions arrived from southeast Virginia, the Army of Northern Virginia numbered just under 80,000 men. By then, Lee had gathered sufficient wagons and supplies, and he was ready for his long-awaited advance.

In the aftermath of the Battle of Chancellorsville, Union troops held their heads low. "The roads and fields are filled with troops going back to their old camps," moped a sergeant, "but a more disheartened set of fellows I never saw. All because we were ordered to retreat." In the minds of soldiers in the Army of the Potomac, leadership at the top snatched defeat from the jaws of victory.[7]

Morale did not suffer for long, at least among cavalrymen. In early June, while on a mission to determine whether Lee had begun to shift his army, Federal horsemen surprised J. E. B. Stuart's mounted troops at Brandy Station (or Beverly Ford). The two-pronged attack penetrated Stuart's screen and ascertained that Lee had maneuvered his army to the northwest, perhaps as a springboard for a northern raid. Equally important, Union cavalrymen had surprised Stuart and his men. Confederate infantrymen rushed to the aid of their stunned comrades, adding more in the way of emotional support than actual firepower, and Rebel horsemen eventually drove the Yankees back across the Rappahannock River. But the Federals had shattered the aura of invincibility that Confederate cavalry had earned, and Stuart took a beating in the press for his lack of preparedness. "The battle at Beverly Ford had stiffened up the troopers wonderfully, increasing their morale and confidence," assessed a Yankee officer. "A new era began to dawn upon our hitherto somewhat disorganized cavalry force, for it was seen that the Confederate cavalry, with its easily accumulated prestige, was now slightly on the wane, more especially because they could no longer rely upon blooded remounts." A member of Stuart's staff pithily summed up the affair when he noted that the Battle of Brandy Station "*made* the Federal cavalry."[8]

While the Confederate horse soldiers endured a taste of humility, the rest of the Army of Northern Virginia rode a wave of conviction. "I am sure there can never have been an army with more confidence in its commander than that army had in Gen. Lee," recalled the multi-talented Edward Porter Alexander. "We looked forward to victory under him as confidently as to successive sunrises." Barely a month and a half ago, they had bested a massive Union force without two of Longstreet's division. With their return, nothing could stop them.[9]

Certainly, they had lost Jackson. He was irreplaceable. But the Dick Ewell–Jubal Early combination seemed to measure up well as a substitute. At the Battle of Second Winchester, in mid-June, Ewell's troops crushed a Federal command, inflicting heavy losses and capturing well over three thousand Yankees. A Union officer claimed that the Confederates had lied about Jackson's death. Referring to Early's flank attack, he insisted, "there was no officer in either army that could have executed that movement but 'Old Jack.'" Richmond newspapers, too, joined the chorus, proclaiming Ewell the Second Jackson. Troops rejected such labels as hyperbole, yet his handling of the affair impressed most soldiers and boded well for the war effort.[10]

On the march northward, troops stirred up clouds of dust that coated clothing and hair and caked on faces. Everyone, it seemed, had doused their hair, eyebrows, and eyelashes with white. Only streams of perspiration disrupted the uniform pale facial mask, creating a macabre appearance. "A demon or ghost could not have looked worse," a soldier jotted down. Mile after mile they trudged, as scorching June heat and choking dirt particles sucked energy from the men in gray.[11]

The Potomac River offered an opportunity to cleanse themselves of Virginia soil. In a frolicsome event, thousands of buck-naked men hoisting clothing and accouterments aloft, plunged into the brisk, waist-deep river, "yelling & screaming like school children." The crossing shattered the monotony and refreshed the body-weary. When they emerged on the opposite bank, soldiers occupied Maryland soil.[12]

Plundering among resource-scarce soldiers had already become a problem. In mid-June, Ewell had warned his corps that "this plundering must be repressed or our discipline is gone." Three days later, when the provost marshal entered Martinsburg, "there was a mob breaking open stores," committing all sorts of depredations. While local citizens huddled in their homes "nearly frightened to death," according to an officer, "the streets were crowded with hundreds of drunken men as there are any number of bar rooms & distilleries in town." Across the Potomac in Sharpburg, "our boys have nearly all supplied themselves with articles of some use or necessity." Whether troops liberated items is unclear, but a soldier did admit, "The stores have been opened & the prices have been to us 'Dixie boys' remarkably moderate."[13]

Although Maryland had remained in the Union, it was a sister slave state, and many Confederates believed that Northerners coerced Marylanders into retaining their loyalty to the old Constitution. Pennsylvania lay above the Mason–Dixon Line. It was the undisputed land of the enemy, and Lee's troops eagerly anticipated an opportunity to cross over into Pennsylvania and invade the North. For two years, nearly all fighting by Lee's Army had taken place in Virginia. It had been Virginia homes invaded, Virginia livestock confiscated, Virginia fences dismantled, and Virginia fields trampled. Now, it was time to exact some retribution "The wrath of southern vengeance will be wreaked upon the pennsilvanians & all property belonging to the abolition horde which we may cross," vowed a soldier. "We will try & pay them for what they have been doing to the innocent & helpless in our good southern land."[14]

As Confederates pushed on into Pennsylvania, the countryside startled them. For most, this was their first trip to the North, and the natural beauty of the region and the level of opulence among northern farmers shocked these southern boys. They had accepted unquestioningly arguments about the superiority of slave labor. What they saw, however, belied those tales. Soldier after soldier wrote home of stunning landscape, with hardwood forests atop hills and lush pastureland and tidy fields scattered along the gentle slopes and valley floors. In Pennsylvania, the soil was rich and the livestock fat. Impressive stone homes and enormous barns dotted the panorama. Evidently, these middle-class farmers in a free labor society did quite well for themselves.

Not nearly as impressive were the local inhabitants. Typical was the comment of a private, who wrote to his sister, "We passed through some of the prettiest country that I ever saw in my life they has [some] of the finest land in it in the world and some of the ugliest women that I ever saw." Soldiers usually treated the residents respectfully, except when locals were a bit too forceful in their support of the Union. One Pennsylvania woman, adorned with a miniature flag affixed to her blouse, cast contemptuous glances at Confederate troops as they marched past. Finally, a Texan had enough. Pointing his finger at the woman, he announced, "Take care, madam, for Hood's boys are great at storming breastworks when the Yankee colors is on them." She retreated into her home.[15]

It was Lee's intention to disburse his forces, drawing on the local population for foodstuffs, fresh horses and fodder, and any other equipment that his army might need. Plundering was unacceptable behavior. He directed officers to pay Northerners for goods, and those who refused to sell would have the necessary property confiscated and a receipt issued to them. Any citizen who attempted to conceal or remove food or useful equipment would have the property seized and their name submitted to headquarters. Clearly, Lee wanted no mob activity.[16]

Instead, deprivation, temptations, and hostility toward Northerners bred misconduct. Quartermasters and soldiers alike took all they could carry or consume, stretching Lee's directives to the breaking point. "There was, in short, a good deal of lawlessness," confessed an officer, "but not as much as might have been expected under the circumstances." Another soldier declared that he and his comrades "enjoyed ourselves finely." He went on to admit that "although positive orders were issued prohibiting soldiers from disturbing private property, they paid no attention to any order of the kind, and took everything they could lay their hands on in the eating line."[17]

Pennsylvanians, like Southerners in Georgia and the Carolinas in the face of William T. Sherman's march, tried their best to conceal livestock and other items. Despite their ingenuity, efforts failed. "They were hidden in most extraordinary places," explained a Carolinian. "Some in upper stories of barns & others in cellars of houses Some even in haystacks all of which was very ludicrous."[18]

Troops plundered abandoned buildings and occasionally took items from civilians. "Numbers of our soldiers exchanged hats with citizens to day, without a willingness on part of citizens," a soldier confessed. "Some of them who were bare footed made citizens pull off shoes and boots." Quartermasters, commissary personnel, and individual troops scoured the region for horses, mules, and cows, impressing all they could lay their hands on. Officers indulged their men and even joined in the process. Almost everyone seized what they wanted. "In short, we killed, captured, and destroyed everything that came our way," boasted a Rebel.[19]

For many Confederates, it was simply a matter of giving Pennsylvanians a taste of real conflict. "They have Known nothing of the war heretofore," justified a Virginian, "and I believe unless we do bring it home to them in this manner they would be willing to carry it on indefinitely." Another Virginian, writing to his father, expressed similar sentiments: "I hope these people may be taught the horrors of war—may be made to feel its deep effects both upon their pockets and persons."[20]

The repercussions of such conduct were subtle, yet grave. For two years, Confederates in the Virginia Theater had repulsed overwhelming Union forces. While superior leadership had been an instrumental factor, victory demanded more. It required tenacious fighting. Beyond their ramshackle look, the men in the Army of Northern Virginia were an aggressive, disciplined, focused, seasoned combat command. That ability to execute in battle had saved them time after time. They carried critical works, held on to key pieces of terrain, delayed their opponents at vital moments, and laid down their lives at pivotal junctures in order to win. In time, they developed an unflagging confidence in themselves and their officers.

Yet it was more than merely a belief in their capacity to fight. Confederates tapped into an extra incentive by battling in defense of their civil rights and for the protection of their loved ones and homes. This additional motivation provided unusual direction. It instilled in them an ability to focus deeply on the problem at hand. Amid the external jollity, these troops possessed a capacity to concentrate, a mental keenness that enabled them to endure untold hardships and execute in the face of unusual adversity. On numerous fields, the margin for victory was slim. That focus provided them with just enough edge to triumph in battle after battle.

On the raid into Pennsylvania, foraging and plundering dulled their edge. The campaign adopted a festive tone, as discipline slipped and concentration lapsed. In essence, the Army of Northern Virginia lost that focus. The excitement of invading the North, the necessity of roaming the countryside and rummaging through homes for essentials, and the opportunity to seize goods that sacrificing soldiers and their loved ones at home had done without for so long was too much for the troops. Officers succumbed to the wishes of the men and their own desires. "Stringent orders have been issued against such conduct by our generals," recorded a company-level officer, "though it is rather a hard matter to restrain our troops when they remember the devastated plains of Virginia and the conduct of the Federals in other portions of our country." In enemy territory, with novel experiences and unusual distractions, Confederate troops needed to elevate their level of concentration, to strengthen their fix on the campaign and its execution. Instead, it dwindled.[21]

Hooker, for his part, responded slowly to Lee's advance. Stuart's cavalry disguised Rebel movements temporarily, and his raid northward further confused the picture from the Union perspective. The Union army commander also seemed a bit reticent to lock swords with Lee. More than anyone else, Hooker had failed at the Battle of Chancellorsville. He had designed an excellent plan, and executed well initially, but at the critical moment he lost courage in himself, his scheme, and to some extent his army. Lee exploited the opening, and Hooker and his command, beaten by vastly inferior numbers, withdrew to safety.

Fortunately for the North, morale suffered only a brief decline among Union troops. In their minds, they had not lost at Chancellorsville—their generals had. Faith in one another and their cause remained unshaken. And they chastised those at home whose belief wavered. "Mother, you said you was down harted," private Jerome Farnsworth penned. "now ma I just tell you that you must not get discouraged for Every thing will be Well." He reminded her that all her sons in the army were alive and in good health and urged her, "remember that they are a fighting for to put this Horrible Rebellion down and to Save our Country."[22]

The thrill of soldiering had vanished long ago; warfare was serious business. As Union troops began their sluggish pursuit northward, a veteran from the Iron Brigade spotted some men from the 22nd Corps, garrison soldiers for the Washington defenses, all attired in fresh, clean uniforms. He and his comrades admired the new garb, "But those days of 'fancy soldiering' had long since passed away and we were now on a real military campaign loaded with dust, our clothes appearing as if we had never used a brush on them, and we careing little how we appeared."[23]

In late June, as the Union army pursued tentatively, troops received some good news. Hooker had locked horns repeatedly with General in Chief Henry W. Halleck and Secretary of War Edwin M. Stanton over strategy and other military policies, and when he offered his resignation, authorities in Washington accepted it. His replacement as commander of the Army of the Potomac was Maj. Gen. George G. Meade.

Meade was a West Point graduate and a topographical engineer in the Old Army. A bright, hard-working man and an excellent tactician, Meade had an explosive temper that earned him the nickname "Old Snapping Turtle." He had risen steadily from brigade to corps commander based on his accomplishments. Unlike many general officers in the Army of the Potomac, Meade refused to play politics or criticize superiors. He concentrated on his job, performed it well, and won the respect of officers and men alike. "Meade was our corps general," a captain commented to his mother after the selection. "You may know perhaps,—a grumpy, stern, severe, and admirable soldier."[24]

With Meade at the helm, pursuit suddenly took on a sense of mission and urgency. He had orders to target Lee's army, all the while shielding Baltimore and Washington. At Pipe Creek, some twenty miles southeast of Gettysburg, Meade laid out a strong defensive position, in case his army had to retire, and then pushed beyond it. Skillfully, he fanned his forces out in all directions in search of the enemy, always keeping his seven corps in support of one another. On June 29, the 1st Corps marched thirty miles in mid-summer heat. "About half the corps fell out," recorded a New York private, "many of them coming up afterwards." The next day, early morning rain created hot and muggy weather. Again it was a long, fatiguing jaunt for the Federals. By the morning of July 1, Meade's corps were anywhere from five to twenty-five miles from Gettysburg, and he had instructed Maj. Gen. John Reynolds to take charge of the three forward corps and be prepared for offensive or defensive operations.[25]

On crossing north into Pennsylvania, a transformation took place among the soldiers in the Army of the Potomac. No longer were they in enemy territory or a state like Maryland, where slavery existed and support for the Union cause was mixed. In Virginia, the women "are our bitterest enemies, where they never look on us except with contempt and never speak but in derision," noted a soldier. Guerrillas infested the countryside, and soldiers always had to be on their guard. Anyone who wandered away from camp carelessly did so at his peril. Maryland was not nearly so dangerous, but soldiers had to act cautiously there, too. In Pennsylvania, they were among friends. Soldiers could concentrate exclusively on the Confederate army.[26]

More important, they gained a psychological boost by campaigning in Pennsylvania. Now, they were fighting to drive an invader from their own soil, to protect their own hearths and homes. The notion gave added impetus to their spirit and strengthened their will to defeat Lee's army. As the 41st Pennsylvania crossed into its home state near midnight on July 1, "The col[onel] Halted us at the line and the boys gave 3 cheers for old Pa[.] and we vowed never to leave the state until we had driven the rebels out," explained Edwin Benedict. "We all felt enthused and showed our determination by increasing our speed." He concluded by reporting, "There is no nonsense about us." Crowds gathered outside shops and homes to cheer on their defenders. In reply, "Many a fervent 'God bless you!' and 'Good for you!' were uttered by the tired and weary soldiers, and many, too, forgot their weariness and their loads, feeling that for such they could fight and endure any hardship without grumbling," a Minnesotan penned home. A fellow named Russ Allen then called out to his buddies, "Boys, who wouldn't fight for such as these?" The commitment of the troops firmed. "Just that little expression," recorded a witness, "and the way it was expressed, seemed to put new life into all of us, and we resolved, if possible, to give them yet more pleasure by driving the invaders from their soil." Days later, Allen gave his life in the attempt.[27]

Federal soldiers perceived a major battle in Pennsylvania as a great opportunity for them. With the Confederates such a long distance from home, a decisive victory and a vigorous pursuit by Union forces could devastate the primary secessionist field command. "We hope to capture or so cripple the confederate army here on northern soil that the south will give up the contest and an honorable peace restored," an optimistic Connecticut soldier jotted down in his diary. "But," came the great caveat, "time will determine." In the recesses of their minds, many Federals sought to end the war here, as did their Confederate counterparts.[28]

The Battle of Gettysburg was an encounter engagement. Neither side anticipated a large-scale fight there. It began almost by accident, with some skirmishing on June 30 and full-fledged combat the following day. Confederates in Maj. Gen. Harry Heth's Division of A. P. Hill's Corps trudged into town in search of plunder; Federal cavalry under Brig. Gen. John Buford opposed them. Once the two sides exchanged fire, reinforcements poured into the area, deploying and joining the fray without any specific plan in mind, merely to take advantage of visible openings.

Heth parcelled his two lead brigades on either side of the Chambersburg Pike. Buford's men, supported by some artillery, fought aggressively and held their position until infantry supplanted them. The weary horsemen then passed rearward through town.[29]

Federals in the 1st Corps arrived on the scene and filtered through cavalry lines. Among those forces, the famed Iron Brigade of Wisconsin, Michigan, and Indiana troops caused the greatest impact. These men crashed through some woods and overwhelmed James J. Archer's Brigade of Tennesseans and Alabamians in front and flank, capturing a sizeable portion of the command, including Archer. On the other side of the Chambersburg Pike, where New York and Pennsylvania troops had their hands full against Joseph R. Davis's Brigade of Mississippians and North Carolinians, the 6th Wisconsin of the Iron Brigade dealt the heavy blow. Ordered to "'move to the right' and 'go like hell,'" these Badgers waded through a withering fire and stormed a railroad cut to dislodge those "kowardly sons of bitches." In the end, they seized the prized ground and a few hundred Confederates along with it. The price, however, was immense. The names of over one-third of the 6th Wisconsin appeared on the casualty list.[30]

To the north, Maj. Gen. Robert Rodes's division of Ewell's Corps suddenly materialized on Oak Hill. One of Lee's premier division commanders, Rodes had received orders the previous day to withdraw from Carlisle and concentrate at Cashtown. With the fight well underway, he deployed three brigades in front and two in support and pressed forward without skirmishers. The troops on Rodes's right helped to clear the railroad cut and drive the Federals back to a gentle slope near town. The Rebels east of the road attacked feebly and fell back rapidly, thus opening the door for a Union concentration on the middle brigade.

After the Yankee 1st Corps, men from the 11th Corps arrived on the scene. They secured Cemetery Hill south of town with their artillery and rushed to the sounds of gunfire, forming part of an L-shaped position that shielded Gettysburg on the north and west sides. As Brig. Gen. Alfred Iverson's North Carolinians in Rodes's center advanced, Union troops who had opposed the weak attack east of the Mummasburg Road swung around and concealed themselves along a stone wall directly on Iverson's left flank. The Tar Heels stepped right into the trap. Federals rose up and poured a devastating fire into the Confederates. The next morning, a Rebel artilleryman recorded the tragic sight. Seventy-nine North Carolinians lay dead in a perfectly straight line, apparently killed by a single volley. Other victims were scattered across the field. The scene was "perfectly sickening" and "would have satiated the most blood-thirsty and cruel man on God's earth," he moaned. It was a turkey shoot with human targets. "Great God!" he recorded in exasperation, "When will this horrid war stop?"[31]

With Rodes's Division stalled, victory on the first day seemed within Union grasp, until a Confederate division under Jubal Early rolled around the Federal right wing. Down the road from Heidlersburg, northeast of Gettysburg, Early's troops pressed, penetrating the Yankee rear and threatening to cut off the retreat route through the town. Panic gripped thousands of bluecoats from the 11th Corps, who broke ranks and raced rearward. That compelled soldiers of the 1st Corps to flee also. In the confusion, a Wisconsin man was knocked down and trampled by his comrades. Some Federals passed through town to safety, while others were cut off or tried to hide. Many, though, were not so fortunate. A Confederate thought they "draged as many as five hundred from the cellars." All told, over three thousand Yankees fell into Confederate hands that day.[32]

South of town, Federals formed a new line, anchored at Cemetery Hill. One month earlier at Chancellorsville, it had been men from the 11th Corps who had buckled under Jackson's flank attack. For some time after the event, Yankees jeered members of the 11th Corps, calling them "Coward" or "Flying Dutchman" in reference to its large number of German regiments. Now, they had done it again. As soldiers emerged from the town, an officer directed them by corps positions. When a man with a German accent asked for the 11th Corps, some embittered soldier shouted over the voice of the directional officer, "1st Corps to the right & 11th Corps go to *hell*."[33]

That evening and throughout the night, Federal forces streamed into the Gettysburg area, anchoring the right and extending along a ridge to form a fishhook-shaped position. Amid the darkness, soldiers on their own initiative piled logs, branches, and stones to form barricades or exploited existing walls as protection against Confederate advances. The lucky ones caught a few hours of sleep, but many rested little more than an hour. By sunrise, five of the seven Union corps, along with the army commander, were on the scene.

Although Lee arrived in the vicinity of Gettysburg in mid-afternoon, he could not organize his army well enough to strike again before nightfall. Losses were so severe that regiments and, in a few cases, brigades almost dissolved. Confederate units had converged from the west, north, and northeast on the Yankee position, and, in the rout, commands got mixed up. Structure disintegrated as units searched house to house. Soldiers uncovered pockets of resistance, crushed them, and gathered and escorted prisoners to the rear. Even worse, Confederates continued their pillaging activities. Many broke into shops and homes and appropriated so many items that a soldier boasted, "I assure you that city is well plundered. The Louisianians left nothing that human hands could destroy." Other Confederates complained about how their comrades dropped out of ranks to rob Yankee killed and wounded. A Maryland man grumbled, "Very often you could see some of our boys go down on a dead yank and take his money out of his pocket." An officer on Early's staff scanned the battlefield and was disgusted with what he saw. "The Yankee dead were stripped, almost to utter nakedness," he wrote with shame. "It seems strange that the champion of liberty, can be the prostitute of avarice. Yet such is the case." He went to state, "The hand that shoots from the front rank of battle is frequently the first to find the pockets of the dead and this pilfering of the fallen is by no means confined to the skulkers, & followers in the rear." Thus, casualties, chaos, a breakdown of discipline, and darkness prevented the Confederates from mounting a strong attack that evening on the new position.[34]

As the sun rose, Union soldiers observed their commander, Meade, surveying the line. With the eye of a topographical engineer, Meade examined it carefully. The position his forces had laid out impressed him. One soldier heard him utter, "We may fight it out here just as well as anywhere else." Meade's decision to stand and fight complimented the army. By implication, it indicated his belief in their ability to slug it out with Lee's troops.

On the Confederate side, Stuart's cavalry, on its grandiose raid around the Union command, was still unaccounted for, but most of Lee's army had concentrated the night before. Early the next morning, after a reconnaissance indicated that the Union had neglected to secure its south wing, Lee ordered two of Longstreet's divisions to swing around to the south and roll up the Federal left flank. To position themselves properly for a surprise attack, Confederate troops began the march and had to backtrack, wasting all morning and much of the afternoon. The lengthy trek under a roasting sun and stifling humidity drained the attackers of precious energy. By 4 P.M., when the attack finally began, Longstreet's troops were tired.

In defense, Maj. Gen. Daniel Sickles, commander of the Federal 3rd Corps, had foolishly projected his forces out from the original line to occupy some high ground where locals had planted peach trees. The new bow in the Union position doubled the length of his defense, forcing him to commit all his reserves and to pull troops away from a natural southern anchor, Little Round Top, to maintain a contiguous line. Meade's Chief Engineer, Gouverner K. Warren, noticed the problem, and a division from the 5th Corps raced over to secure the position as the assault began.

On the Confederate right flank, Hood's men rumbled through difficult terrain just to reach Union lines. At Devil's Den, a rocky outcropping guarded by huge boulders several hundred yards north of Little Round Top, Union guns poured such an effective fire into the attackers that it drew front-line and follow-on units like a magnet. Eventually, Confederates carried Devil's Den, but carefully positioned artillery and infantry to the rear prevented the attackers from exploiting the gain. The resistance, moreover, detracted from the strength of the extreme Confederate right by drawing away two Alabama regiments from the initial assault and a brigade of Georgians who composed the second wave.

Over at Little Round Top, Alabamians and Texans attempted to seize the position by storm. They had carried such difficult places before; this time, they failed. Disorganized from the cut-up terrain, and fatigued by a long day in a broiling sun, these Rebel attackers launched several assaults late that afternoon. Lacking reinforcements, they were too few in number and too weary in body and spirit to wrest the position from the Federals. Even had they gained Little Round Top, Federal reinforcements approaching the area most likely would have snuffed out the penetration, as they did elsewhere on the field that day. So exhausted and demoralized were these Confederates that four hundred of them surrendered to a counterattack by perhaps two hundred men with fixed bayonets.

Aiding the defenders, too, was a severe water shortage among the troops from Alabama and Texas. The exhausting march in intense heat sapped liquids from their bodies, and as soldiers ripped apart cartridges with their teeth, the gunpowder sponged up all moisture in their mouths. The brigade commander later admitted his men "suffered greatly for water," believing it "contributed largely to our failure." Yet it was not simply a matter of thirst that injured the attacker's cause. Without water, Confederates could not clean their weapons of the black powder residue that caked the inside of their rifle barrels. After firing a dozen rounds, the grimy buildup prevented them from ramming down charges. Armed with unusable muskets, their weary bodies drained of fluids, and spirits flagging, they were nearly defenseless against the Union counterattack.[35]

Much credit has gone to Col. Joshua Chamberlain of the 20th Maine for his leadership in the valiant defense of Little Round Top. Yet it was Chamberlain, a historian with exceptional writing skills, who prepared the dramatic report. Soldiers in the regiment who wrote home immediately after the battle scarcely mentioned Chamberlain. It was his troops who stood tall that day, resisting the Confederate onslaught superbly. Amid the smoke, noise, and fright, few in the regiment probably noticed their colonel. The men in the 20th Maine, like so many other Union soldiers that day, reached deep within themselves and found the character and fortitude to do what was necessary for victory. When ammunition ran out, soldiers remained at their post, rather than fall back. Chamberlain may have ordered them to fix bayonets, but evidently the critical counterassault was either spontaneous or directed by a subordinate officer.[36]

Elsewhere on the field that day, Union and Confederate forces battled with similar results. Several times Confederates pierced the Federal line, only to falter at the critical moment. Tired from the prolonged delays, drained by the heat, and lacking that sharp edge of focus and discipline that had sustained its charges in the past, Confederate columns fought aggressively at first, but failed to exploit the advantage. Casualties and straggling soldiers eroded the power of their assault, and lacking the mental toughness to see the attack through as they had done so many times in Virginia, Federals hurled them back. Lee's army suffered some 6,500 losses that day, all in vain.

Despite being overwhelmed at the initial point of attack, Union troops fought an inspired battle on July 2. Two days earlier, Meade had requested subordinates explain to the troops "the immense issues involved in the struggle" and that "The whole country now looks anxiously to this army to deliver it from the presence of the foe." He believed the Army of the Potomac "will fight more desperately and bravely than ever if it is addressed in fitting terms." The men responded. Before Brig. Gen. John Gibbon's division entered combat, officers read Meade's circular to the troops, reminding them what was at stake and urging them to do their duty. One of Gibbon's soldiers, in the 1st Minnesota, applauded the decision, insisting "one thing our armies lack is enthusiasm, and no efforts are made to create it, when, in many cases, it would accomplish more than real bravery or bull dog courage." That day, the 262 men who composed the 1st Minnesota suffered 82 percent casualties, but drove back Cadmus Wilcox's Alabama Brigade in a desperate fight. Genuine enthusiasm and bulldog courage marked their conduct.[37]

No other Yankee units endured the losses of the 1st Minnesota, and perhaps none accomplished as much with such limited manpower, but the Army of the Potomac had never fought better. Some 9,500 Federals fell on July 2. Nevertheless, the Union troops had held, despite some generals' blunders. That day, they were a focused, motivated combat force. Often in the past, with their line shattered, they had fled to the rear. This time, they battled desperately, fell back and regrouped, and fought again. On several occasions, at critical moments, determined bluecoats repelled superior numbers of Lee's troops. They reached deep within themselves and discovered the courage, fortitude, and sheer force of will to bend, but not break.

After moments of indecision on the night of July 2, Meade elected to remain right there and slug it out with the Confederates the next day. Again, he had made a statement to the troops that he believed in them.

The entire affair had frustrated Lee. It was an encounter engagement on a field not of his choosing. Despite great success on July 1, his army had not completed its work. The Confederates had squandered too much daylight on the second day, and had failed to exploit opportunities. He could withdraw in the face of an undefeated enemy, a risky proposition at best that would most likely end the campaign, or he could attempt one more desperate fight. Audacious to the core, Lee placed his faith in the Army of Northern Virginia to win the next day.

Lee's plan for the third day was to place pressure on the two Union flanks and crack through the Federal center. Near success in the middle of the Union line convinced Lee that Meade had weakened the center to fortify the wings. Ewell's Corps, on the northern end, would strike at Culp's and Cemetery Hills. Stuart's cavalry, which had only reached Gettysburg on the afternoon of July 2, would swing around both Big and Little Round Top and threaten Meade's rear. An extensive bombardment, followed by a massive assault, would rupture the Yankee line.

At 1 P.M., the Confederates fired a signal salvo, followed by a barrage of shot and shell. One hundred thirty-eight guns under the command of Brig. Gen. Porter Alexander blasted away at the Union defenses, sustaining a tremendous fire for nearly three hours. Federal artillery replied vigorously at first, but gradually tapered off to conserve ammunition. A Mississippian recalled that "the smoke was so thick that I could not see our battery horses between our lines and the guns." Nor could the troops tell the difference between the reverberation of Rebel guns and the explosion of Yankee shells. Both shook the ground terribly.[38]

From Culp's Hill, a Connecticut soldier reported, "All at once it seemed as though all the artillery in the universe had opened fire and was belching forth its missiles of death and destruction." The thunderous sound, recorded a Yankee officer, reminded him of Niagara Falls. Soldiers along Cemetery Ridge hunkered down as best they could, to shield themselves from the deadly projectiles. Solid shot struck among the Federals or in front and bounced through the lines, as Rebel gunners intended. But exploding shells, the ammunition that Confederates depended on for success, failed them. Only those shells that struck well up in the trees rained chards and chunks of lead on the defenders. According to a Minnesotan, the enemy "tried to explode their shells directly over us, but fortunately, most of them just went far enough to clear us." Although some Federals were killed or wounded in the bombardment, no one in his regiment suffered an injury. "Many more were killed in the rear than in the front," he insisted, "though their fire was directed at the front line and batteries nearly altogether." Wagons, rear-area personnel, and Meade's headquarters, hundreds of yards behind the front line, endured a blistering fire, while the Confederates had neglected to soften up the Union defenders. Smoke and clouds of dirt obscured the view. The attackers did not know that the greatest bombardment since the origin of mankind had not fulfilled its designs.[39]

As his ammunition began to run out, Alexander sent word to open the assault. Soldiers rose to their feet and aligned. Eleven brigades joined in the attack, led by troops in George Pickett's and J. J. Pettigrew's Divisions. Alexander supported them as best he could with the artillery, but problems with premature explosion of shells negated any hope of indirect cannon fire to assist them.

"I never was scard as bad in my life," confessed a Mississippian in Pettigrew's Division. Over several fences and up and down gentle slopes elegant formations of Confederates marched. Union rounds carved gaping holes in these ranks, only to have them close up rapidly. The various angles of approach and the different distances that the attackers had to cover began to disrupt formations. At a range of approximately 250 yards, Union infantry opened fire. Rather than continue the charge, pockets of Confederates halted in open ground and exchanged rifle fire, exposing themselves horribly and detracting from the power of the assaulting waves.[40]

On the Confederate left, brigades converged on the target area. Gradually, however, strength on the wing withered away. Federals concentrated effective fire on the outer flank of the attackers, first compelling Brockenbaugh's Virginians to fall back, then Davis's Mississippians. As the remainder of Pettigrew's Division struck the principal Federal line, Yankees poured fire from two and sometimes three directions. The Confederate left buckled. "Suddenly the column gave way," described an Ohioan, "the sloping landscape appeared covered, all at once, with the scattered and retreating foe. A withering sheet of missiles swept after them, and they were torn and tossed and prostrated as they ran. It seemed as if not one would escape."[41]

Among the defenders, a New Yorker "thought that our line would give way as I noticed the uneasiness of some of the men." At a critical moment, "some of the men began to cheer and the spirit was soon spread along the line." Within seconds, "cheer on cheer rent the air and we all fought with increased vigor and the ranks of the foe became confused and broken and they were forced back."[42]

The stalwart Union defense, accompanied by a devastating fire on the flank and even rear, demoralized many attackers. "Rebels laid down their arms & came in and no one to make them," described a Federal soldier. His regiment alone claimed five Confederate flags that day. One of the heroes, his brother Morris, led a party of ten Union troops who counterattacked and seized the 14th North Carolina's flag. Morris received a Medal of Honor for his efforts.[43]

In the center and on the Confederate right, miscommunication caused serious problems. Pickett's brigades angled sharply to the left, while Wilcox's Alabamians and Perry's Brigade of Floridians charged directly ahead, splitting the assault columns. Some Vermonters seized the opening. On orders from their brigade commander, they struck Pickett's men on the flank and damaged that attack. Then, the 16th Vermont pivoted and poured a wicked fire on Wilcox's and Perry's Brigades, shattering their charge.

Led fearlessly by their brigade commanders, the bulk of Pickett's troops rushed onward. With a shout, they raced at the double quick toward the works. Blasts of canister and volley after volley of Federal rifle fire struck down Confederates by the hundreds. Some halted in the open field and blazed away at the Yankees, and then continued the advance. Others dropped to the earth, shielding themselves from the hail of lead. To them, the situation was hopeless; the risk was too great.

Yet, somehow, a portion of the wave pressed on. At twenty yards from the wall they endured a burst, recoiled, and then surged forward. The sight of this seemingly irresistible mass panicked the defenders. Suddenly, some Pennsylvanians broke and raced rearward, leaving a handful of their comrades to repel the onslaught. Several hundred intrepid Confederate souls crashed over a low stone wall and penetrated the Union works. Remnants of the Pennsylvania regiments battled them with rifle butts and bayonets, as if they were warring for sacred ground, but the Northerners were outmanned.

In reality, the Rebels were too few in number, and too far from support, for this small band to have held the break for long. To an unlikely hero like Lieut. Frank Haskell, however, the situation appeared perilous. A Wisconsin volunteer on Gibbon's staff, Haskell coaxed adjacent brigades into lending support, and then helped rally the troops for a counterattack. With Haskell in the thick of it, Yankee reinforcements smashed into the Southerners. The struggle lasted just a few minutes. These Confederates fought brilliantly, but their numbers were too small. Many fell right there; others yielded to the Federals. And some foolishly attempted to run the gauntlet back to Confederate lines, where they made easy targets.

Lee's attack had failed. Bodies littered the field, and those who had broken or laid down now had to race back across "no man's land." Union riflemen and artillery picked them off as they worked their way rearward. As one soldier described, "many noble spirits who had passed safely through the fiery ordeal of the advance and charge, now fall on the right and on the left." A few Confederates backed their way out, fearing the mortification of their family had they been shot in the back while retreating. Thousands lay still or groaning with wounds. As Pickett rode off the field, tears rolled down his cheeks. "Taylor," he sobbed to a staff officer, "we've lost all our friends."[44]

A few weeks after the battle, tests undertaken by the Confederate Ordnance Department indicated some problems that may have been an influential factor in the outcome of the fight on July 3. Complaints of the premature explosion of some shells during the Battle of Chancellorsville led to an investigation of ammunition produced at all Confederate arsenals. From mid-July through January the next year, disturbing results trickled in: There was a lack of regularity in the performance of artillery shells and fuses. When artillerists fired shells and case shot, they cut the fuses a particular length. The blast that hurled the projectile forward also ignited the fuse, which burned down and caused the shell or case shot to explode over the enemy position. Fuses produced in Charleston, Atlanta, and Augusta, however, usually burned slower and performed more inconsistently than those made in Richmond. Confederate artillerists simply assumed a level of uniformity in manufacture, that all fuses burned at roughly the same rate. As experienced gunners, they had estimated the distances correctly. Although some batteries may have cut the fuses a bit longer, to protect themselves against premature explosions, in most instances they employed fuses for the proper length of shells manufactured in Richmond. But because many of the shells and fuses had come from the other arsenals in the aftermath of the Richmond Arsenal explosion, the fuses burned more unevenly—often slower—, and the explosive projectiles carried far beyond the Union line before they burst. Clouds of smoke and dirt obscured visual confirmation of the gunners' accuracy, but the explosion of Yankee caissons and damage to Federal guns by solid shot convinced them that they had determined the range properly.[45]

As darkness settled over the battlefield, Union forces engaged in the horrible task of attending to the dead and wounded. On Culp's Hill, where fighting had begun before sunrise and lasted into the early afternoon, Federal troops built fires to light up the field. They buried gray and blue alike and carried the injured to hospitals. "The groans and moans of the wounded were truly sadning," recorded a Connecticut soldier.[46]

Over the next few days, soldiers gazed at the battlefield in utter shock and dismay. "Such a sight I never want to see again," insisted a man from New Hampshire. "The men had turned black, their eyes had sweled out of their head and they were twice the natural size and the stench of the field was awful and dead men were thick. You may as well believe," he concluded, "I had rather go in to a fight than to see the effects of it." A New Yorker confirmed the horror when he penned his sister, "The look of their bloated, blackened corpses was a thing to murder sleep." The aftermath of battle haunted him.[47]

Confederates, too, had no immunity from such visions. "Part of the field, across which I had occasion to ride twice, presented a horrible spectacle," recorded Campbell Brown. "Corpses so monstrously swollen that the buttons were broken from the loose blouses & shirts, & the baggy pantaloons fitted like a skin—so blackened that the head looked like an immense cannon ball, the features being nearly obliterated."[48]

Soldiers initiated the search for friends and loved ones. The heartbreak was nearly unbearable. An officer and his buddy went searching for two friends, presumed killed in action. "We did not look long," he explained to his mother, "it was too sad and horrid a piece of business."[49]

Physicians poured into the Gettysburg area to lend a hand. They had no idea what awaited them. The foul odors and ungodly sights prompted many to lie down and vomit. Without adequate facilities, wounded lay on the field for days and even weeks, until doctors and nurses could care for them. In many cases, the situation was hopeless. "I went to bid good bye to Capt. Barré— of our regiment, but he was unconscious, and died in half an hour after I saw him." Barré lived near family friends and had a wife and two children. Soldiers knew him for a beautiful singing voice. Balls shattered his leg and arm and two more lodged near his spine. For a moment, he awoke and sang, "'I wish I were a child again, just for tonight.'" Soldiers around him on the ground, wounded and healthy alike, "cried like babies."[50]

Suffering from pain, and slowly expiring, soldiers made amends to their God. A few also had the privilege of jotting some final words to loved ones. "I am here a prisoner of war & mortally wounded," an Alabamian wrote his mother. "I can live but a few hours more at the farthest—I was shot fifty yards [from] the enemy's lines. They have been exceedingly kind to me." After expressing the hope that he would live long enough to hear Confederate shouts of victory, he called on his mother, "Do not mourn my loss. I had hoped to have been spared, but a righteous God has ordered it otherwise and I feel prepared to trust my case in his hands." He concluded with the words, "Farewell to you all. Pray that God may receive my soul. *Your unfortunate son John.*" He was buried in an unmarked grave on the outskirts of Gettysburg. Born with an identity, he rests in oblivion.[51]

After the repulse on July 3, Lee expected to continue the battle. He waited a day, hoping the Yankees would come out of their works and offer an open-field fight. Meade refused to take the bait, and by nightfall Lee began the evacuation.[52]

On July 4, Federal forces had much to celebrate. It was the

anniversary of the day of the nation's birth, and they had just won their first true victory in the war. Soldiers felt good about themselves and also their commander. The leaders "are now practicing war not theorizing it," exclaimed a Yankee. Meade did not throw them into battle piecemeal. He let the army fight as an army.[53]

But as they dawdled, and Lee's army escaped, Union troops became more and more disillusioned with their leader. "We do not understand why we do not start in pursuit," wrote a soldier in dismay several days after the battle. "Meade was no longer equal to the situation," concluded a New Yorker. As it became more and more apparent that Lee's damaged army was escaping, soldiers became downright hostile. "The Prisoners that come in this morning say that we might have took their whole army just as well as not," complained an annoyed soldier. "it is just as I expected Mead was very fraid of A little rain and laid over 24 hours to long and they sliped away from him evry Solgier is growling about it because we might just as well had him as not and now they will march us like light[n]ing to catch him again but Shit let it go." Soldiers would pay the penalty for Meade's mistake. They would have to fight more campaigns.[54]

For many Federals, the unsatisfactory pursuit placed the Battle of Gettysburg in clearer perspective. Senior leadership had not won there; they had. Never before had the Army of the Potomac fought so well. Campaigning in defense of Union soil had compelled these men to reach deep within themselves, to draw more on their courage, experience, discipline, and commitment than they had ever done before. It aided them just enough to win all the critical engagements within the larger battle. They now knew what it would take to defeat Lee's army, and they felt confident in their ability to replicate that level of focus and performance.[55]

By the time Lee's army returned to Virginia soil, the Confederate troops were absolutely exhausted. It had been a long and demanding campaign, with a merry entrance into the North, a calamitous battle, and a hasty retreat. "We had a nice time going into Pa.," a veteran wrote a friend in early August, "but comeing out was quite to the contrary." Another soldier insisted this was easily the most demanding expedition of the war. "I thought I knew it all, but this last campaign exceeds in hardships anything I ever experienced. I have been cold, hot, wet, dry, ragged, dirty, hungry & thirsty, marched through clouds of dust, waded mud knee deep & suffered from fatigue & loss of sleep." He was glad to be "home," on Confederate soil.[56]

In evaluating the campaign and its results, some refused to acknowledge defeat. They equated victory with driving the opposing forces from the field. Since the Confederates retreated voluntarily, they had not lost. "The truth about Gettysburg is that we were *repulsed* at the *final* position of the enemy, & that the *want* of *success* was a *terrible calamity;* but we were *not defeated,*" insisted Robert Stiles. "Our men were very much mortified at the result—but say they can whip the Yanks—have done so and can whip them still," justified another soldier. "At no time during the engagement were our men panic stricken or routed." Gettysburg was merely a setback on the road to independence—nothing more.[57]

Yet in their state of exhaustion, quite a number of troops admitted to dissatisfaction, verging on demoralization. With food and rest, however, spirits revived. Others took "french leave"— unauthorized absence—or threatened to do so, but with time to recuperate, they returned to their commands or realized how foolish their thoughts had been. Morale recovered.

Some Rebels blamed their failure on the strength of the Union position. "The Enemy occupied a Gibralter of a position," commented brigade commander Dodson Ramseur. "It was a second Fredericksburg affair," asserted a perceptive captain, "only the wrong way." They chided their leaders for their conduct of the battle. "The insanity of our Generals led them to attack," argued an Alabama officer. Confederate tactics at Gettysburg made no sense. The Yankees "are as mere chaff before the wind when ever they come out in the open country and this but makes the policy of attacking them when they are entrenched more criminal." Another soldier called it a "sin" to kill experienced troops in such numbers because "his place could not be filled."[58]

For the first time since he took command in early June 1862, criticism spilled over on Lee, although most of it was indirect. Soldiers grumbled that the loss was at the general's level, or that "I don't think we made much by going into Pennsylvania." When they did target Lee specifically, it was done so gently. They now admitted that the campaign proved Lee was *"human."* Even those who were more direct in their objections to the way he handled the battle expressed them gingerly. "Gen. Lee was too confident in his men—," conceded a soldier, "expecting them to overcome difficulties too great." Lee himself corroborated that opinion. Assuming full responsibility for the failure of the campaign, he stated in his official report, "More may have been required of them than they were able to perform." In fairness to Lee, however, his army had always carried the critical positions. No doubt, he believed they could crack the Union line.[59]

The attack on July 3 may have been unwise, but Confederate troops had certainly seized more difficult positions than those they attacked on July 2. Part of the explanation for failure, as one soldier pointed out, was that "the enemy had the advantage over them in position, & supplies, and were encouraged to fight, because we were invading their soil." Yet a more determined foe was not the sole reason for the repulse. Another factor rested with the Confederate troops. Throughout the campaign, the distractions of invasion—amid a hostile populace and novel surroundings, living off the countryside and plundering Yankee households—may have stripped the Confederate troops of their fighting edge. The distractions and festivities of the raid eroded their discipline and focus. As one Confederate pinpointed in a letter home, "I felt[,] when I saw how our men were going on[,] that nothing but disaster would follow and in truth I was associated with an armed mob with the broadest license and not with a disciplined army such as General Lee has had under his command." Walter Taylor, Lee's aide-de-camp, employed different words to ratify the same argument, that the soldiers fought better in Virginia than in Pennsylvania. "I will not hide one truth—that our men are better satisfied on this side of the Potomac," he divulged to his brother. "They are not accustomed to operating in an enemy country where the people are inimical to them & certainly every one of them is today worth twice as much as he was three days ago."[60]

For two years, Confederates had dominated the war in Virginia. Time after time, they had pulled out victories, despite overwhelming Union advantages in men and matériel, by drawing on peerless leadership and superiority in battle. There was a focus, a level of concentration, and eventually a confidence among Confederate troops that Federals lacked. But in the Gettysburg Campaign, roles reversed. Fighting on Northern soil, Union troops exhibited an unusual degree of commitment and tenacity, which enabled them to hold on during the most desperate moments of the battle, to win the critical fights within the fight. And for the first time in the war, Confederates lost those decisive encounters. Distracted by the complexities, hazards, and temptations of invasion, and the ensuing slippage of discipline that widespread foraging and plundering wrought on them, detracted just enough from the fighting effectiveness of Lee's troops to swing the outcome of the battle to the Federals.

For all the casualties, the impact of Gettysburg was more dramatic for Federal soldiers than for Confederates. In a series of major engagements, Lee's army had won all except one, and in that instance the Federals had failed to drive them from the field. No one doubted they would win again. But for the Union troops, the victory at Gettysburg was more important. For the first time, they had bested Lee's army in a campaign. The triumph provided proof positive for soldiers' claims that they were "good stuff" from which to build an army. With proper army leadership, they could defeat the Army of Northern Virginia. This newfound confidence, born of experience, helped to sustain them through that last, decisive year of war.

# 2

## Joshua Chamberlain and the American Dream

GLENN LaFANTASIE

THERE was an air of expectation that filled the Boston Music Hall as the audience waited for Joshua Lawrence Chamberlain, the incumbent governor of Maine and "The Hero of Little Round Top," to be introduced. Chamberlain was going to speak on one of his favorite subjects, "The Left at Gettysburg," and his skill as a public orator had already brought him considerable fame in his home state and throughout New England. It was "the celebrity of Gen. Chamberlain," said one newspaper, that had drawn the sizeable crowd to the music hall that November evening in 1868. The people of Boston wanted to see for themselves this great hero of the war and hear him tell his tale.

He did not disappoint them. Chamberlain described in vivid detail the bloody afternoon of July 2, 1863, when he had saved the Union army by ordering his regiment—the 20th Maine Infantry—to make a desperate bayonet charge down the slopes of Little Round Top in the face of a superior Confederate force. For more than an hour, the audience was entranced by his "glowing eloquence" and "graphic power." The lecture, said one reporter, was "a masterly production."[1] No one who saw his performance that night could have ever doubted that Joshua Lawrence Chamberlain was a true American hero.

Today Chamberlain enjoys an even loftier status as a hero than he did in his own lifetime. Over the past three decades, he has become a household name, a role model, and the subject of a popular novel, television documentary, and theatrical movie. The story of his courageous defense of Little Round Top has been told over and over, and with each telling his reputation seems to grow by leaps and bounds. His bravery on that hillside and his stouthearted service throughout the war have earned him a permanent place in America's gallery of honored heroes.

What appeals to us most about Joshua Lawrence Chamberlain is his simplicity and purity. Unlike heroes from our own time whose greatest achievements invariably become tainted by disappointing character flaws and inconsistent actions, by secret vices and unsavory motives, Chamberlain is an unsullied champion who seems never to have let himself or his contemporaries down. When events called for him to be intrepid and steadfast, as they did that summer afternoon on the jagged slopes of Little Round Top, he neither faltered nor failed. Later in life he did not damage his hard-earned reputation by becoming morally or politically corrupt. He stayed the course; he remained true to himself. He was, quite frankly, what we'd like to think we all are or could be: a hero for all seasons.

Yet there is more to Chamberlain than meets the eye. He is remembered today precisely as he wanted to be remembered during his own lifetime. If Chamberlain could return from Valhalla, where no doubt he resides with all the other great heroes of the Civil War, he would surely be quite pleased with his celebrity. Although there is no denying that he was brave and daring, and that his deeds at Gettysburg were truly remarkable, the fact is that our image of him as a hero is derived from his own image of himself. The Chamberlain we know is the Chamberlain he wanted us to see, and while there is nothing particularly wrong with that, it does tend to give us pause if we happen to scratch the veneer and encounter something odd or unexpected about him that doesn't quite fit the image. Beneath the surface of the polished past, the hero and his deeds take on a different luster—not unimpressive, by any means, but not exactly shiny either.

When the Civil War broke out, Chamberlain was a professor of Rhetoric and Oratory at Bowdoin College in Brunswick, Maine. Although his passions were aroused in support of the Union, he did not rush to enlist in the first wave of Bowdoin students and other young men from Brunswick who dashed to defend their country's honor. Having already arranged a sabbatical from the college to study in Europe for two years, he suddenly felt "an irresistible impulse . . . to have a hand" in the fighting and offered his services in the summer of 1862 to the governor of Maine. When the governor told him that he was forming a new regiment, Chamberlain decided to use his sabbatical to extricate himself from Bowdoin and accept a commission as lieutenant colonel in the 20th Maine Infantry.[2]

He soon began to act very much like a soldier. After the battle of Antietam, Chamberlain wrote home to his wife, Fannie, complaining about the monotony of camp life and the desolation of the countryside. Yet he took to soldiering quickly, without real effort, and he suddenly discovered that there was something about army life that greatly appealed to him. He wrote to Fannie: "A dashing rain & furious gale in the night makes me put on a skull-cap (given me by the major) & pull the talma over me—head & all—curl up so as to bring myself into a bunch, & enjoy it hugely."

Chamberlain found out, too, that there was something about war that was oddly to his liking. At the battle of Fredericksburg in December 1862, when the 20th Maine was one of the endless line of Union regiments raked by the merciless enemy fire that swept across the broad fields below Marye's Heights, Chamberlain came face to face with the horrors of war. The ground, he remembered years later, was slippery with blood. Pinned down by the Confederate guns, he spent a long, macabre night huddled between the bodies of two dead soldiers, resting his head on the body of a third and using the flap from the dead man's coat to protect his face from the chilling wind. All night he listened to the dreadful moans of the wounded on the field. "It was heart-rending," he said. "It could not be borne."[3] Yet he lived through the Fredericksburg ordeal and saw for himself the worst that war could bring.

He did not let the brutality of war torment him. As some men can do, he was able to shut out the ghastly realities of battle and put its frightening horrors out of reach. It was not that the human misery of war failed to touch him. He saw all its bloody consequences plainly, and he lamented the suffering and loss that each battle brought with it. It was rather that he began to regard war from his own perspective, one that enabled him to see it not precisely as it was, but as he thought it really should be.

Claiming that he never felt afraid in battle, he scoffed at those who admitted their fear. "A soldier has something else to think about," he said. Most men might flinch a little at the thought of their "present peril," but as a rule, "men stand up from one motive or another—simple manhood, force of discipline, pride, love, or bond of comradeship"—to face the blazing guns without trepidation. Officers, said Chamberlain, are far too busy to think about their own personal welfare on the battlefield. "The instinct to seek safety," he maintained, "is overcome by the instinct of honor."

For Chamberlain, war was mostly chivalry and honor. Like the knights of old, he saw the two contending armies as representing good and evil, white knights battling black knights in epic duels that would determine the fate of the United States. In his eyes, officers displayed knightly countenances as they rode by on noble steeds. He named his favorite horse Charlemagne and marveled that his mount suffered almost as many wounds as he did before war's end. The effects of warfare on its participants, he wrote in his history of the Army of the Potomac's last campaign, were salutary, not hellish: "In the privations and sufferings endured as well as in the strenuous action of battle, some of the highest qualities of manhood are called forth,—courage, self-command, sacrifice of self for the sake of something held higher,—wherein we take it chivalry finds its value."[4]

No episode captured for Chamberlain all the chivalry and honor of the entire wartime experience more than did the surrender of Gen. Robert E. Lee's Army of Northern Virginia to the Army of the Potomac at Appomattox Court House in April 1865. Having been given the honor of officially receiving the Confederate surrender on April 12, Chamberlain took the opportunity to pay homage to his former enemies. As Gen. John B. Gordon, the Confederate officer in charge, approached the stretch of line where Chamberlain and his staff waited, a Federal bugle sounded, the first Union regiment stiffened to attention, and each regiment down the line did the same. Gordon, recognizing the salute, immediately swung his horse around to face Chamberlain and, giving a slight kick of his spurs, managed in picture-book style to have his horse bow in front of his victor as the southern general lowered the tip of his sword to his toe. "Honor answering honor" was what Chamberlain called it. For the rest of his life, he was praised in the South for his gallantry.[5]

His Victorian sense of self-sacrifice and self-discipline enabled him to see the war in these rosy shades, through the romantic lenses of chivalry and honor. "War," he said, "is for the participants a test of character; it makes bad men worse and good men better."[6] There was no question into which category he should be placed. Judging his own war record, Chamberlain concluded that he had passed the test of war with flying colors. All the promotions and accolades he had earned throughout the conflict proved that the Civil War had changed him for the better.

His faith was not only in himself. He believed that the real test for every person came from a clash from within one's self, from the conflict of warring spirits. "There is," he explained in his later years, "a two-fold nature in us, or perhaps two natures, I should rather say two souls." One soul acts exclusively in the interest of the individual self. The other soul looks to a "life associated with others." This latter soul, he thought, was truly the "better soul," which found its ultimate source in love. When a person was sorely tested, as Chamberlain had been in battle after battle during the Civil War, "this better soul of man sinks self and sense and moves and acts in the communion of a larger life." His own experience had shown him that "great crises in human affairs call out the great in men." They rise up to reach their better souls.[7]

As an army officer, Chamberlain sought to grab hold of his better soul by using all his self-control and self-determination to put his men first, assert his leadership through personal heroism, and demonstrate his willingness to suffer great privations for the cause of the Union and the sake of his command. According to one contemporary account, Chamberlain made sure that on forced marches or in bivouacs "he never took rest for himself until he had seen his men made as comfortable as possible." He was wounded six times during the war, twice almost fatally, and in every instance he showed great courage in moving his men forward or fighting on despite his injuries. At Petersburg, where he was shot through both hips and was believed to be dying, Gen. Ulysses S. Grant promoted him on the field to the rank of brigadier general.[8]

Chamberlain survived, of course, and his victory over death only added to his illustrious reputation. Gen. Charles Griffin, commander of the Army of the Potomac's Fifth Corps, once remarked that "it is a magnificent sight to see Chamberlain in battle," and Chamberlain's men wholeheartedly agreed with the general's assessment. One private in the 20th Maine wrote to the state's adjutant general after the war to say, rather grandly, that Chamberlain was "one of those rare individuals thrown conspicuously out to our admiring view by the revolution and evolution of the stupendous enigma of War."

His men loved him. His superior officers loved him. Even his enemies loved him. He was, said General Gordon after the Appomattox surrender, "one of the knightliest soldiers of the Federal army." There seemed to be no doubt among nearly everyone who knew him that he had succeeded in embracing his better soul. Wrote Theodore Gerrish, a 20th Maine veteran: "There were but few officers who displayed greater bravery, faced more dangers, and shed their blood on more battle-fields than did Gen. Joshua L. Chamberlain."[9] He was a perfect hero in everyone's eyes.

So he was in his own eyes, too. As he explained in a Memorial Day address delivered in Springfield, Massachusetts, in 1897, he believed that "everyone has in him, slumbering somewhere, the potencies of noble action, and on due occasion these are likely to make themselves manifest and effective." The secret to unlocking those potencies could be found in the two souls residing in each person, for by striving for one's better soul, the soul of love and community, one could thus find the path toward greater glory, the road toward true heroism. "Every man has in him the elements of a hero," he said. His own heroism sprang from an assertion of will, a conscious effort to put others before himself and to achieve, as he put it, a "largeness of action." In all of this, there was something lofty and spiritual, the fulfillment of divine destiny.[10]

In fact, he based his conception of a true hero not on a knightly archetype out of Sir Walter Scott but on a divine model—Joshua, the Old Testament warrior and his own namesake. In a long article published in 1883, Chamberlain delineated, with a fair amount of discursive argumentation, ten qualities "of nature and character" that had made Joshua an outstanding military commander. Each of the ten traits—inspiration, resolution, straightforwardness, severity of discipline, justice, prudence, sagacity, promptness of action, thoroughness of execution, and balance of character—allowed Joshua to meet the many challenges involved in moving his people to the Promised Land, conquering their enemies, and establishing a nation.

But these traits did not belong to the hero of Jericho alone. Most of them were qualities that Chamberlain prized in himself. When he spoke of Joshua as "a man tried and true," he could just as easily have been speaking about himself. "Here stands the man," wrote Chamberlain of the Biblical commander, "clear in the light of his mission,—his traits almost suggested by the situation, correlated to the demand."[11] That was precisely how Chamberlain thought his own virtues had surfaced through his character—tested by the necessity of the moment, forged by the emergency at hand. In Joshua the commander, Chamberlain saw a clear reflection of himself.

The battle of Gettysburg gave Chamberlain a perfect opportunity to prove to himself and the whole world that he was, like his Old Testament exemplar, a hero of extraordinary merit who could—and did—defeat the Canaanites swiftly and decisively. At Gettysburg, he was able to call on all the virtues—the ten traits of Joshua—that made a military commander great. As a result of what he and the 20th Maine accomplished on the slopes of Little Round Top, Chamberlain received the praise and thanks of his superior officers, and his reputation for bravery and skill began to grow. The fame that came to Chamberlain from his actions at Gettysburg did not emerge overnight; it spread slowly over time, like the plodding movement of clouds across the sky.

Chamberlain got to tell the story of his regiment's defense of Little Round Top for the first time in the official report he wrote after the battle for his superior officers. Writing the story out helped him organize his thoughts, put events in their proper order, and figure out how much—and how little—he wanted to share with his superiors. Not surprisingly, Chamberlain cast himself in a role that fit his picture of himself—his conception of what a heroic field officer should be. He seems not to have worried about appearing boastful or vain, for he freely portrayed himself as the hero of the day. More to the point, the story of Little Round Top that he told in these reports would be the story he was to tell over and over for the rest of his life.

It was the bayonet charge, that great lunge into uncertainty, that stirred everyone's emotions, including Chamberlain's. His official report to Col. James C. Rice, the brigade commander, dramatically narrates the story of the charge and the events leading up to it, replete with flourishes and crescendos. Having been placed on the extreme left of the Union line along the southern slope of Little Round Top, Chamberlain's men held off a powerful Confederate force for over an hour until their ammunition was nearly exhausted. "It was imperative," he wrote, "to strike before we were struck by this overwhelming force in a hand-to-hand fight, which we could not probably have withstood or survived." He ordered the bayonet, and the word "ran like fire along the line, from man to man, and rose into a shout." The left wing moved down the hill, swinging in a great right wheel, and swept the surprised Confederates before it. His men, who wanted to press on all the way to Richmond, took 400 Confederate prisoners. One hundred fifty of the enemy had been killed or wounded on the hillside. Out of his regiment of 386 men, Chamberlain lost 136, including 30 dead and many seriously wounded.[12]

He knew they had accomplished a wondrous thing. The day after the battle, he wrote to Fannie: "The 20th has immortalized itself." With an understandable delight in himself and his marvelous deeds, the kind of glee and swagger that is allowable between husband and wife, he wrote to Fannie again a few weeks later and repeated most of the information he had already told her about Little Round Top. To the governor of Maine, he wrote a lengthy letter telling how the regiment had "won distinguished honor" at a place on the battlefield "where the fiercest attack was made." And he pointed out to both wife and governor that his little regiment had defeated a whole Confederate brigade.[13]

When word of what he and his men had done reached the high command of his corps, the top brass could not restrain themselves from heaping praise on him, and certainly he deserved every good word of it. After the 20th Maine was relieved on July 3, Chamberlain reported that his corps' brigade commanders greeted him by shaking his hand and telling him, "Your gallantry was magnificent, & your coolness & skill saved us." Both Colonel Rice and Brig. Gen. James Barnes, the brigade's division commander, singled Chamberlain out for favorable mention in their official dispatches. Barnes even included a long, rather melodramatic description of the 20th's defense of Little Round Top. Chamberlain wrote Fannie: "I am receiving all sorts of praise but bear it nicely."[14]

It was a very honest thing to say. One of the reasons people liked Chamberlain so much and enjoyed praising him for his accomplishments was because he never went fishing for the compliments or asking for advancement or any special consideration. To Fannie, he once said: "I hate to see a man always on the spring to get the best of everything for himself. I prefer to take things as they come." People could see that he was not a self-seeker. "Never was," said one newspaper of him thirty-five years after Gettysburg, "and never will be."

Yet in the weeks following Gettysburg, his ambition did begin to get the better of him and his hopes were raised about the possibility of promotion. In August, after assuming temporary command of the Third Brigade of the Fifth Corps, he was given permanent command of the brigade by Gen. Charles Griffin. With his new responsibilities, Chamberlain worked to gain some prominent support for winning a higher rank. After receiving a letter of commendation from General Barnes for his "gallant charge upon the enemy" at Gettysburg, Chamberlain sent the general an unofficial "memoranda" that told, in terms similar to the ones he had used in his official report, his version of the events that had transpired on Little Round Top. A few days later, Colonel Rice wrote an unsolicited letter to William Pitt Fessenden, U.S. senator from Maine, recommending Chamberlain for promotion to brigadier general and attributing the victory on the army's left at Gettysburg to Chamberlain's "moral power" and "personal heroism."[15]

The wheels were in motion. By the end of October, Chamberlain had received support for his promotion from Gen. O. O. Howard (a fellow Mainer), Gen. Adelbert Ames (the former commander of the 20th Maine), Congressman John H. Rice of Maine (who wrote his letter of recommendation directly to President Lincoln), Israel Washburn (the former Republican governor of Maine), Gen. Charles Griffin (Chamberlain's Fifth Corps division commander after Gettysburg), Col. Charles Gilmore (who assumed command of the 20th Maine after Chamberlain's elevation to brigade command), and Hannibal Hamlin, the vice president (who also wrote to Lincoln). The not-so-luminary also endorsed Chamberlain's promotion. E. B. French, an obscure auditor in the Treasury Department, sent papers to Secretary of War Edwin S. Stanton commending Chamberlain as "highly cultivated" and "patriotic." Most of the letters, especially the ones from the military men, mentioned his bravery at Gettysburg.[16]

Although it was all made to look like spontaneous combustion, Chamberlain was the heat behind this firestorm of endorsements. To his regret, however, the campaign for his promotion failed. He attributed its lack of success to a prejudice in Washington against the Fifth Corps, a bias that kept many colonels commanding brigades throughout the corps, but it was also apparent that politics had also worked against him. He had marshaled plenty of support, and much of it from all the right places, but it was simply not enough to push the promotion through. "I was without political influence in Washington," Chamberlain explained in his later years, "without which, in those days, no military merit in the field could claim attention among the many nearer interests that pressed upon the Government." Although he had been elevated to command of a brigade, without promotion, the honor was not much appreciated by him. Without extra pay or allowance, he complained, the elevation to command without rank was an "injustice" that "quite cancelled the compliment" of having been given responsibility for the brigade.[17] Nevertheless, his bid for higher rank did win some rewards. It affixed in the minds of many people his heroic action on Little Round Top, and his name became more widely known in military and political circles.

During the remainder of the war, his heroics helped spread his name and build his reputation even more. He distinguished himself at Petersburg in June 1864, where he was critically wounded (and received, at last, a brigadier general's commission). In several battles in March and April 1865, as the war rushed to its dramatic finale, Chamberlain performed brilliantly at Quaker Road (where he was wounded again and received a brevet rank of Major General), at White Oak Road, and at Five Forks. He was a hero, plain and simple. Years later, in his home state of Maine, crowds would welcome him to their town halls and auditoriums by having the band strike up "See the Conquering Hero Comes."

The public knew him best, however, for what he had done at Gettysburg. After the war, when he served three terms as governor of Maine and twelve years as president of Bowdoin College, he labored hard and deliberately to forge that association more solidly in people's minds. On the campaign trail in Maine or the lecture circuit around New England, Chamberlain told his story over and over about the desperate fight and the bold bayonet charge on Little Round Top. By 1868, he was widely known in Maine as "The Hero of Little Round Top."[18]

He told his story often, and he told it very well. Occasionally he spoke about the surrender of Lee and the chivalrous moment when he and General Gordon exchanged salutes, but mostly he told the people of his state about Gettysburg and the brave deeds of the 20th Maine. He often spoke without notes to packed halls, and his Gettysburg lecture could sometimes last as long as an hour and a half—sometimes longer. When he gave his Gettysburg talk in Boston in the fall of 1868, a reporter commented on Chamberlain's effective delivery: "The Governor's voice is full, rich and sonorous; his manner bright and interesting, and his gesture free, graceful and impressive. . . . He writes with a considerable degree of elegance, and, what is more important, with an uncommon amount of vividness and graphic power." In the 1880s, one newspaper account described Chamberlain's ability to bring the Little Round Top engagement to life: "The interest was positively painful at times, so real did the lecturer make it by his eloquent speech." His audiences loved every minute of it.[19]

Chamberlain's thoughts never seemed to be very far away from Gettysburg. He returned to the battlefield several times after 1863. While serving on court-martial duty in Washington during the spring of 1864, he took Fannie to Gettysburg to show her the places he had defended, and he visited the field again in the autumn of 1865. Four years after Appomattox, he went to Gettysburg for a reunion of officers who had served in the Army of the Potomac. Organized by the Gettysburg Battlefield Memorial Association and John B. Bachelder, a former civilian observer with the Army of the Potomac whose interest in the battle was becoming his life's work, the reunion was intended to help locate and mark where each unit had been positioned on the battlefield. Chamberlain walked the ground, pointed out where his line had been formed, told the story of the 20th Maine's daring counterattack, and watched as wooden stakes were driven into the soil to show where his men had stood.[20]

In October 1889, Chamberlain was back in Gettysburg—this time to participate in the dedication of two monuments to the 20th Maine that had been erected on the battlefield by the survivors of the old regiment. He was the man of the hour. At the dedication ceremonies, held on October 3, he delivered two of the many speeches made that day—the first, in the afternoon on Little Round Top, went into the details of the fight and the gallant charge that had occurred twenty-six years before; and the second, in the evening at the Adams County Court House, explored the meaning and importance of the Union cause in the context of his theory about each individual's two souls. For the evening program, Chamberlain closed by saying: "In great deeds something abides. On great fields something stays. Forms change and pass; bodies disappear; but spirits linger, to consecrate the ground for the vision-place of souls."[21]

But even as Chamberlain spoke at Gettysburg it was becoming less certain if his own great deeds, his heroic actions on Little Round Top, would endure precisely as he wanted them to. Since the end of the war, other veterans of the fight for that rocky hill had given their own versions of the story in speeches, books, newspapers, and other publications, and while these authors did not necessarily set out to challenge Chamberlain's account or question his credibility, their reminiscences sometimes presented a different picture of what had occurred on that hillside.[22]

Sounding uncharacteristically defensive, and more than a little peevish, Chamberlain took note of the fact in his afternoon address, which was delivered at the site of the 20th Maine monument on Little Round Top, that the remembrances of some veterans did not comport with the story he had been telling for years. He tried, however, to dismiss the inconsistencies and their importance. Several of the regiment's former officers, he said, had claimed the distinction of being the one who notified Chamberlain, as the fighting began to heat up on Little Round Top, that a Confederate column was moving around the 20th's left flank. Without setting the record straight, one way or another, as to the identity of the officer who did bring him the news that day, Chamberlain attempted to reconcile the contradictory claims by declaring that "they are all right; no one of them is wrong." He took issue, though, with those who had maintained that at the moment of the charge, the men of the 20th Maine had hesitated, ever so briefly, before moving forward down the hill. "No man hesitated," he insisted, although he did admit—for the first time, publicly—that his order to charge "was never given, or but imperfectly," and that the men had begun to move even before he had finished uttering, "Bayonet! Forward to the right!" These conflicting accounts, he said, were "all of them true in their time and place, and so far as each actor is concerned." Truth, in other words, was in the eye of the beholder.

But the discrepancies could not be so easily cast aside. The facts about Little Round Top seemed suddenly slippery, and Chamberlain could no longer hold on to them as if they were his exclusive property. Nonetheless, he did what he could to sustain his version of the Little Round Top story. For the most part, he simply ignored the inconsistencies and kept telling his own tale, just as he always had. In one instance, when he learned that an author of "a graphic account of the Little Round Top incident in brief," which was intended to be published to raise funds for a Grand Army of the Republic post, had entirely omitted any reference to the 20th Maine's moment of glory at Gettysburg, Chamberlain hounded the poor man until he received an apology and assurances that the missing episode would be included in the author's larger work in progress.[23]

When several friends and supporters decided in 1893 to ask the War Department to award Chamberlain a Medal of Honor for his bravery on Little Round Top, the formal application included a description of his courageous acts that adhered in all its particulars to Chamberlain's account of the battle, drawn largely from the official reports that he and his superior officers had written at the time. A few important persons—including former Army of the

Potomac generals Alexander S. Webb and Fitz John Porter, and Governor Henry B. Cleaves of Maine—wrote letters recommending Chamberlain for the medal. There were, however, no letters from anyone in his command, a surprising fact given the active role that the Twentieth Maine Regimental Association otherwise played in sustaining the good name of the regiment and the high standing of its veterans. The man who submitted the application, Gen. Thomas Hubbard, a friend and former student, pointed out that Chamberlain, who was suffering badly from his old wounds, "has still many friends and admirers; but in his sickness and advancing years he is less in the public eye."[24]

The War Department awarded him the Medal of Honor on August 11, 1893, "for distinguished gallantry at the battle of Gettysburg, Penna., July 2, 1863." Chamberlain cherished the medal and made sure that he received new issues and ribbons whenever the government changed the design slightly. He considered the medal itself a "sacred" honor, something "not to be bought or sold, or recklessly conferred."[25] He had every right to feel proud, and every reason to believe the medal would elevate his fame higher.

As it turned out, the Medal of Honor did not make him a national hero, although he did win some acclaim from the fact that his name was mentioned repeatedly in a fair number of books during the postwar years that described, either briefly or sometimes at surprising length, the charge of the 20th Maine down the slopes of Little Round Top.[26] Mostly Chamberlain himself kept his version of the story going—less so by lecturing than he used to do, for his old wounds bothered him more and more as the years went on, but more by keeping his name before the public and making sure that no one, at least in Maine, forgot what the 20th Maine had done or who "The Hero of Little Round Top" was. He was quite pleased when the War Department constructed a new road on Little Round Top and named it "Chamberlain Avenue."[27]

He happily complied when the state commission established to erect the Maine monuments on the Gettysburg battlefield asked him to rewrite a "historical sketch" of the 20th Maine that had been drafted by Ellis Spear for its final report. Besides writing the short history of the regiment, Chamberlain also supplied the report's editors with his field notes for a detailed description of the fight at Little Round Top, and though the evidence is awfully sketchy, he may have actually drafted the Little Round Top account himself. At the very least, the editors relied heavily on his knowledge of Little Round Top and his memory of the events surrounding the battle. In return, Chamberlain worried about the completeness and accuracy of the regimental rosters that the commission intended to publish, and he worked hard to reduce the possibility of error in those lists.[28]

He was worried about some other matters, too—so much, in fact, that he decided to get in touch with William C. Oates, his former adversary, because, as Chamberlain put it, he was "having some controversy with some of the 'Gettysburg Commission' of this State in regard to points of our respective movements on the Round Tops." Taking exception with an article Oates had published nearly twenty years earlier in the *Southern Historical Society Papers,* Chamberlain argued that it was not possible, as Oates had claimed, for the Confederate troops to have passed over the summit of Big Round Top before attacking the 20th Maine on Little Round Top. He also tried to convince Oates that, contrary to what the former Confederate colonel had written, the Rebel force could not have hit Chamberlain's men as soon as it had emerged from the woods at the foot of Big Round Top, for it was Chamberlain's contention that his regiment was already heavily engaged in the fighting before Oates's troops arrived on his left flank.

Oates answered Chamberlain within a friendly fourteen-page letter that confirmed in detail that the Confederates under his command had indeed scaled Big Round Top's peak and that they did not engage the Federals until after coming out of the woods in the valley between the two Round Tops. No doubt Oates's reply did not help Chamberlain in his dispute with the Maine commissioners. How Chamberlain resolved that controversy with them is uncertain, but it was not the last time he would become entangled in disagreements over what actually had taken place on Little Round Top. Although he professed a few years later to be uninterested in the sordid little squabbles that many Civil War veterans took so seriously, Chamberlain found himself nevertheless in the center of two very heated quarrels that called into question his version of the Little Round Top story.[29]

The first of these disagreements, as anyone might have predicted, was with William Oates. Their exchange of letters in 1897 appears to have simply set the stage for a more vigorous disagreement that heated up in 1902, when Oates sought to erect a monument to the regiment he commanded at Gettysburg, the 15th Alabama, in the proximity of the existing memorial to the 20th Maine on the southern slope of Little Round Top. The battlefield was then under the administration of three park commissioners who reported directly to the Secretary of War, Elihu Root. For a variety of reasons—including a rule that required monuments to be placed on the battlefield at the "battle line" rather than the spot where a unit engaged its enemy (which meant that most Confederate monuments could only be erected on Seminary Ridge) and a suspicion that Oates's account of his assault on Little Round Top was factually unreliable—the commissioners initially approved Oates's request, then later changed their minds. When Oates filed a formal application to Secretary Root for approval of his monument in June 1903, the Gettysburg commissioners turned to Chamberlain for help and asked him to comment on the extent to which Oates's description of the fight for Little Round Top was "at variance with the records."

Chamberlain told the battlefield commissioners he did not object to a monument for the 15th Alabama, "but I expect it to be placed on ground where it [i.e., the regiment] stood at some time during the battle." And that was the rub, for Oates argued that he had turned the 20th Maine's right flank and had pushed its left wing so far up the hill that he was justified in placing the Alabama monument on a prominent boulder behind the 20th Maine lines that Chamberlain had so carefully marked for Bachelder in 1869. Chamberlain declared that Oates's description of the battle differed "widely from the well established record of facts in the case." John P. Nicholson, chairman of the battlefield commission, agreed with him and sent Chamberlain's assessment off to Secretary Root. "Chamberlain is not accurate in his statements," Oates complained to William M. Robbins, the Southern member of the three-man commission, "[and] his memory is at fault in some respects." Worse, said Oates, was Chamberlain's egotism about the battle: "He is like many others on both sides at this late date who are disposed to make themselves the whole push."[30]

As the dispute dragged on, wearing everyone down, the battle-field commissioners tried to persuade Oates to revise his statements about the battle and submit them for review to Chamberlain—all in an effort, they told Oates, "to avoid any controversy in the matter." Oates refused to do so, but he did visit the battlefield in the summer of 1904 and showed Commissioner Robbins how deeply the Alabamians had penetrated the wings of the 20th Maine. Angry and frustrated, Oates finally wrote directly to Chamberlain and said that the commissioners had claimed that Chamberlain was opposed to the monument. He asked Chamberlain to reconsider the events and acknowledge that some aspects of the battle might have unfolded as Oates believed they did. "No man can see all that occurs in a fight," he said, "even between two regiments." Chamberlain answered with a stern letter, one might even call it grumpy, saying he was sorry that his earlier correspondence had impressed Oates so little and denying that he had played any part in the commissioners' decision. "It is really my desire to have your monument set up," he wrote, "only let us make sure of our ground for the sake of historical fact." When Chamberlain sent copies of the correspondence to Nicholson, the Gettysburg commissioner was elated. Oates, declared Nicholson, "has not the slightest idea of admitting the views of any one in the controversy except himself."[31]

The irony, of course, was that just the opposite was true. Chamberlain's unwillingness to even consider the possibility of Oates's differing views had sounded the death knell for the Alabama monument, which was never erected. In another disagreement over Little Round Top (a deeper, more personal conflict than the one he had had with Oates), Chamberlain chose to handle it in pretty much the same way. When Ellis Spear, a good friend who had served as an acting major at Gettysburg and had commanded the left wing on Little Round Top, painted a different picture of what had transpired on July 2, Chamberlain stood his ground and refused to take Spear's perspective into account.

During the years after Appomattox, Spear's various writings about Gettysburg seemed to support Chamberlain's description of the action, and the two men remained close friends and sometimes exchanged new information they had acquired about the battle and the old regiment. But in a Memorial Day speech, given in May 1888, Spear said he had never received an order on Little Round Top to fix bayonets or charge; instead, he maintained, there was suddenly "a shout of forward on the center from the company or companies next [to] the colors[,] and through the smoke they seemed to be moving forward[,] and the colors lifted up [and] began to advance."

A few years later, Spear told John Bachelder that on July 2 he had informed Chamberlain of the threat to the 20th's left flank and had asked permission to pull back two companies on the left wing, which Chamberlain allowed him to do. He repeated that he never received an order to charge from Chamberlain, but that he had heard the men tell a story about how Company K, near the center of the regiment, had wanted to retrieve some wounded men in front of their lines, called to other companies to cover them, and moved forward; when they did, said Spear, the whole line advanced and the regiment swept down the hill. Concerned that his recollections differed from those of Chamberlain, Spear wrote to his former commanding officer in 1895 and conspicuously repeated the same points he had earlier made to Bachelder—except the story about Company K, which he had told Bachelder he could not vouch for.[32]

Chamberlain dealt with the differing details about Little Round Top, the ones he had heard from Oates and Spear or had read in accounts written by Holman Melcher and Theodore Gerrish, by dismissing them. Spear, who seems genuinely to have liked and respected his former commanding officer, was unwilling to push Chamberlain about the Gettysburg inconsistencies; so "The Hero of Little Round Top" continued to have his day in the sun. But finally Chamberlain stepped over the line, at least so far as Spear was concerned, when he wrote an account of Little Round Top for a book on Medal of Honor winners that presented the victory on that hillside as practically a single-handed act. In telling his story this time, Chamberlain had disregarded all the little details that Spear knew to be true, particularly that Spear had recommended refusing the regiment's line and that Chamberlain had never "sent word to the senior officer on my left [i.e., Spear] to make a right wheel of the charge." Worse still, Chamberlain had painted himself as the solitary hero of the regiment.[33]

While Spear tried to keep up the pretenses of friendship, sending Chamberlain a warm Christmas greeting in 1910, his ire reached its apex two years later when Chamberlain published "My Story of Fredericksburg" in *Cosmopolitan Magazine.* Less than a year after that, another article by Chamberlain—"Through Blood and Fire at Gettysburg"—appeared in a popular periodical, *Hearst's Magazine.* Upset that Chamberlain was perpetrating untruths, Spear publicly challenged Chamberlain's recollections not only of Fredericksburg, but of Lee's surrender and Little Round Top as well.[34]

What bothered him the most—and in later life became something of a strange obsession—was Chamberlain's "egotism," as he called it. He was not alone. Oliver Norton, who also served in the Fifth Corps at Gettysburg as Col. Strong Vincent's bugler, wrote Spear in 1916, two years after Chamberlain's death, complaining that Chamberlain's attitude was "about the same as that of the Texas man who said he was 'a bigger man than old Grant.'" Spear replied that Chamberlain's egotism was indeed "colossal," and he noted that his fellow Mainers called him "The Hero of Little Round Top," implying that Chamberlain had welcomed such public recognition. Norton believed that the only true savior of the hill was Strong Vincent, who had died there. Although Norton's book, *The Attack and Defense of Little Round Top,* published in 1913, evenhandedly related the details of the 20th Maine's charge on Little Round Top, he focused most of his attention on demonstrating Vincent's timely arrival and personal heroism at the summit of the hill. In their old age, both Spear and Norton came to consider Chamberlain a skilled prevaricator and self-promoter.[35]

Not everyone felt about Chamberlain the way that Spear and Norton and Oates did, but it's safe to say that Chamberlain did put people off by his vainglorious demeanor. When it came to Gettysburg, part of the problem—if Spear and Norton can be read between the lines—stemmed from Chamberlain's failure (or inability) ever to share credit with anyone else for the victory on Little Round Top.

Yet nothing could really stop "The Hero of Little Round Top." Chamberlain's heroic reputation, particularly in Maine, did not diminish over time; if anything, it grew stronger. Even when Chamberlain himself was not doing the talking or the writing, his name and great deeds were being frequently praised by others. Books and articles on Gettysburg, which poured forth in abundance in the years leading up to the fiftieth anniversary of the battle in 1913, repeatedly mentioned Chamberlain and the valiant charge of the 20th Maine.[36]

In the public's mind, he was closely connected with Gettysburg and its legacy. He visited the battlefield again in 1909 and 1911. The governor of Maine appointed him to serve as the state's representative on the national committee formed to plan the fiftieth anniversary commemorations at Gettysburg. Chamberlain returned to Gettysburg one last time in May 1913 to attend a meeting of the planning committee; poor health kept him away from the big celebration the following July. In his final years, he planned to write a book on Gettysburg, but he spent most of his time, painfully, laboring on his long memoir about the battles leading up to the end of the war and Lee's surrender, a work that was not published until after his death. When he died on February 24, 1914, his last words should have been "Fix bayonets" or "Forward to the right"; there's no record, however, that he said anything at all in his final moments. Throughout Maine, people mourned the passing of "The Hero of Little Round Top."[37]

His sun began to set after his death, but not for very long. With the fading away of the Civil War generation, Chamberlain's name was no longer known to a very large public, even in Maine. For a few decades, from the time of his death through the years of the Great Depression, he seems to have slipped from view, unheralded and unknown, except perhaps by only a few. Then, suddenly, he was remembered again in a small book by a very famous author. In 1938, Kenneth Roberts, the Maine author of several popular historical novels, including *Arundel* (1930), *Rabble in Arms* (1933), and *Northwest Passage* (1937), published a book called *Trending into Maine,* which included a retelling of Chamberlain's exploits on Little Round Top in a chapter entitled "Maine Stories I'd Like to Write." Roberts approvingly quoted a newspaper reporter who had once remarked about Chamberlain: "The brush of artist never had a grander theme. It should be put on canvas or sculptured in marble and placed in the rotunda of the capitol at Washington to show to the world the stuff of which American patriots are made. As an example to inspire patriotism it would rank with Leonidas and his three hundred Spartans. America is secure against the world as long as she has such sons to spring to her defence in the hour of darkness and danger."

Chamberlain also gained favorable notice from some prominent Civil War historians after World War II, namely Earl Schenk Miers and Bruce Catton. But it was a wonderfully written history of the 20th Maine Regiment by John J. Pullen, who told the story of the unit and its famous commander with lively style and great gusto, that must be given the credit for reintroducing Chamberlain to a modern audience. Pullen's book, published in 1957, presented Chamberlain just as he always wanted to be seen. Wrote Pullen: "He was destined to become one of the most remarkable officers in the history of the United States—a veritable knight with plumes and shining armor."

Although Chamberlain was sometimes missing from popular books about Gettysburg, he became more and more of a mainstay in the literature about the battle after Pullen's book came out. In 1960, the first full-scale biography of Chamberlain, written by Willard M. Wallace, was published. Relying on a good selection of manuscript sources from Maine and elsewhere, Wallace reconstructed Chamberlain's multifaceted life as a mosaic of experiences, public and private. The Chamberlain story was regaining visibility, not unlike in the days when Chamberlain himself would repeat his own tale to audiences around his state and region.[38]

It was, however, a novel that finally thrust Chamberlain onto a national stage—and, later an international one—by portraying his heroism in a grittily realistic manner. When *The Killer Angels,* written by Michael Shaara, was published in 1974, few people had heard of Joshua Lawrence Chamberlain. Shaara's novel, which told the story of the battle of Gettysburg through the eyes of a handful of main characters, Chamberlain one of them, changed that forever. Shaara portrays Chamberlain as a thinking man gone to war, but mostly as an everyman, someone not unlike all of us, caught up in a deadly situation in which he must, out of necessity, rely on his keen wits to get himself—and the men he commands—through the terrible ordeal of Little Round Top. He succeeds, of course, and feels very good about his accomplishment—"an incredible joy," as Shaara describes it: "He looked at himself, wonderingly, at the beloved men around him, and he said to himself: Lawrence, old son, treasure this moment. Because you feel as good as a man can feel."[39]

Although Shaara brings Chamberlain to life as no writer has been able to do before, there is still something oddly familiar about his characterization. To be sure, Shaara draws heavily and rather shamelessly on Pullen's history of the 20th Maine for his information. But mostly Shaara makes use of Chamberlain's own story, Chamberlain's own words. The character in the novel seems so recognizable because it is, quite simply, Chamberlain talking again about Little Round Top, just as he had done for most of his life. Shaara fleshes him out, but it is really Chamberlain come back again, Chamberlain the Old Testament warrior—the student of Joshua—talking about "Man, the Killer Angel," worrying about departing the earth "in a chariot of fire," seeing a vision of the battlefield before him "like a Biblical dream."[40]

Over the past twenty years, Shaara's novel has gained a large and loyal readership. It might have been an obscure work, passed over by all except a few devoted fans, but it won the Pulitzer Prize in 1975 and has gone through scores of printings in cloth and paper editions since then. The book has become a popular assignment as a supplemental reading in high school and college history courses—and even in military-training classes. In 1983, the popularity of the novel led curriculum designers at the U.S. Army Command and General Staff College at Fort Leavenworth back to Pullen's book and convinced them to devote long sections of a field manual on military leadership to Chamberlain and the fight for Little Round Top.[41]

Shaara's novel drove the Chamberlain legend in the years after winning the Pulitzer. Books and articles on Gettysburg featured Chamberlain and the 20th Maine more prominently than many earlier works had done.[42] But in 1990, unlike the results of any earlier telling of the Chamberlain story, his notoriety suddenly soared when Ken Burns, a documentary filmmaker, decided to include Chamberlain as a key historical figure in his epic television documentary "The Civil War," which was broadcast on PBS. Watched by fourteen million viewers, the documentary became the most popular program ever shown on public television. Burns later explained that his inspiration for the film came from reading Shaara's *The Killer Angels*. An accompanying book, *The Civil*

*War: An Illustrated History,* hit the best-seller lists and stayed there through the following Christmas.[43] Chamberlain had truly become an American hero of the 1990s. He was a television star.

Like other celebrities, Chamberlain has successfully made the transition from small screen to big by appearing in 1993 as a prominent character in the motion picture *Gettysburg,* produced by Turner Pictures and directed by Ronald F. Maxwell. The movie is an adaptation of Shaara's novel, so the Chamberlain we see on the screen is, for the most part, Shaara's characterization of him from *The Killer Angels,* although the scenes depicting the Little Round Top fight seem to be based more on Chamberlain's heroic legend than on the novel per se. Chamberlain (and the actor Jeff Daniels, who portrays him) attracted the attention of several film reviewers, whether or not they cared for the movie as a whole. One reviewer wrote: "Mr. Daniels's luminous performance as the heroic colonel dominates the first half of the film. And when the actor all but disappears in Part 2, he is sorely missed." The reviewer praised Chamberlain as a extraordinary leader, with "sad blue eyes," who wins the loyalty of his men and prevents the Confederate army from gaining "a clear path to Washington."[44]

Americans tend to venerate their heroes, and while Joshua Chamberlain stands on a lower tier than some national legends, he has become duly venerated nonetheless. Chamberlain is "irresistible," says one historian, but the simple fact is that he has become too good to be true. The portrait of the man painted by one of his most recent biographers, the late Alice Rains Trulock, is so thoroughly admiring, so laden with excessive homage, so quick to defend and explain away, that the readers yearns for even a tiny flaw in the man, a peccadillo to smile at—anything that would demonstrate conclusively that he was as human as the rest of us. Sad to say, Trulock gives us only the public man, the paladin, the only man Chamberlain wanted his contemporaries or posterity to see.[45] Likewise, numerous military artists have recently depicted Chamberlain in a romantic vein. Artists such as Dale Gallon, Mort Künstler, Don Troiani, Keith Rocco, and several others, have created portraits and prints of Chamberlain and his fighting men on Little Round Top. One cannot walk past the many book shops and galleries in Gettysburg without seeing

Chamberlain's likeness in the window. Not only is Chamberlain irresistible, he is also quite profitable.

Books, articles, and prints continue to spread Chamberlain's legend far and wide, often without much literary grace or artistic creativity. Only two books in the spate of works that have appeared recently manage to present a realistic picture of Chamberlain, the soldier and the man: Michael Golay's lively portrait of Chamberlain (contained in a dual biography that also sketches the life of E. P. Alexander, the Confederate artillerist), and Thomas A. Desjardin's carefully researched and balanced account of the 20th Maine's role in the battle of Gettysburg.[46] But mostly the hero-worshiping goes on and on, for Chamberlain has become the man Civil War buffs love to love.

There is a high price for such veneration. Not only do we lose sight of the man, as has happened with Chamberlain, but we also end up misconstruing his real accomplishments. This has certainly been the case with Chamberlain's charge on Little Round Top. Chamberlain and his superior officers at Gettysburg believed that his counterattack against the Confederates saved the left flank of the Army of the Potomac and perhaps even kept the entire army from destruction, but many others realized that Chamberlain and his 20th Maine played only one small part in winning the day. On the western side of the hill, between the crags and crevices of its rocky face, the other regiments of Vincent's brigade (and, later, Gen. Stephen H. Weed's brigade and Lt. Charles E. Hazlett's battery) fought a desperate battle—a very near thing—and successfully repulsed the formidable Confederate onslaught there.

Even if Chamberlain had failed to turn Oates's Alabamians back on the southern slope, and the gray horde had swept up the hillside, it is unlikely the Confederates would have been able to dislodge the other Union troops that held the heights of Little Round Top. Many years after the battle Oates confessed privately that he could not have held the hill for more than ten minutes if he had overrun the 20th Maine. Col. E. P. Alexander, the former Confederate artillerist, agreed. The Confederates, he said, simply could not have taken Little Round Top and held it against a practically endless ocean of Union reinforcements.

So the Chamberlain we have come to know is, in a sense, the same man Chamberlain saw in the mirror every morning. That man knew what the stakes at Gettysburg were, and it was just no use trying to tell him otherwise. He was, as he liked to be called, "The Hero of Little Round Top." Once, at a Bowdoin commencement exercise, he passed a student who remarked to a friend, "There goes the man who took Little Round Top." Without stopping or turning his head, Chamberlain replied in a loud voice: "Yes, I took it and I held it."[47]

There is, after all, no getting around the fact that the charge of the 20th Maine was remarkable—brave, effective, and deadly. Somehow it doesn't seem to matter much whether it truly saved the Union left or not, whether Chamberlain gave the order or not, or whether the men began flying down the hill before Chamberlain could say anything at all. What's important, in the end, is that the charge did happen, and on that gray summer's evening, when hope seemed to be in especially short supply, the men of the 20th Maine put their courage behind the muzzle of a .58 caliber musket and the point of an eighteen-inch bayonet.

Like nothing else in his life, the charge at Gettysburg defined who Joshua Chamberlain was and who he would always be. But his greatest achievement—greater than any assault he led, any wound he survived, any medal he earned, any obstacle he overcame—was how he had lived his dreams and made them come true. He wanted to be a chivalrous knight and an Old Testament warrior, and so in his own eyes and those of his contemporaries he became those things. The Civil War gave him the opportunity to turn his deepest aspirations into reality. But it is our need for heroes, our admiration for those who are able to rise above their own limitations to turn their dreams into reality, that has enabled Chamberlain to achieve the glory he longed for throughout the war and most of his life. All in all, he accomplished what few men, either in his own time or in our own, can ever honestly claim: he lived his dreams to the fullest.

# 3

## *"Old Jack" Is Not Here*

HARRY W. PFANZ

"**T**ELL Gordon, Hays, Avery, and Smith to double-quick to the front," shouted Maj. Gen. Jubal A. Early to his staff, "and open the lines of infantry for the artillery to pass." It was one of the dramatic moments of the Civil War. Early's division had arrived at Gettysburg on the afternoon of July 1 at just the right time to bolster the Confederate attack, and, in response to Lt. Gen. Richard S. Ewell's urging, Early ordered his division into the fight. The Union Eleventh Corps was in its front, and John B. Gordon's Georgia brigade swept toward the blue line, "moving forward through a field of yellow wheat like a dark gray wave in a sea of gold." Confederate batteries galloped into position and opened fire, and Early's Louisiana and North Carolina brigades swept forward along the Harrisburg Road and around the Union flank. Early struck a smashing blow that the poorly posted Eleventh Corps could not long withstand. "The Federal flank had shriveled up as a scroll," and the men in blue retreated south, past Gettysburg College into the town.[1]

Captain Fred Winkler of Wisconsin saw the gray line coming on and called to a staff officer for orders. "Fall back," the officer shouted. Winkler's men fired a volley at the gray line and retreated into the town. Winkler thought it "the most humiliating step" that he had ever taken. But Maj. John Daniel of Early's staff was ecstatic: he looked to the right, and there were victorious Confederates advancing as far as he could see. He rode to Early's side and shouted, "General, this day's work will win the Southern Confederacy."[2]

The Union forces crowded back through the town from their positions west and north of it. There had been harder fighting in the fields west of town, but it was the arrival of Ewell with two divisions of his corps from the north that had precipitated the Union retreat. Ewell had shared most of Stonewall Jackson's victories, but this ought to have been his finest hour. Since Ewell is not a familiar figure to everyone, I will say something about his life and career and then review his part in the Gettysburg Campaign. Following that, I will mention the treatment given him and his conduct on July 1 by some historians and close by submitting my own present assessment of Ewell's performance in the first day's fight at Gettysburg.

Stonewall Jackson was shot accidentally by his own men on the evening of May 2, 1863, during General Robert E. Lee's brilliant but Pyrrhic victory at Chancellorsville. His death eight days later forced General Lee to find a replacement for him and prompted a needed reorganization of the Army of Northern Virginia. The result was that its two corps of infantry and its supporting artillery commanded by James Longstreet and "Stonewall" Jackson were changed into three, each with three divisions and about 20,000 men. The First was still commanded by Longstreet; the Second, Jackson's old corps, Lee gave to Ewell; and the new Third Corps, two of whose three divisions had been under Longstreet and Jackson, now was commanded by A. Powell Hill. Each of these corps commanders held the grade of lieutenant general.

Richard Stoddert Ewell, though born in Georgetown, D.C., was reared a Virginian. Despite being a grandson of the first secretary of the Navy and possessed of important family connections, he spent his boyhood in near poverty on a farm near Manassas, Virginia. Fortunately, young Ewell was an apt student and was able to secure an appointment to West Point's class of 1840. After graduating from the academy, Ewell joined the 1st Dragoon Regiment in which he served on the plains, in the Mexican War, and in the Southwest, particularly against the Apaches. When Virginia seceded, Ewell resigned as captain in the dragoons and became a lieutenant colonel of cavalry in the Confederate army. Ewell lost much when he followed Virginia from the Union. He had gained a favorable reputation in the Old Army, but this, the promotions, and the security it promised, he forfeited for Virginia and the Confederate gamble.

Ewell commanded a brigade of infantry at First Manassas, and became a major general and a division commander in early 1862. As a division commander he served effectively under Stonewall Jackson in the Valley Campaign, was a dutiful subordinate, and apparently got along well with him—something that A. P. Hill and others did not do. Later, he served with Jackson on the Peninsula, at Cedar Mountain, and then at Second Manassas, where he was shot in the left knee and lost the leg. By then he was Jackson's chief lieutenant.

Ewell, a bachelor, had rivaled Stonewall in eccentricity. But Ewell lacked Jackson's religious zeal and some of his forbidding sternness. He could swear mighty oaths, but suppressed this talent during his convalescence, when he courted and married a wealthy and widowed cousin, the mother of his staff officer, G. Campbell Brown. Thus, in May 1863, when he returned to duty, he was minus a leg but had gained an imperious wife and command of a corps.[3]

His former comrades and new subordinates welcomed his appointment. Jedediah Hotchkiss, the map maker, wrote that the entire corps desired him as Jackson's successor and that his appointment gave general satisfaction. Maj. Alexander (Sandie) Pendleton, Jackson's brilliant young adjutant, who now served in the same capacity under Ewell, wrote that Ewell was in fine health and spirits and rode a horse well. The more Pendleton saw of him, the more he liked him. He found him to be much like Jackson in his disregard of his own comfort and in his inflexibility of purpose. Pendleton looked for great things from his new corps commander.[4]

Lee launched his Pennsylvania Campaign on June 2, 1863. Two stated purposes for the campaign were to disrupt Federal plans for 1863 and to remove the war from Virginia if only for that summer. Lee's plan called for the Army of Northern Virginia to shift from its positions near Fredericksburg to the Shenandoah Valley, march down that valley, cross the Potomac, and follow the Cumberland Valley into Maryland and Pennsylvania. Ewell and his corps were to lead the march, gobbling up the Federal forces in their front, foraging in Pennsylvania for horses, cattle, and supplies for the use of the Confederacy.[5]

And so Ewell, with about 20,000 troops divided into three divisions commanded by major generals Robert Rodes, Jubal Early, and Edward Johnson, marched into the Valley and removed the Federals from it, winning victories at Winchester and Martinsburg, and capturing many men and an abundance of needed supplies. Ewell's corps crossed the Potomac at mid-month, and by the end of June, Early's division had passed through Gettysburg, Pennsylvania, and reached the Susquehanna River at Wrightsville. Ewell, with Rodes and Johnson, was in Carlisle and preparing to capture the Pennsylvania state capital, Harrisburg. It had been a grand march, conducted without a hitch, and Ewell's men had harvested much booty. Stonewall Jackson could not have done better.[6]

In the meantime, General Lee with Hill's and Longstreet's corps had reached Chambersburg, Pennsylvania. There on June 28 he learned that his foe, the Army of the Potomac, was now under the command of Maj. Gen. George G. Meade; that it also had crossed the Potomac and was at Frederick, Maryland. (Because he had lost contact with Maj. Gen. J. E. B. Stuart and the cavalry that was to have screened his right, Lee knew little of the enemy's movements.) Lee thereupon ordered his army to concentrate east of South Mountain in the Gettysburg–Cashtown area to draw Meade's army away from his line of communications in the Cumberland Valley. Ewell received these instructions on the 29th and immediately complied. Johnson's division and Ewell's huge wagon train would return down the Cumberland Valley, and Johnson would approach Gettysburg from the west. Early would march west to the concentration point via Hunterstown and Mummasburg, while Ewell, traveling with Rodes's division, marched south to Heidlersburg and then west via today's Biglerville to Cashtown at the east end of that pass through South Mountain.[7]

Both Rodes's and Early's divisions reached Heidlersburg about ten miles northeast of Gettysburg on June 30. Ewell received orders from Lee instructing him to move to Gettysburg or Cashtown "as circumstances might dictate." Such imprecise orders, according to Maj. Gen. Isaac R. Trimble who was with Ewell, bothered Ewell, who knew little of what was going on elsewhere in his own army and less of the whereabouts of the enemy. Nevertheless, on July 1 he started Rodes's and Early's divisions for Cashtown over two parallel roads north of Gettysburg. At about 9 A.M. he learned from A. P. Hill that Hill was moving to Gettysburg, and he ordered Rodes and Early to do the same—Rodes marching to Gettysburg from what is now Biglerville over the Carlisle Road and Early over the Harrisburg Road.[8]

On the morning of July 1, Hill had sent the divisions of Henry Heth and Dorsey Pender from Cashtown eight miles west of Gettysburg toward that town in a reconnaissance-in-force. Union cavalry, screening the left of the Army of the Potomac, had reached Gettysburg on the day before and had picketed the roads to the west and north. Also on the morning of July 1, Maj. Gen. John F. Reynolds, commander of the left wing of the Army of the Potomac, was marching toward Gettysburg with his own First Corps and the Eleventh Corps commanded by Maj. Gen. Oliver O. Howard. The advancing Confederates had encountered some cavalry pickets west of the town, pressed them back, and when they reached the fields just west of the town and Lutheran Seminary, they collided with the leading two brigades of Reynolds's infantry.

It was a meeting engagement, and both forces grew stronger as additional troops hurried to the field. Two Confederate brigades attacked the two leading brigades of Union infantry on McPherson Ridge (brigades numbered 1,500 or so men each), there was a fight, and by noon the Rebels had been driven back to Herr Ridge a mile and a half west of the town. There Heth formed his four brigades in line of battle, supported by Pender's division, which deployed in a line in their rear. On the Union side, Reynolds had been killed early in the fight, and General Howard took command of the Union forces in the field. They included three divisions of the First Corps, which formed on McPherson's Ridge and Seminary Ridge between the Confederates and Gettysburg, plus three divisions of Howard's Eleventh Corps, which were just coming into the area. Howard posted Brig. Gen. Adolph von Steinwehr's division and a battery on Cemetery Hill just south of the town in reserve to provide a Union rallying point in case one should be needed. The other two Eleventh Corps divisions hurried through town to the fields just north of the college grounds. There they would try to protect the right of the First Corps and the town from Ewell's troops, who were known to be coming from the north.[9]

After turning his two divisions toward Gettysburg, Ewell sent Maj. Campbell Brown to Lee at Cashtown to tell of his intentions. Brown gave Lee Ewell's message, and Lee responded by emphasizing that a general engagement *was to be avoided until the arrival of the rest of the army.* Brown then hurried back to Ewell, and General Lee continued his ride toward Gettysburg and the morning's battle.[10]

During Brown's absence, Ewell accompanied Rodes's division toward Gettysburg over the Carlisle Road. About four miles from the town they heard the sounds of the battle, and instead of following the road onto the lower plain east of Oak Ridge, they kept to the high ground of the ridge itself. In due course, Rodes's skirmishers broke from the woods on Oak Hill near where the Eternal Light Peace Memorial stands. There Ewell and Rodes saw the morning's battlefield spread before them. They saw Heth's and Pender's divisions formed on Herr Ridge to their right front and the Union First Corps on McPherson Ridge and on Seminary Ridge at the seminary directly in front them. Ewell and his two divisions had arrived at the right place at the right time.[11]

Without delay Ewell and Rodes hurried the four batteries of Carter's Battalion of artillery forward, and their guns opened with "fine affect." At this time too, Maj. Gen. Abner Doubleday, now commanding the Union First Corps, deployed brigades to his right, some to the Mummasburg Road, to face Rodes's troops, and two divisions of the arriving Eleventh Corps were taking position in the fields north of the town. Here it must be said that the Union commanders were thinking primarily in defensive terms—Howard's goal was to hold Gettysburg until the rest of the Federal army arrived. At the same time Lee did not want a "general engagement" until most of his army was at hand.[12]

But Ewell took matters into his own hands. He interpreted the Federal deployment across his front as preparation to attack him. His comment on this in his report was: "It was too late to avoid an engagement without abandoning the position already taken up, and I determined to push the attack vigorously." He suited his action to the word, and Rodes's division advanced. Certainly, at this point in the battle, Ewell, who believed that Lee was not yet on the field, was acting decisively and aggressively. Lee, in fact, had reached Hill's Corps on Herr Ridge west of the town and had denied Heth permission to attack. Then, when he saw that Ewell's Corps was engaged, he gave Hill's Corps permission to advance as well—this in spite of his knowing no more about the enemy than he could see.[13]

Rodes's attack began in an uncoordinated way, but his brigades continued to press the Federal units in their front on Seminary Ridge and east to the Carlisle Road. At the same time, Heth's division attacked toward Seminary Ridge from the west. As soon as Major Brown returned from seeing Lee, and after the fight had opened, Ewell sent him and a second messenger to Early, whose division was known to be marching toward Gettysburg over the Harrisburg Road. Each told Early to hurry along, but Early needed no prompting. He could hear the firing, and when he reached high ground northeast of the town, he could see the Union and Confederate forces locked in battle. As stated above, his artillery rushed into position and opened fire, and he deployed three of his four brigades to strike the Union right. By this time the Confederate forces on the field outnumbered those of the Union, something on the order, perhaps, of 27,000 to 18,000 men; their lines were longer and could envelope the Union flanks. With hard fighting they drove the Union forces from their positions west and north of Gettysburg and forced them back through and around the town to their rallying point on Cemetery Hill.[14]

After seeing that Rodes's attack was under way, Ewell rode east down onto the plain north of the town. As he passed Carter's Battery, a shell exploded near him, a fragment struck and killed his horse, and the one-legged general plunged to the ground. He protested that he was not hurt, secured another horse, and continued east.[15]

By this time, Early's division was driving the Federals into the town. Ewell and his staff paused on a rise, likely that west of Carlisle Road and north of today's Howard Avenue, about a half mile north of the college, and watched the attack. While they paused there, Maj. Henry Kyd Douglas, whose book, *I Rode with Stonewall,* is a Civil War classic, reached Ewell with a message from General Johnson saying that his division was about an hour's march away and would be ready to attack as soon as it arrived and was put in position. At this Brig. Gen. John B. Gordon, whose *Reminiscences of the Civil War* has also been much quoted and whose brigade had just done most of Early's successful fighting, in his enthusiasm claimed that, if his brigade was allowed to attack with Johnson, they could take Cemetery Hill before dark! This claim has been quoted often as an indication of what could and ought to have been done, but there was little basis for it. It is unlikely that Gordon had any personal knowledge of what was happening on and around Cemetery Hill, and Johnson's division would not arrive early enough to make such an attack.[16]

Critics have said that Ewell's response to the bravado of his young officers was to ponder in silence rather than take aggressive action. He asked Douglas to tell Johnson to bring his division "well to the front, to halt and wait for orders." He was also said to have remarked that General Lee was in Cashtown six miles to the rear, that he, Ewell, had brought his corps to Gettysburg as required, and that he did not wish to attack again without orders. (Actually, as we now know, Lee was not in Cashtown at this time but was somewhere just west of Gettysburg.) Ewell's caution disappointed Douglas and some of the young men of Ewell's staff, and one, presumably Sandie Pendleton, is said to have muttered the often-quoted remark, "Oh, for the presence and inspiration of Old Jack for just one hour!"[17]

Ewell followed his troops into the town and to the square. In one article, Lt. James P. Smith, a staff officer inherited from Jackson, wrote that Ewell sat on his horse in the square, chatted, and did nothing while valuable time slipped by. In a later article, Smith described Ewell differently, writing that he was "earnestly engaged in receiving reports from all his command, giving direction as to the disposition of his troops, directing supplies of ammunition and making disposition of a large number of prisoners that had fallen into our hands." Ewell talked with Rodes and Early, and he learned that they favored a continuation of the attack if Hill would attack on their right. He agreed and sent Lt. Smith to tell General Lee this. He then received a message from Lee through Capt. Walter H. Taylor saying, as Taylor remembered it, that the enemy was fleeing in confusion and that it was only necessary for Ewell to press him to take the hill. Neither Lee nor Ewell recalled it that way—Lee said that Ewell was to attack if *practicable* but was to *avoid a general engagement.* Ewell understood that he was to attack only if he could do so *to an advantage.* Lt. Smith returned in due course and reported that Lee could not aid him with troops from Hill and Longstreet.[18]

In the meantime, the generals rode south along Baltimore Street until they were fired on and then left it to examine the Federal position. Ewell saw that an attack could not be made from the town, it would take time for Rodes to reorganize his division to attack, and Early had but two brigades at hand; the other two, Smith's and Gordon's, were to the east, guarding against a threat reported on the York Pike. By this time, it was apparent that an attack should not be made with just the troops at hand. The three generals rode out the York Pike a piece to examine the reported threat there and discovered that it was probably a false alarm. Still, Ewell and Early chose to leave both brigades east of the town for the time being instead of returning at least one to a position in front of the hill. It was at this time also that Ewell sent a scouting party to Culp's Hill, which is to the east and rear of Cemetery Hill. (Its occupation in strength would probably have made the Federal position on Cemetery Hill untenable.) The party returned later with the false report that the hill was unoccupied. The generals then rode to Ewell's headquarters along the Harrisburg Road to await Johnson's arrival.[19]

Johnson's division entered Gettysburg over the railroad bed to the west just before dusk. Ewell asked Johnson to attempt to take Culp's Hill. It was long dark by the time Johnson's division was able to file east of the town, take position, and begin preparations to seize Culp's Hill.[20]

At dusk also, General Lee visited Ewell at his headquarters and talked with Ewell, Rodes, and Early. From them Lee learned that the terrain east of Gettysburg was not suitable for a major attack; instead they believed that any attack should be made from Seminary Ridge. Lee then considered moving Ewell's corps left to that part of the field. Later Ewell, who did not want his corps moved left, went to see Lee, told him that Culp's Hill was unoccupied, and convinced him that Johnson should be allowed to try to take it.[21]

On his return to his headquarters sometime after midnight, Ewell sent Lt. Tom Turner to tell Johnson to take Culp's Hill, if he had not already done so. Turner found Johnson preparing to advance, but learned that Johnson had sent a reconnaissance party to Culp's Hill and found that it was occupied. Even as Turner and Johnson talked, they learned more bad news. Johnson's men had captured a courier bearing a dispatch revealing that the Union Twelfth Corps was at Gettysburg and that the Union Fifth Corps was approaching the town over the Hanover Road. This news called for a change in plans. Johnson called off his attack, and Ewell later wrote in his report, "Day was now breaking, and it was to late for any change of place."[22]

Ewell made diversionary attacks to assist the main Confederate assaults against the Union left and center on the evenings of July 2 and the morning of the third. These attacks, that of Rodes's division excepted, though subordinated to the efforts led by Longstreet, were vigorous and obtained some temporary successes. But all was for naught. On the night of July 3, after Pickett's Charge had been repulsed, Ewell's Corps moved from its positions near the town and at the base of Culp's Hill to Seminary Ridge at the Seminary and north to Oak Hill. This signified the end of the Confederate initiative at Gettysburg.[23]

July 4 was a dismal day for the Confederates of Ewell's Corps, a day of lowering skies and rain. The Confederates knew that their army had not been victorious and wondered why. They were loath to blame General Lee, and they deemed the Army of Northern Virginia invincible. Therefore, others were culpable. Major John Daniel of Early's staff, who had been ecstatic with the success of July 1, was in despair—he thought that they had made a fatal mistake by not continuing the attack of July 1. He wrote that "had we pushed thru the town & charged Cemetery Hill without halting, none can doubt that complete success would have rewarded us." We can well wonder if he was not voicing Early's view at this time. Early wrote that he had been anxious to advance against the hill at the time, but later conceded that such an attack by Rodes's and his divisions would have been repulsed. Many other Confederates adopted Daniel's opinion. They would attribute the Federal victory primarily to Longstreet's alleged failures, but many would blame Ewell for not seizing Cemetery Hill and possible victory on July 1.[24]

The view that its defeat at Gettysburg was a result in part, at least, of Ewell's not assaulting Cemetery Hill on July 1 must have permeated the army. Correspondent Francis Lawley of the London *Times* reported in an article published on August 18 that many soldiers of the Army of Northern Virginia believed that if Ewell had not halted his pursuit on the evening of July 1 the Confederates would have camped on the high ground occupied by the Federals. A correspondent of the Richmond *Enquirer,* who signed his report as "X," echoed Lawley when he wrote in an article published on July 11: "The great mistake which was made by Gen. Lee [and therefore Ewell] seems to have been in not pushing his advantage at the close of the first day's fight, so as to have seized the wooded heights beyond Gettysburg." "X" elaborated by reporting that General Early was said to have wanted to do so for the task then would have been "quite less difficult and far more advantageous in event of success."[25]

Ewell died in 1872. Although fully conscious of the criticism that was directed toward him, he wrote nothing to rebut it. His relief by Lee from corps command after the Wilderness battle in 1864, allegedly for reasons of health, to which he objected, must also have rankled. In 1878, Harriot Stoddert Turner, Ewell's niece and wife of his former aide, Tom Turner, wrote Early a letter of thanks for his defense of Ewell. She stated that Ewell had suffered from "ignorant censure and unjust criticism" and had felt "bitterly the injustice and unkindness of his treatment." She referred particularly to the writings of Col. William Allan, once Ewell's chief of ordnance and later Lee's secretary at Washington College. I do not know with certainty which writings she was referring to, for Allan's articles seem not to have been published until after Ewell's death. However, in 1872, Allan wrote in a letter to Early that General Lee had said that the Confederates could have won the battle if he had managed a simultaneous attack along his whole line, and that he could not get Ewell to act with decision. Allan also wrote later that, had Hill and Ewell followed the Union forces promptly (which they probably could not have done), they could have taken Cemetery Hill, but the more serious mistake was made by Ewell when he did not send a brigade to Culp's Hill before Johnson's division arrived.[26]

Many histories of the war and accounts of the battle written in the nineteenth and early twentieth centuries have little to say of Ewell's failure to take Cemetery Hill one way or the other. Seizure of the hill is mentioned only as something that was not done. Perhaps this was because few of these accounts were written by Southern writers for whom the reason for not doing so required explanation.

Yet, there were some who addressed the matter. The Count of Paris surmised that Jackson would have continued the attack and that Lee, who had confidence in him, would have been willing to have Hill make a diversion. However, he observed that Ewell did not have Lee's confidence to the degree enjoyed by Stonewall Jackson and that Ewell had valid reasons for not pressing ahead. Jesse Bowman Young, who was an officer of the Third Corps at Gettysburg, later became a minister and resided in the town for a time and wrote a history of the campaign, believed that Ewell was right in stopping at the foot of Cemetery Hill. Young faulted Ewell for not having been more aggressive in occupying Culp's Hill with Johnson's division later in the evening. Gen. Henry J. Hunt, commander of the Union artillery at Gettysburg, observed in a *Battles and Leaders* article that a Confederate assault was not practical until 5:30 P.M., at which time the Federals were ready to meet it, and Armistead Long, an artilleryman and colonel of Lee's staff, thought it inadvisable. Cecil Battine, the English soldier–author, stated in 1905 that no one gave the *coup de grace* after the fight of July 1 and that Cemetery Hill could have been taken if an attack had followed sharply on Early's victory.[27]

John B. Gordon, whose writings reflect hindsight and self-promotion, agreed with Battine. In his 1904 reminiscences, he quotes The Reverend J. William Jones as saying that after the war Lee once slapped a table and said: "If I had had Stonewall Jackson at Gettysburg, I would have won that fight!" Gordon bemoaned Early's order for him to halt his attack on July 1, but fails to add that Early did this because Early knew it was better to attack the troops confronting Gordon on their right flank with the brigades of Hays and Hoke rather than head-on with Gordon's brigade.

Instead, Gordon wrote that Early and Ewell could not have been fully cognizant of what was happening, and that he at first refused to obey the order. Since both his seniors were on the field and Early must have had better knowledge of the general situation than Gordon, this statement is hard to credit. Gordon wrote also that, had Lee and Jackson been there, they presumably would have seen the situation as he, Gordon, saw it, and that they would have urged him forward.[28]

No author has had greater influence on the interpretation of matters relating to the Army of Northern Virginia than Douglas Southall Freeman. His *R. E. Lee* and *Lee's Lieutenants,* which were written in the 1930s and 1940s, were among the first modern studies of the war. They have been deservedly regarded as an authoritative word on matters relating to the Army of Northern Virginia and its senior commanders. Freeman, who was not blessed with some of the source materials and the scholarship that we have available today, based his comments on writings in the *Official Records,* supplemented by commentary on Ewell's generalship by several Confederate officers, including Gordon, Isaac R. Trimble, Walter H. Taylor, James P. Smith, Randolph A. McKim, and Jubal A. Early. He trusted some of their writings too much.

Some remarks on Freeman's sources are very much in order. As mentioned above, Smith changed his 1905 commentary about Ewell's dawdling in the town in a 1920 article and presented Ewell there in a much more favorable light, but Freeman seems not to have used the latter source. McKim's article on this phase of the battle was based not on his own observations but on comments of Trimble and Gordon. Taylor, I think, might simply have remembered Lee's orders wrongly, but why Freeman and others who used his writings as a source did not square them with Lee's and Ewell's reports I cannot say. Early's egotistical writings had to do with the evening meeting with Lee and seem not intended to be critical of Ewell even though they make him appear to have been in Early's shadow.[29]

The writings of Gordon and Trimble seem to be another thing. Both were highly critical of Ewell, and I must wonder why Freeman did not question their credibility. The writings of each are obviously self-serving. I have commented on Gordon's already. Trimble's relate primarily to the march to Gettysburg and Ewell's failure to take Culp's Hill.

Maj. Gen. Isaac R. Trimble of Maryland, who had led a brigade under Ewell, had been wounded at Second Manassas, but he had not sufficiently recovered at the time the army was reorganized to command a division in it. Therefore, he joined the army at his own volition in mid-campaign as a general without a command. After Lee chatted with him about Pennsylvania and Maryland geography, Lee suggested that he join Ewell, which he did. Trimble would become an oft-quoted source of information on some matters relating to Ewell and his corps through articles written ten or so years after the battle. In these writings, he described Ewell as an indecisive and bumbling commander lacking the sense to listen to his advice and, with the advantage of hindsight, would claim credit for some correct decisions made in the course of the march to Gettysburg. Because of a lack of other accounts dealing with Ewell in this phase of the campaign, Trimble's writings have had considerable weight. Although Trimble's articles were published after his death in 1888, we know that he was expounding the views contained in them as early as 1883, twenty years after the battle. Trimble was about eighty at the time, and his recollections might have been askew. Certainly, his alleged offer to Ewell late on July 1 to try to capture Culp's Hill if given a division, brigade, or regiment, mirrored his urging General Lee earlier in the campaign to send a brigade from Hagerstown to Baltimore to capture that city. These offers, plus another reported offer to take Harrisburg if given a brigade, do not inspire either confidence in his memory or his good sense. Further, his uncharitable remarks about Ewell seem to be based on hindsight.[30]

What then does Freeman have to say of Ewell at Gettysburg on July 1? Since Lee had little contact with Ewell during the fighting on July 1, Freeman made little mention of Ewell in *R. E. Lee,* Volume III, until he told of Lee's sending Walter Taylor to him with the order to "push those people" and take the hill. Freeman returned to Ewell five pages later, saying that no attack had been made, and discussed the conference Lee is said by Early to have had with Ewell, Rodes, and Early. His conclusion was that the

Second Corps "was operating very clumsily," citing Rodes's attack and Early's concern with a threat coming over the York Pike as examples. He went on to say, in accordance with Trimble's writings, that Ewell had been irresolute and had been thrown off balance that morning by the discretionary orders that had made little sense to the corps commander. Then, according to the first article by Lt. Smith and not the second, which seems more accurate to me, Freeman wrote that Ewell had "remained passive" in the streets of Gettysburg. By his delay after taking the town, "He had lost an opportunity of seizing easily the position on Cemetery Hill that was the key to victory." Later, in summing up the reasons for the Confederate defeat at Gettysburg, he cited Ewell's failure to take Cemetery Hill on July 1.[31]

Freeman did not change his mind greatly in the nine years between his discussions of Gettysburg in *R. E. Lee* and in *Lee's Lieutenants*. In his focus in the latter, in the chapter titled "Ewell Cannot Reach a Decision," he stated, "Inwardly something had happened to the will of Richard Ewell" because, in the field north of Gettysburg, Ewell did not give the nod to Gordon's alleged request to continue his attack. At almost the same time when Ewell failed to express enthusiasm for Gordon's offer to attack the hill alongside Johnson's division (which did not arrive until shortly before dark), Freeman saw fit to present without comment Pendleton's supposed remark, "Oh, for the presence and inspiration of 'Old Jack' for just one hour!"[32]

Freeman then took Ewell into the town, where, as before, he said that Ewell wasted time in the square before being persuaded to go to what became his headquarters site near the almshouse. There Freeman told of two conversations between Trimble and Ewell—in the first Trimble urged Ewell to continue the attack without success, and in the second he urged that Ewell occupy Culp's Hill and, when Ewell did not take his advice, stomped off in "an insubordinate display of temper."[33]

Freeman's censorious treatment of Ewell that was based on an uncritical use of heavily biased sources was not challenged directly until the publication of Edwin B. Coddington's *The Gettysburg Campaign* in 1968. Coddington observed that Ewell's corps contained a number of articulate and intelligent officers (those named above) who wrote of Ewell's activities on July 1. These men, according to Coddington, did not write of the activities of Hill and Lee and discussed the events of July 1 with the advantage of hindsight; they overlooked the circumstances that made an attack on Cemetery Hill impracticable at the time. Coddington held that it was the judgment of these officers, whose writings were published in the *Southern Historical Society Papers,* that Freeman accepted "without much question."

Coddington believed that their statements regarding Ewell raised three important questions: What troops did Ewell have at his disposal for an immediate attack? Was Culp's Hill unoccupied for a considerable period as Ewell's critics believed, and why was the onus of the failure to attack placed on Ewell? Coddington concluded that in time (a long time, judging from Rodes's efforts on July 2) Ewell might have been able to organize an attack force of 6,000 to 7,000 men, and that failure for the Confederates to attack Cemetery Hill should rest with Lee. I concur wholeheartedly with Coddington's opinions and would even add to them.[34]

And now, having sprinkled the preceding discussion with my opinions about the work of several writers about the battle, I will close with what may be taken as fallible observations.

First of all, although new sources on the war are continually cropping up, I doubt that any additional authoritative ones relating to these events will appear. Instead, we will have to make do with what we have and use them as critically as we can.

Many Confederate soldiers and veterans had opinions on what might have happened if they had pressed their attack and it had been successful. Obviously, this was speculation. Had a successful attack been made and the hills taken, the battles of July 2 and 3, as we know them, would not have occurred. But many believed, as I do, that there would have been a battle elsewhere, perhaps along Pipe Creek or, more likely, near Emmitsburg, for after Stuart arrived, Lee would probably have tried to move around or against the Union left, staying close to the mountain passes as he did so. Certainly, whatever done would have been done without great delay—the pressure of an aroused North would have been too much for Lee to withstand, and Meade, tarnished by a Gettysburg defeat, if not relieved, would have been goaded into action by the warriors of Washington and the press.

For my own part, if my reconstruction of events is correct, I must agree that Ewell's decision not to attack was the correct one, and, except for leaving two brigades on the York Pike, I believe that he did well on July 1.

The first question is what were Ewell's orders and did he carry them out? In effect, he had three—he was to bring his corps to the Gettysburg–Cashtown area; he was not to provoke a general engagement until the army was assembled; and, after his troops had taken Gettysburg on July 1, he was told to carry Cemetery Hill, if practicable, but he was not to bring on a general engagement. In response, he had moved his corps to Gettysburg without a hitch, and Rodes's and Early's divisions had arrived in a most timely fashion. Once at Gettysburg, he had opened the afternoon's battle because he believed that the Federals were preparing to attack Rodes's division and had smashed the Eleventh Corps. Then, after the Federals had been driven to Cemetery Hill, he heeded Lee's warning about not bringing on a general engagement. He made this decision in part because he did not consider an assault on Cemetery Hill with those of his troops available to be practicable. In addition, although he did not say so, we can assume that he believed that, if Lee wished him to attack, he would have so ordered.

Why did he deem an attack against Cemetery Hill not practicable? Obviously, he believed that the Union position was too strong for his troops to take alone. The hill is a hundred feet high, its slopes were laced with fences and walls. Union soldiers were positioned behind those walls, in the buildings at the foot of the hill, and in nearby houses in the town. Further, the hill was crowned by a line of over forty cannons. They alone would have been enough to have given him pause. Ewell himself wrote nothing of his opinions of the Union position on July 1, but others did. Rodes reported that the enemy displayed a "formidable line" of infantry and artillery in his front extending "smartly" to his right and to his left in front of Early as far as he could see. Col. Armistead Long, who examined the Union position for General Lee, wrote that the hill was "occupied by a considerable force, a part strongly posted behind a stone fence near its crest, and the rest on the reverse slope." In Long's opinion, an attack with the troops at hand would have been "hazardous and of very doubtful success."[35]

Ewell did not say why he did not attempt to occupy Culp's Hill prior to Johnson's division's arrival at dark. It is likely that he did not occupy it because he believed that he did not have enough troops at hand to do so. Probably he thought that even a brigade sent so far from the main body in the face of the enemy would court destruction. Since he did see fit to comment on the matter in his report, he might well have assumed that the reason for not occupying the hill before Johnson's arrival was so obvious that it needed no explanation.

Ewell did not know the location of Meade's army and how much of it was close at hand. We do. Two brigades of Buford's cavalry division were in the area, together with the infantry that had fought west and north of the town—perhaps 10,000 men in varied conditions had retreated to the hill. Then there was Orland Smith's brigade of 1,600, which had been left in reserve and had done no fighting. In addition, two divisions of the Twelfth Corps had reached the field, and Stannard's brigade of the First Corps and the Third Corps were not far away. An attack against Cemetery Hill could have met great opposition.

What forces had Ewell? First, he had learned that there would be no help from Hill's Corps, apparently not even from its artillery, which should not have been damaged much in the day's fight and could have gone into position on Seminary Ridge opposite Cemetery Hill. The remainder of Rodes's division was at hand, but it had suffered nearly 2,900 casualties and was guarding 4,000 prisoners. As stated by Coddington, it could have become available for an attack in time—too long a time, I should think. Early had only two brigades, those of Hays and Hoke. His other two were off on the York Pike and would not be available for the remainder of the day. In addition, unlike the Federals, Ewell's front had no good artillery positions from which his batteries could support an attack. Beyond that, as Ewell stated in his report, he could not attack from the town, and his brigades could not form for the attack in front of the hill and under the muzzles of the Union batteries on the hill.[36]

Ewell was not a perfect general; he did not trust his instincts, and at times he seemed indecisive. It might be that his service under Jackson had conditioned him to await orders when his superior officer was at hand. There is ample reason to believe that he was tired when on the field—most generals were, I think, and I continue to wonder if the loss of his leg and his fall from his horse when it was shot soon after his attack began might not have sapped his vigor. Yet, apart from his leaving two brigades on the York Pike, I can see no major errors that he made on July 1. Surely, the facts, as we know them, seem to support his decisions. But past opinion, perpetuated in part by critical, self-serving writings, has held otherwise. And, to use the vocabulary of Dr. Richard N. Current, long-held opinions, even when fallible, tend to wear the uniform of incontrovertible fact.

# 4

## The Chances of War:
## Lee, Longstreet, Sickles, and
## the First Minnesota Volunteers

KENT GRAMM

THE field at Gettysburg where the First Minnesota monument now stands was hot and smoky as the sun set, sometime around 7 P.M., that July 2. Some of the men from Red Wing, Winona, St. Paul, and places north and west lay on shuddering ground as the battery immediately behind them thundered, shooting flame and streams of acrid smoke. Until now these men had watched safely for hours—but with growing unease, then alarm— as the battle of Daniel Sickles's Third Corps against the two big Confederate divisions assailing it spread toward them. Facing west, the Minnesotans had stood by the battery, seeing, across a half-mile of mostly open country, long blue lines stretching north along the road ahead, and away southeast into some woods at least a mile from their left. The apex of this bent line was at a peach orchard. Way off to the left a rocky hill and a stony prominence in front of it had been swept by a pandemonium of smoke, volumes of musketry fire, and cheers of thousands of men—not to mention the unnerving Rebel Yell; the roar and smoke had traveled up that line until the peach orchard had been drowned in smoke. The men could, at first, see Union gunners frantically but systematically working their artillery pieces; then smoke had whisped, clouded, and filled the air; then the sounds of battle changed, coming closer, as the blue lines unravelled, and artillery dashed back, and new lines of guns, closer now, formed and opened on the pursuing enemy. Sounds from the bald, rocky hill on the far left did not come closer, however; that anchor of the line seemed to be holding. But the division previously occupying the ground where the First Minnesota regiment now waited had been sent over left of the orchard, leaving the midwesterners alone, their front only a hundred yards wide, to occupy a quarter-mile in support of Thomas's battery—and still the blue line, they could see, was crumbling. Between them and the bald hill thousands of blue soldiers streamed to the rear.

Even worse, the battle had spread along the road a half-mile in front of them as two Rebel brigades swept across the orchard. The position held by Humphreys' Union division along the road had disintegrated during the last few minutes. Most of the line was retreating in orderly fashion diagonally across the Minnesotans' front, across the farm fields this side of the road, opening away from those fields like a door; and now stragglers by the hundreds, not following their units, were rushing in disorder toward the First. Behind them, two heavy Rebel brigades in two long battle lines, with ten or a dozen red regimental flags waving in the smoke: the Minnesotans were ordered down as the battery opened at the Confederates. With Humphreys' infantry drifting northward, there was nothing except the First Minnesota and these crowds of stragglers to defend the batteries placed across this quarter-mile of open fields. Already the long, long Rebel skirmish line was coming through a thin wooded swale three hundred yards in front.

As the first stragglers ran between the Minnesotans, Colonel William Colville—a big man, at six feet five inches he was taller than President Lincoln—shouted for the fugitives to stop. His men, rising and scuffling to help him, realized that another tall officer had just ridden up and dismounted. Even before noticing the striking military bearing and familiar white collar through the dusky smoke, the Volunteers knew it was their corps commander, General Winfield Scott Hancock—the best general and best bellower of profanity in the Army of the Potomac. In a minute, Col. Colville shouted that trying to stop the stampeding fugitives was doing nothing but disordering his own regiment, and Hancock agreed to let the panic-stricken men through. The Minnesotans saw that behind them, a quarter mile away, a dark blue line of battle was coming up to help. But they were too far off. The Rebels would be here on the crest of this slope in five minutes—you could see their first line of battle entering the swale. General Hancock looked along the crest and cried to Colville, "My God! Are these all the men we have here?"[1]

In command of this half of the battlefield since General Sickles's wounding over two hours ago, Hancock had been everywhere, steadying lines, going back to order up troops, placing artillery. He had seen within pistol range what the Minnesotans knew only from battle sounds and indistinct lines: that the Round Top area on the far left was holding firm, but the mile between Little Round Top and the Copse of Trees six hundred yards to the right faced catastrophe. Minutes ago, a Confederate brigade had been thrown back on the Minnesotans' left—where Hancock had just ridden from—but here, with reinforcements five minutes too far away, gaped a wide-open section, a quarter-mile broad, with nothing but sulphurous air between these exposed batteries and those long enemy lines—nothing except this understrength regiment. Looking back toward his reinforcements, Hancock mounted, wheeling his horse; seeing the first enemy regimental flag emerge from the twilight of the swale ahead, Hancock pointed to it and shouted to Colville, "Take those colors!"[2]

> Every man realized in an instant what the order meant [wrote a survivor]—death or wounds to us all; the sacrifice of the regiment to gain a few minutes time and save the position, and probably the battlefield—and every man saw and accepted the necessity for the sacrifice.[3]

Hancock said after the battle,

> I had no alternative but to order the regiment in. We had no force on hand to meet the sudden emergency. Troops had been ordered up and were coming on the run, but I saw that in some way five minutes must be gained or we were lost. . . . I knew they must lose heavily and it caused me pain to give the order for them to advance, but I would have done it if I had known every man would be killed. It was a sacrifice that must be made.[4]

Colville jumped forward and faced his men, shouting, "Will you go along?" Yes, they answered simply. Immediately the colonel ordered, "Forward, double-quick!"[5] The regiment, preserving what witnesses agree was an almost perfect line, trotted forward with rifles at right-shoulder shift. At least three regiments of Alabamians, more than one thousand men, had entered the swale from the other side in two lines. The first line was stepping into the dry creek bed, a meandering S-shaped depression of two to three feet deep, with a fork, surrounded by rocks and a narrow belt of trees.

With perfect discipline, and without a shout or cheer, the narrow line of Minnesotans began to run faster. But of the 270 or so who started, over 100 would not even make it to the trees. Confederate artillery in that peach orchard, a slight elevation, had focused on the charging Yankee regiment. The Rebel skirmish line was firing steadily.

> Bullets whistled past us; shells screeched over us; canister and grape fell about us; comrade after comrade dropped from the ranks; but on the line went. No one took a second look at his fallen companion. "We had no time to weep.". . . It seemed as if every step was over some fallen comrade.

They cross a Virginia rail fence. Their colors have gone down three times.[6]

The Alabama line is jumbled getting across the tortuous little stream bed; not yet reordering their formation, the first battle line comes out of the swale in groups as the second line enters behind them. Still silent, the Minnesotans break into full run, then at thirty yards Colville shouts "Charge!" and the men lower their bayonets as they plunge forward.

> . . . Men were never made who will stand against leveled bayonets coming with such momentum and evident desperation.

The Alabamians in the first line clear out, quite a few being shot as the line behind them fire at the Yankees. The Minnesotans stop at the creek bed and fire their first volley; it is nearly dark down in the swale, but the range is only a few yards. To one Minnesotan, the Rebels seem to be swept from the earth. But they reform just across the dry run; their line overlaps the Minnesotans, extending even past the end of the swale.[7] Now, as the Yankees jump into the dry bed and stop behind trees and rocks for cover, Brig. Gen. Cadmus Wilcox can order his line forward again, brush the hundred Yankees away, sweep onward and take those batteries ahead. The Union line needed five minutes' delay, but Wilcox's men have been stalled for only one or two. It has come down to this. The plans of Robert E. Lee, the field leadership of James Longstreet, the decision of Dan Sickles, the defense of Winfield S. Hancock and George Gordon Meade: they have all come together at this small place in half-darkness.

Hancock was trying to defend the midpoint of the shaft of a defensive line shaped like an upside-down fishhook. After the previous day's fighting, the Army's commander, George Gordon Meade, had found that the hook portion of the Union line had been solidified by his ablest corps commander, Winfield Scott Hancock. The barb was on Culp's Hill, the bend on Cemetery Hill. Hancock's Second Corps defended the near part of the shaft, upper Cemetery Ridge. In the darkness, Meade had ridden along the low rise, misleadingly called a "ridge," perceiving that all of it must be defended, and it must be anchored by a hill (Little Round Top) that we now call the eye of the hook. Robert E. Lee, who knew his Union generals very well, predicted that the Army of the Potomac's new commander would make no mistakes. George Meade knew a strong position when he saw one.

As Daniel Sickles and his Third Corps arrived, Meade ordered him to extend the line from the Second Corps' left onto Little Round Top. The Fifth and Sixth Corps, marching hard toward Gettysburg, would soon be available to support the Second and Third Corps along the shaft of the Federal line. Sickles was not a professional soldier but a politician from New York City—courageous, controversial because of a scandalous past, volatile, apparently erratic, craving the limelight. Sickles's men loved their fighting corps commander. Though one of the army's best fighters while in charge of the Fifth Corps, Meade was in other respects Sickles's opposite. Modest, responsible, careful, well trained, the Pennsylvanian could get irritable and nobody was said to love the "goggle-eyed" "snapping turtle" Meade.

Lee, meanwhile, was trying to think of a way to get at the strong Federal position. He had three corps, each containing three divisions. (Because the Southerners put four or five brigades into a division—whereas some Union divisions contained only two brigades—a Confederate division was the rough numerical equivalent not of a Union division but of a small Union corps.) The Army of Northern Virginia's Second Corps extended around the barb of the Union fishhook; its Third Corps faced the bend of the hook and the near section of the shaft. Lee, not aware of Meade's intent to man all of Cemetery Ridge and Little Round Top, decided to use his First Corps to attack the lower ridge next day.

But the First Corps, under Lt. Gen. James Longstreet, had not arrived on the battlefield. While Lee waited during the morning and early afternoon of July 2, Daniel Sickles moved his Union Third Corps forward from Cemetery Ridge, uncovering Little Round Top, to establish a line a half-mile out in front of his army, extending along the Emmitsburg Road, bending back across a peach orchard, continuing toward but not onto Little Round Top. The two classic Gettysburg controversies are whether Sickles should have moved so far forward and whether Longstreet let Lee down by delaying his arrival and attack.

On the board, Lee's plan looks simple and formidable: threaten the opponent's right with the Second Corps, deliver a right hook with the First, hold the Third Corps ready to assist both wings and crush Meade's center when the time comes. The Second Day's fighting, therefore, mainly consisted of Longstreet's three-hour assault on the Cemetery Ridge line. Because his third division had not arrived, Longstreet used his two, in fragile concert with one Third Corps division, Anderson's.

Longstreet was Lee's doubt and redoubt: the man on whom Lee most relied, after Stonewall Jackson's death, was strongly skeptical of Lee's plan, preferring not to attack Meade's present position at all, but rather to move the whole army around toward Washington and await attack on ground of the Confederates' choosing. Attack he did, nevertheless, but when Longstreet went forward at 4 P.M., the board had changed. A line of pugnacious pawns (the Union Third Corps) stood between him and his objective, Cemetery Ridge. During the next three hours Hood's and McLaws's divisions pounded Sickles's Corps and reinforcements from the Fifth and Second, failing to capture Little Round Top but smashing up Sickles's whole position. By 7 P.M., the southern end of the battlefield was deadlocked, but Meade had stripped the center of his line to achieve the stalemate there. Now two

Confederate brigades saw virtually nothing between them and Cemetery Ridge.

When analyzing an historical battle, we tend to think of war as a game of chess. One player—a general—brings a piece against his opponent's, and one piece by rule takes the other. But in real battle the pieces fight. There might be order over the board as a whole, but in that disputed square there is chaos. (It is easier to manipulate the past than to control the present.)

To continue with the situation in the Plum Run swale:

Seeing the hesitation of the outnumbered Yankees, Wilcox bellows the order for his second line to charge. The Alabamians comprehend the disadvantage to the enemy and, also sensing the Yankees' sudden misgivings, respond with a ragged but irresistible dash into the swale, carrying with them most of their first line.

The Minnesotans, faced with the howling onrush, recoil. Realizing that his flanks would be enveloped almost immediately, Colville saves his regiment from useless slaughter or capture by shouting, "Out of here, boys!" followed by the famous statement, as he turns toward Cemetery Ridge, "Home, boys! Home is across that hill."

The Minnesotans are compelled to share the fate of the Army of the Potomac despite their narrow escape from the swale along Plum Run. Federal regiments marching toward Wright's Georgia Brigade, a quarter-mile north of the First Minnesota's position, are countermarched by an alert Hancock and thrown with temporary success against Wilcox's Brigade—only to be caught in flank and rear by the Georgians as they widen their breach of the Union Cemetery Ridge line. The brigades of Lane and Posey, behind the Georgians, deepen the lodgement and hold it as night darkens. Mahone's Brigade, arriving within a half-hour to support Wright, and the propitiously timed Confederate assault on Cemetery Hill, affirm the military commonplace that a small disaster can breed geometrically accelerating disaster. The Union army, pierced, demoralized, its Cemetery Hill bulwark shattered and its best general, Hancock, wounded by Posey's men, commence the rapid dissolution that results in the July 17 Armistice. From one hundred thirty-five years away, it all looks inevitable.

Of course, the preceding account of what happened after the initial contact between the Minnesotans and Alabamians is fiction—contrary to fact, but how contrary to possibility, or even probability?

Not every historian would agree that those few minutes were the extremity of the Union army. Coddington, for example, downplays the moment, partly on the ground that no real support existed for a breakthrough: "Posey's and Mahone's men would merely have broadened the front but not the depth of his [Anderson's] attack." However, it must be observed that, *contra* Harry Pfanz, for example, Coddington does not believe that Wright actually reached the crest of Cemetery Ridge: "Wright's story of the battle of July 2 should be included among the better Civil War romances." True, Wright's description of Cemetery Ridge is fouled up, his description of "gorges" and "boulders" is "literally beyond belief," but Pfanz observes,

> The important thing is not Wright's fanciful description of the terrain but that the Georgians did go beyond the wall that marked the main line of Gibbon's division on to the crest of the ridge.
> . . . the Third and Twenty-second Georgia regiments, on the Georgia brigade's right, were opposite the gap [between the Seventh Wisconsin and Fifty-ninth New York] and had little opposition in their front. They could have charged onto the ridge somewhere between one and three hundred yards south of the Copse of Trees, and many of them would have penetrated much further than Pickett's men did the following day.[8]

The point is worth belaboring because all this was happening at about the same time, or barely after, the First Minnesota charged.

Regardless of what historians say, we have the opinion of a highly qualified person, General Winfield S. Hancock, that this was an extreme emergency. He had a better view of the battle than any human being had, or has had since. He knew both the large picture and the local conditions, and he understood Civil War battle better than most Civil War soldiers, not to mention twentieth-century observers. He viewed the panorama of the southern battlefield sector from horseback, with information constantly brought to him as he ranged the field, often at a gallop. He knew what was going on not only in the Wheatfield Road and peach orchard and along the Emmitsburg Road, but comprehended the significance of what was happening right in front of him. At one point, riding up to the 19th Maine, Hancock "vaulted from his horse, grabbed the first man on the left of the regiment's front line, and led him a couple of yards forward to the left. He planted the soldier . . . firmly on the spot and shouted, 'Will you stay here?'"

> Hancock loomed magnificently above the smoke of battle as he rode up and down. . . . He seemed to be everywhere at once, and nothing escaped his notice.[9]

Let us, then, submit the question to Hancock. Was the emergency genuine? "I had no alternative but to order the regiment in," he answers. According to him, the battle not *might* have been lost, but *would* have been lost, had he and the First Minnesota failed.

The Minnesotans, contrary to the fanciful "history" perpetrated above, never did flinch or hesitate, and Wilcox's veterans were too shocked, fatigued, and disorganized to pull their ranks together for an immediate countercharge. Losing about two-thirds of their men,[10] including Colville (wounded), the Minnesotans dodged behind rocks and small trees, hugged the two- to three-foot-deep creek bed, and fought it out with the Southerners. As friends were hit all around them, the Minnesotans stayed and fired into the smoky red sunset. They didn't retreat; they didn't surrender; they stayed through the end of a long day's dying and fought it out. For two minutes, four minutes, five minutes, through their private eternities, for seven minutes then ten minutes, they fought, fewer and fewer—fate, Providence, the chances of war devolving on each of them, funneling life and death down into their busy little places on the ground—chaos or the will of God coming too fast for their fumbling hands, too slow for their beating hearts, until they got the order to fall back.

From that perspective, the issues of who was right, Lee or Longstreet, Meade or Sickles, seem both easy and inconsequential. What we students of Gettysburg and war often forget, thinking we can assign victory and defeat to the personalities and plans of generals, is that sometimes it simply comes down to a fight. You can't ask more from a general. It is rare for a plan to assure victory. If a general deprives his soldiers of the proper results of their fight, as Union generals had done before Gettysburg, he has failed. But Robert E. Lee had brought it down to a fight, and his boys almost won it. His plan could not have been foolish. If 270 Minnesotans hadn't offered their own lives and blood, every bit of unselfish courage a human being is capable of, Lee's tactics would have worked. He would not have asked more than to have his splendid infantrymen come to a point where it was finally in God's hands, as Lee would have phrased it, or in the hands of chance or fate—that is, brought down to a fight. At four-to-one odds.

We students of war rightly do not like violence, so we try to eliminate it from battles. It is a matter of maps and movements, in our books; it is a matter of ballistics and tactics, failures and brilliance—but from Marathon to Gettysburg we are shown men and women who fought, who endured and perpetrated chaotic violence, men and women who sweated and stabbed and bled and were shot, who slashed and screamed and shouted, who lived and died like us, contingent and dependent not on plans or anything we can think through, but dependent on the dark, the beyond, we being not gods but mortals subject to accident or intention or chance or absurdity that we cannot see through. This is how we live, for as Martin Luther said on his deathbed, "We are all beggars."

Robert E. Lee has been rightly called "the central character of the battle."[11] The wisdom or error of his plans and his ability or failure to have them executed have made the bulk of Gettysburg controversy—whether one is ostensibly talking about Longstreet, Ewell, Hill, Early, or even Meade. We subject Lee's complicated and apparently contradictory personality to our distant analysis because his actions seem baffling. One of the tersest examples of such analysis is Eisenhower's remark to Montgomery as the two World War II generals gazed at the field of Pickett's Charge: "The man must have got so mad he wanted to hit that guy [Meade] with a brick."[12] From a man who should know why generals do what they do, the remark is suggestive of a profound possibility, namely, that Lee made the supreme error because at the supreme moment he couldn't control his anger.

Perhaps more to the point regarding the first two days' fighting is one of the reasons why Lee tried to control that temper: his religion. Bluntly stated: at the center of Lee's failure are his delusions. That, anyway, is an unspoken implication. He underestimated Yankees disastrously, though he had served with them in the Mexican War. He overestimated his own men. He thought the battle was in God's hands.[13]

Now, Robert E. Lee is famous for his ability to understand his opponents. Who else would have left a skeleton force in front of Hooker twice at Chancellorsville while taking his main body elsewhere? Lee is also the general who inflicted more casualties on U. S. Grant than Lee had in his own army. Robert E. Lee probably gave the Confederacy the three years of life it had beyond the early summer of 1862. It seems a bit of a stretch, in view of all this, to conclude that at the supreme moment at Gettysburg Robert E. Lee simply got goofy.

On the other hand, "Whom the gods would destroy, they first make mad." The most delusionary aspect of General Lee invites some analysis. If it turns out to be a delusion, then the rest of his behavior falls into place. His basic delusion, if it was one, was expressed to a Prussian officer who observed the battle from Lee's lines:

> I plan and work to bring the troops to the right place at the right time; with that, I have done my duty. As soon as I order the troops forward into battle, I lay the fate of the army in the hands of God.[14]

It doesn't matter for the moment whether we agree or disagree that God is present on battlefields. From the times of Homer and the Old Testament, people have believed, and soldiers have felt, that the gods, or fate, or the Lord, intervene. Whether a battlefield is less righteous a place than a house or a ship at sea is quite irrelevant to a faith that believes where God is, and only there, is complete righteousness. While we might not allow ourselves personally to be overborne by three millennia of premodern Western people, we must at least concede that Lee was not an ignorant chump to believe what his tradition held to be a certainty.

It must also be noted that it's a mistake to interpret Lee's philosophy, as stated to that Prussian major, as an excuse for being negligent in making his subordinates carry out his orders, or in anything else. *To bring the troops to the right place at the right time* includes everything. No general does more, unless he steps in beside his privates and fights. When Napoleon, or Stonewall Jackson, or Robert E. Lee brings his troops to the right place at the right time, he has done all he can do; he has done his whole duty.

Beyond that lies the essence of war. Not the panorama of war, and not the war that is subject to historical analysis, but the very essence. Winston Churchill said that anyone who goes to war thinks he can win. Only later do analysts decide that an outcome was inevitable. But *at the time* who knew, for example, that a few colonies could defeat the British Empire, that the greatest technological, economic, and military power on earth could not defeat North Vietnam, or that human beings would invent an atomic bomb? Glenn Tucker quotes Oliver Cromwell as saying, "God would by things that are not, bring to naught things that are."[15] This is exactly what battle is, when it comes down to a fight. Some use the name of God, some refer to fate or chance, but the essence of war is one step beyond the whole duty of generals, as it is one step beyond the knowledge of planners or analysts. In this, Lee was again the realist; he was under no delusion. All generals do what Lee did; some of them just don't realize it.

Did he do his duty well? At several points on July 2, nowhere more so than in the Plum Run valley, the battle came down to a fight. We want our generals to minimize chance by overwhelming the enemy at the point of decision—a Napoleonic principle, Jackson's principle in the valley. What more can we ask than odds of four to one? Jackson never had such odds along the Shenandoah. Did Napoleon have them anywhere? Lee had them in the Plum Run valley at dusk on July 2.

With this in mind we may backtrack to look at the controversy regarding Lee and Longstreet. It is clear—now—that General Lee made a disastrous mistake by continuing the battle after July 1. Gary Gallagher provides an excellent summary of opinions regarding this question. Edwin B. Coddington, Harry Pfanz, and D. S. Freeman accept in varying degrees Lee's decision to continue giving offensive battle. The grounds include the avoidance of demoralizing an army that had won a great victory on July 1, Pyrrhic though it may actually have been; the difficulty of keeping supplied in enemy territory while awaiting an attack; and the difficulty of moving miles of artillery, ambulance, and supply trains around to the south of Meade's army.[16]

The latter is what Lee's First Corps commander, Lieutenant General James Longstreet, proposed: swing around between Meade and Washington City and make the enemy attack us. Alan Nolan in *Lee Considered* observes with Porter Alexander, Longstreet's chief of artillery, that, if the Army of Northern Virginia survived with its trains in enemy country *after a heavy defeat* at Gettysburg, it could have managed to do so before the defeat. Did Lee have good reason for attacking what Alexander called the "really *wonderful*" position Meade's army had been driven into? According to Alexander, "The crisis of this battle, & this campaign, & of all that depended upon it" was not an action on the field but the *decision* General Lee made regarding "the question whether or not to resume offensive battle on the morrow."[17]

Longstreet proposed breaking off battle and moving to the right. Gallagher points out that this would have endangered Lee's supply lines and exposed his flank to Federal troops in Washington. Alexander's idea was that both alternatives were wrong. The best thing to do was line up on Seminary Ridge, "a fine defensive position" that "could never have been successfully assaulted." Meade, Gallagher argues, would have had to attack because his orders were "*to give* battle rather than simply await the enemy's moves." Lee's overconfidence in his army, along with his underestimation of the Yankees, reinforced Lee's native aggressiveness, however, and the "crisis" of the battle issued in Lee's offensive on July 2. However, Gallagher quite correctly adds,

> Had Southern infantry solidified the first day's victory through successful assaults on July 2, as they almost did, many of Lee's critics would have been silenced.[18]

Criticism of Lee regarding July 2 depends, in effect, on whether we think it was possible for the Union army to lose that day— whether we think there was no contest, no *fight*, on July 2. In this respect, Winfield S. Hancock is one of the best friends General Lee ever had. Does anything in the history of warfare entitle us to expect a walkover, even if all Lee's decisions and plans had been correct?

Critics of General Longstreet claim that he felt himself impaired, as Milton says of Satan, when Lee did not adopt his proposal, and so Longstreet in effect sabotaged his own attack. This accusation was first leveled in a noticeable way by General Jubal Early, who wrote in his *War Memoirs,* "Errors were undoubtedly committed, but these errors were not attributable to General Lee."

> . . . we were given to understand that, if the rest of the troops could be got up, there would be an attack very early in the morning on the enemy's left flank . . . there was great delay in the arrival of Longstreet's corps.

Later, Early's attacks became nastier.[19]

Lee's biographer, Douglas Southall Freeman, adopted Early's point of view, likewise defending Lee by attacking Longstreet: "In plain, ugly words, he sulked." Longstreet was "disgruntled because Lee refused to take his advice for a tactical defensive." To force a different situation, Longstreet, alleges Freeman, "delayed the attack." "Longstreet's slow and stubborn mind rendered him incapable of the quick daring and loyal obedience that had characterized Jackson."

By accusing Longstreet of disloyalty and disobedience in his great, indispensable, but not entirely reliable *R. E. Lee,* Freeman established the Lee–Longstreet controversy for more than a generation of historians. Adding to the accusation, Freeman believes Early's highly questionable recollection of Lee's saying, in Early's presence, during the battle, that Longstreet was a good fighter when everything was ready, but that "he is so slow." Longstreet's "sulking" meant that he was late getting his divisions to the field, that he dragged his feet getting them into position for the advance, and that he didn't fight well once in. In *Lee and Longstreet at Gettysburg,* Glenn Tucker quotes Freeman as saying that he had done Longstreet an injustice and wished to "re-write or revise" *R. E. Lee.* But the damage to Longstreet had been done, at least for the time being.[20]

Tucker rescued him. His argument was popularized by Michael Shaara's novel *The Killer Angels* and the movie *Gettysburg*. Tucker shows the dawn attack order to be a fiction relying on the testimony of Lee's bumbling chief of artillery, William N. Pendleton, who had his own inadequacies to divert attention from, and whom few in the army took seriously. "Even Lee ignored him," an officer said, expressing disgust at Pendleton's "presuming to know anything about the battle of Gettysburg." Tucker argues that there could have been no "dawn attack order" because:

(a) plans were still being made the morning of July 2; Lee didn't decide to attack on the right until his visit to the left that morning;
(b) Lee was not impatient concerning Longstreet's arrival but concerning the delay in Ewell's attack (and diarrhea put an edge on that impatience);
(c) Longstreet was on hand and could have advanced at 8 A.M.;
(d) Lee ordered Longstreet not to march until the reconnaissance party returned, which was not until 2 P.M.[21]

Tucker's defense of Longstreet does not cover all the squares: one wonders, for instance, why Lee was impatient for Ewell to attack but not for Longstreet to advance, since both events were supposed to happen together. Still, key accusations against Longstreet are refuted. Take the idea that the First Corps approached the field slowly. Hood's orders from Longstreet were "so imperative"[22] that Hood marched nearly all night, allowing his men only two hours sleep, and reached the field at 6 A.M. During the morning no comment was made by Lee or any other general complaining of a late arrival by Longstreet. Nobody was in a hurry—except Early, in 1880.

As to Longstreet's "dragging his feet,"[23] there is a persuasive argument against it. He requested to delay his march to the jumping-off point until Law's brigade arrived. A hundred years later, General Eisenhower observed that Longstreet, without Law, did not have sufficient strength to attack before 3 P.M.[24] (The actual events seem to be reflected in Ike's judgment.) Lee approved the request, and in fact was with Longstreet during the march.

We have been left with the impression that Longstreet's march was sluggish. However, as Tucker puts it, "Anyone who traverses the ground will realize that the accusation by Early that Longstreet was dragging his feet is unfounded." Some of Longstreet's men marched more than eight miles "over broken country."[25] They were ready at 4 P.M.—surprised to see Sickles confronting them at the peach orchard. But before we turn to Sickles, two more accusations regarding Longstreet should be dealt with.

One is that he was acting like a sullen, fuming little boy when Hood requested three times to be allowed to march farther to the east, circumambulating Round Top, and attack the Federal army—and wagon train—in the rear. It is tempting to believe that Hood's idea would have won the battle, since the defense of Little Round Top was essential to the Army of the Potomac's survival. But the actual attack was made by the east end of a continuous Confederate line going all the way to the peach orchard and, in terms of communications, back to the main line. Hood was asking to put a mile's distance, not to mention a big wooded hill, between himself and McLaws's Division. Not only that, as Tucker points out, but two Union corps were close enough back there to "chew up" Hood's division. I would also imagine that getting in among the Union trains would not have been good: it would have disorganized Hood's men. Lee probably took these possibilities into consideration when he refused Hood's request—for, Tucker claims, Lee was present with Longstreet.[26]

As for Longstreet's not fighting well, we can turn once again to General Eisenhower, who believed "Longstreet was too good a soldier to botch an attack."[27] Hancock, I think, can also rescue Longstreet on this point.

The case concerning Longstreet is not simple. Testimony exists for Longstreet's acting out of sorts—"exceedingly overbearing" and "giving contrary orders to everyone," in the words of Lafayette McLaws.[28] The division commander also thought Longstreet's attack was poorly managed. But Longstreet's abilities and reliability during the war should say something about whether Lee's "war horse" should be accused of irresponsibility and disregard for the lives of men he at all other times valued and cared for, or be accused of disobedience to orders, and, in effect, of treason against the cause he was putting his life forward for. Events that late afternoon should be testimony enough. Longstreet's corps nearly broke the Federal line in more than one place, fighting greater numbers (though they were thrown in piecemeal), and using up thirteen Federal brigades in several hours of the hardest fighting of the Civil War. As Coddington points out, however, Longstreet's two divisions had the advantage of some Federal mistakes, and they "could not have hit the Union left flank at a more inopportune moment for Meade."[29] The man responsible for the largest portion of this inopportune situation was the commander of the Union Third Corps, Daniel Sickles.

"You will see from the statement of General Longstreet that I won the great and decisive battle of Gettysburg," Sickles wrote in 1911, referring to Longstreet's 1902 letter to him, which contained the former Confederate general's opinion that "the advanced position at the Peach Orchard, taken by your corps and under your orders, saved that battlefield to the Union cause."[30] Sickles was writing to a New York City sheriff who almost had to arrest the ninety-year-old general for misappropriation of state funds— the general who had become a multimillionaire and lost it all. The situation typified "Sickles the Incredible," as his biographer calls him: surrounded by scandal, controversy, and friends, the millionaire lost or stole money that was supposed to go for monuments to his beloved fellow veterans at Gettysburg and elsewhere, and was rescued when others came forward with money. One of those who offered was James Longstreet's widow, who telegraphed: "I will raise money among the ragged, destitute, maimed veterans who followed Lee."[31]

Sickles and Longstreet were in cahoots, all right. Helen Longstreet's *Lee and Longstreet at High Tide* included her husband's 1902 letter to Sickles, as well as a preface by Sickles supporting Longstreet's moves on July 2. It might seem that both of them had "made the battle" on July 2 and in a sense had been in an odd, shifting embrace for forty years. But the real force behind Longstreet's assault was Robert E. Lee. Had anything been behind Sickles?

First, how reliable is Sickles's claim that he "won the battle"? If it came from Sickles only, we would alternate between doubt and applause, as did his contemporaries. He was, on one hand, amazingly likeable and energetic: he had impressed and therefore become friends with Presidents Pierce, Buchanan, Grant, and (within limits) Abraham Lincoln. On the other hand, there would have been no shortage of contemporaries to agree with George Templeton Strong: "One might as well try to spoil a rotten egg as to damage Dan's character."[32]

He had a gift for deceiving others. Sickles's greatest notoriety came when, while a second-term congressman, he shot and killed a man having an affair with Sickles's very young wife. His defense, managed by future Secretary of War Edwin Stanton and seven other high-profile attorneys, was the first "temporary insanity" defense in American history. It was successful. But the next day Sickles commented to friends, "Of course I intended to kill him. He deserved it."[33]

The fact that, as the New York *Evening Post* said, "It is certain that the man who makes no scruple to invade and destroy the domestic peace of others—he who, in his own practice, regards adultery as a joke . . . has little right to complain"[34] seems to have troubled Sickles very little. His wives had to get used to his idea of wedlock being, well, one-sided. The point, as Strong wrote in his diary, is that "Sickles is not the man to take the law into his own hands."[35] This is the issue at Gettysburg. He ignored legal authority in shooting the adulterer; he exceeded his authority when he was Minister to Spain after the war; he ignored the federal courts when he administered the Carolinas during Reconstruction; and he violated General Meade's orders at Gettysburg. But there was always a question: in each of the cases mentioned, many thought Sickles did the right thing, from right principles.

Sickles was a violent Tammany Hall libertine with colossal nerve and ambition who happened to have a winning personality. He was also a man of principle, taking back his contrite young wife, whom he loved deeply, after he had spread her titillating letter of confession across the nation's newspapers for his own defense; he would remain unforgiven by the righteous for forgiving such a sinner, his political ambitions virtually ruined. He was capable, in that instance, of a nobility beyond that of his contemporaries and contrary to his selfish interests.

Mark Twain, who lived near the old general in New York City around the turn of the century, said Sickles's conversation was "always about himself" but "he spoke with dignity and courtesy." His talk, along with his self-referential home museum of war relics, was "sweetly and winningly childlike." Like the lifelong child he must have been, "He had . . . everything but a deep sense of responsibility," according to W. A. Swanberg, his biographer. As with King Lear, it could perhaps be said of Sickles that "he hath ever but slenderly known himself." "His mind, so quick and brilliant in appraising others, had a blind spot when it came to self-analysis." If he made a mistake at Gettysburg, he would have been the last to acknowledge it; if he had a responsibility to obey his commanding general's orders (Longstreet comes to mind here), he didn't feel it.[36]

Like the insistent boy he was, Sickles pushed his way through the crowds and marched right out to the center of the Gettysburg battlefield, where we cannot ignore him. It is as if he had the patronage of a goddess to get him there, because he had no business by experience, knowledge, or any of the usual rules, being in command of an army corps. Back in 1861 when the war came, ex-Congressman Daniel Sickles had raised a regiment, which according to the practice of the day entitled him to a commission as its colonel. But the governor wanted a whole brigade, and so Sickles raised it, the Excelsior Brigade, and became its commander. (Congress, remembering Dan Sickles all too well, didn't confirm his brigadier generalship for about a year.) Sickles handled the brigade well during the Peninsular Campaign and proved himself to be "the bravest of the brave" under fire.[37] But he missed everything else until Chancellorsville—back in New York recruiting replacements during Antietam, not engaged at Fredericksburg. Nevertheless, because he was well liked by people who counted (such as Joe Hooker), and because the seniority system, ironically, favored this general who had no military training, he found himself in command of the Union Third Corps when Hooker faced Lee and Jackson in the wilderness around the Chancellor clearing. What happened there prompted Sickles to do what he did at Gettysburg—including the disobedience of orders.

Sickles's corps was positioned at the upper end of a long clearing called Hazel Grove. Sloping upward away from the center of the Union position, Hazel Grove was the key to the Union position because if Lee could put artillery there the Rebels would blast Hooker's center. On the other hand, if Sickles held Hazel

Grove with his own guns, he could enfilade the long gray lines sweeping toward Chancellorsville from the west. Hooker, now unnerved by everything, ordered the dismayed Sickles to abandon his position and come back into the main defensive line. Sickles, being new at this and being a friend of the commanding general, obeyed: he was not up to fighting Joe Hooker.

So Lee took Hazel Grove, put his artillery hub to hub up there, and blew Chancellorsville to rags. Sickles correctly saw himself as a man who had been willing to fight, curbed by a suddenly timid commander despite the acuity of his tactical ideas. Sickles incorrectly thought he was in the same situation at Gettysburg.

The line Meade ordered Sickles to occupy extended along Cemetery Ridge from the left of Hancock's Second Corps, about one and a half miles, ending with, *and including,* Little Round Top:

> Sickles should take up the position from which Geary's division was to withdraw. . . . These instructions [to extend the army's left across Little Round Top] Geary had intelligently carried out, some of his troops passing the night on Little Round Top. . . . Troops do not occupy ground without leaving palpable evidence of their presence. . . . Sickles' orders were repeated to him, by General Meade in person, to extend his command from the left of the Second Corps over the ground previously held by Geary.[38]

The elevation dips rather low as the "ridge" flattens to a level with the surrounding fields before rising to Little Round Top. Looking toward the Emmitsburg Road, Sickles noticed that a peach orchard, where the major road from Maryland and Wheatfield Road intersected, was on a significantly higher elevation than was his own position. The orchard was not on a hill, but the ground sloped down toward the Union position along Cemetery Ridge. Hazel Grove again.

But there were differences. The countryside was open—no flank protection afforded by woods. (Artillery could enfilade this bare salient from both sides.) Also, to get out there, the Third Corps would have to break contact with the Second Corps and leave a half-mile gap between them. At Chancellorsville, Sickles's corps could cover the position they were in, but here at Gettysburg the new line would be twice as long as what the Third Corps could adequately occupy. Most significant of all, there was no position at Chancellorsville that dominated Hazel Grove. But the peach orchard could be pounded from Little Round Top. That hill, and not the peach orchard, was the key to the Federal position. The peach orchard was key not to Meade's position but to one that Sickles had in mind. Sickles, of course, was a salient sort of person.

Daniel Sickles was not a dolt. According to a capable Third Corps general, Regis de Trobriand,

> He was gifted in a high degree with that multiplicity of faculties which has given rise to the saying that a Yankee is ready for everything. . . . He had a quick perception, an energetic will, prompt and supple intelligence. . . . When he has determined on anything, he prepares the way, assembles his forces, and marches directly to the assault. Obstacles do not discourage him.[39]

Sickles, afterwards, must have realized that abandoning Little Round Top to move his line forward had been a terrible error, because he lied to cover the mistake:

> Fortunately, my left had success in getting into position on [Little] Round Top and along the commanding ridge . . . and those positions were firmly held by the Third Corps.[40]

The second part of that statement is as shameless as the first, unless by it Sickles meant the line was firmly held until Longstreet attacked it.

Valiantly defended it certainly was, however. And Little Round Top was held, but by the Fifth Corps. While taking full responsibility for the move without authorization, Sickles claimed that Meade had given him no orders. The evidence does not support Sickles:

> Meade had . . . given Sickles orders to post his corps at least four times. He had provided general orders at midnight at the gate house; very specific orders came in the form of Captain Paine's drawing; Captain Meade had relayed his father's orders again earlier that morning; and now at his meeting with Meade, Sickles' orders came straight from the commanding general; Sickles literally had his orders pointed out to him.

At best, Sickles had acted like an intelligent little boy who refused to get straight what he didn't want to do. In the words of a colleague, Sickles "failed properly to subordinate his views and acts to the instructions of his commander." He had trouble with the truth regarding himself. There is evidence that when he arrived on the battlefield after the first day's fighting, Sickles said, "This is a good battle-field," but some years later Sickles—here certainly "the incredible"—was to write that the person who had actually selected Gettysburg as a battlefield was "perhaps himself"! Shortly after the battle, Sickles wrote that "invincible resistance . . . under Sickles . . . saved the army."[41]

Regardless of whether Sickles was insubordinate, or disingenuous, or wrong about *how* the Third Corps affected the battle's outcome, the question remains: Did his move save the army? His advance to the peach orchard line was made for the wrong reasons. Sickles had neither the authority nor the military qualifications to make it. The move itself was made improperly, in that he reported the advance to no one—not his commanding general, and not to anyone in the Second Corps, whose flank he was abandoning.[42] Even if Sickles had known exactly what he was doing, it would not have made sense unless the whole army aligned on his peach orchard salient. And if that had been done, it would have meant moving off Cemetery Ridge to the Emmitsburg Road—giving up the high ground that John Reynolds and the Union First Corps had fought and died for on July 1.

Yet the question persists. Did Sickles's move force Longstreet to wear out his attack before reaching Cemetery Ridge; and *was it necessary that he do so?* There is disagreement by historians as to whether Meade had been attentive enough to his left,[43] but there is little doubt that once forced to defend that portion of his line, George Meade did an excellent job. This does not mean that Sickles's action was to thank for Meade's attention. One imagines that Longstreet's Corps in full view sweeping to the Emmitsburg Road and across Wheatfield Road would have prompted even a bemused Meade to similar activity.

If Sickles's Third Corps had still been on Cemetery Ridge at 4 P.M., would he have had sufficient support, or did his advanced position buy time for reinforcements to arrive, just as the First Minnesota did on a smaller scale? The Third Corps in effect made a defense in depth, such as Reynolds had positioned the First Corps to make the day before. The persistent question is whether it was necessary to prevent Longstreet from hitting Cemetery Ridge.

Had he done so, his artillery would have been able to shoot at Sickles from the peach orchard; he would have been able to attack in tight formation, in depth, where Lee wanted to land the blow. If he had pushed the Federals off Cemetery Ridge, there would have been no place for the Yankees to fall back to.

On the other hand, unless the high command modified the assault plan, Longstreet would have been raked down his right flank and even rear as his line swept alongside lower Cemetery Ridge; he would have been shelled from Little Round Top; most important, he would not have had to face only the Third Corps. The Union Fifth Corps *could* have reinforced Sickles anywhere along his line almost immediately (they did rush to Little Round Top in time as it was), and other troops were on hand or en route. Meade would have had control over the battle, and reinforcements would not have gone in almost willy-nilly to get ground up in relative isolation. Longstreet's attack would have failed, as happened the next day, without the massive Union losses suffered on the afternoon of July 2. Probably.

The thing is, something *invisible* to armchair tacticians writing a century later *might have happened,* just as it did when, incredibly, Sickles moved his corps forward, or when Chamberlain ordered his bayonet charge, or when the First Minnesota went in with a rush. The most we can say is that Sickles had been alert. Seeing the cavalry desert his left flank, Sickles sent reconnaissance forward—way forward—and discovered "Rebs in rows." He correctly surmised that a big assault was coming his way. But then he did what should not have been done. Generals Meade, Hancock, and others, along with the foot soldiers of the Army of the Potomac, then put together a successful defense. If a boxer drops his guard and is knocked down but then gets up and goes on to win by split decision, should he wonder whether he would have lost the fight if he hadn't been knocked down? Sickles's move at Gettysburg, like his life as a whole, was "the most spectacularly successful failure of the century."[44]

Sickles's enabling error came together with Robert E. Lee's plan, James Longstreet's execution of it, George Meade's defense, and Winfield S. Hancock's acuity, in a dry creek bed where the First

Minnesota Volunteers struck Wilcox's Alabamians. All things had worked together for this, and at that point it could have gone either way.

Chaos theory is a recent trend of study in physics that attends not to simple particles or controlled experiments but to relatively large-scale, complex phenomena that have not received much scientific attention. Chaos theorists are interested in cloud formations and the behavior of molecules in stirred seas of water; they have been attempting to analyze and predict behavior in such chaos conditions as the stock market, heart disease, and the formation of stars. The idea is that chaos is not exactly chaos; it may have properties, or mathematical patterns.

Now, many veterans will tell us that battle is chaos. This is easy for us to understand when we try to imagine a platoon being ambushed in Vietnam: explosions, noise, and lethal projectiles coming suddenly, perhaps from every side, their origins possibly invisible. Essentially the same holds for the Civil War, even though battlefield tactics tried to regularize events in lines, formations, and so on. The soldier is ordered forward; Yankees appear out of nowhere with bayonets fixed, rushing toward us; on the left artillery opens, and in a few minutes bullets are coming from the wrong direction, all while the sun has set and soon we see only muzzle flashes. The learned procedures of a soldier, whether calling in artillery or loading in nine counts, are meant to provide him a productive refuge from the sense of chaos all around him.

Suppose we apply chaos theory to the battlefield. A battle has the complexity of the chaos situation, and—I think this is the chief point—the unpredictability that chaos theory works on. Viewed from above, as in the Russian film version of *War and Peace,* a battlefield is a swirling kaleidoscope of colliding forces behaving like crashing waves and roiling cloud masses; participating from the infantryman's place on the ground, one *feels* the chaos rather than simply views it.

The soldier feels either alarm or invincibility, terror or rage, bewilderment or determination—but were there time for thought (events and training worked against taking time for thought), the soldier would realize that the complex volume of bullets and explosions around him might possibly contain something that will kill him. Maybe it is a sudden and clear insight into the nearly unbearable *contingency* of battle that makes a soldier drop his musket and run.[45]

General Hancock, in the moment before he ordered Colonel Colville to take those Southern colors, saw the awful contingency that the battle around him had reached. In fact, it might be said that Sickles, Meade, Lee, and Longstreet had planned and ordered against each other to a point of equivalency. That point was at the swale in front of the First Minnesota; the point of unpredictability was that minute, as the sun went down.

We apply something very much like chaos theory if we decide that Longstreet, Lee, Sickles, and Meade had delivered the outcome of this fight into the hands of one necessity or another. Chaos, though called a "sensitive dependence on initial conditions," is not quite what Newton meant by the idea of necessity: "Given an *approximate* knowledge of a system's initial conditions and an understanding of natural law [substitute "military principles" here], one can calculate the *approximate* behavior of the system . . . . Very small influences can be neglected." History has known better all along. In chaos, as opposed to Newtonian necessity, there is "instability at *every* point," and a change such as that introduced by Sickles or, possibly, Longstreet is "like giving an extra shuffle to an already well-shuffled pack of cards. You know it will change your luck, but you don't know whether for better or worse." Nevertheless, chaos is also being called "order *masquerading* as randomness."[46] One is tempted to think of Sophia Hawthorne cutting with her diamond on a windowpane at the Old Manse, "Man's accidents are God's intentions."

All theories are subsumed in the very personal contingency of a Minnesotan affixing his bayonet with a hard *clack*. In a second or two the deepest secrets of life and death, will and necessity, choice and fate, of randomness or the "alien work of God" are flashed through a life that up to this moment had seemed a self-contained universe—but now in the smoky red half-darkness is a transparent vessel in the hand of the real force, the real life, whatever it is. Keep silence, Mortal; "Stand in awe and sin not."

Only Sickles blundered. Lee, Longstreet, and Meade did creditable work, which should be all their contemporaries or their posterity could ask of them. But if they cannot be faulted, we are confronted with something human beings don't easily face: mystery. 

From that twilight, in the swale, two roads diverged, one toward Confederate victory, one toward Union victory. The passing there had worn them really about the same. Neither historical, military, nor psychological "analysis" can resolve the mystery. We are about as well off with mathematical analysis—chaos theory—but nothing really works. We are left, finally, with that unanalyzable element present continually in history and in our own lives. We are not left with understanding. We are in the presence of mystery, mystery that has power over great events and over each of us. As the First Minnesota had a choice, so now a choice is ours: despair or awe. We can resign ourselves to the absurd or, like Moses at the burning bush, we can put off the shoes from our feet, knowing that we stand on holy ground.

# 5

## *Eggs, Aldie, Shepherdstown, and J. E. B. Stuart*

### EMORY M. THOMAS

Assistant Adjutant General Henry Brainerd McClellan was perplexed and a little scared as well. His chieftain, Maj. Gen. J. E. B. Stuart, was not himself. Stuart had been riding and fighting with his cavalry command for almost a full month now. Confederate horsemen most recently had the mission of escorting the Army of Northern Virginia out of Pennsylvania, through Western Maryland, and back across the Potomac River into Virginia in the wake of the Gettysburg Campaign.

The day had been one of "incessant fighting," and neither Stuart nor members of his staff had eaten anything for twenty-four hours. At last, about 9 P.M. the commander and his weary staff reached a friendly home near Hagerstown, Maryland. A young woman there adhered to their cause; she had fed them before; she would aid them again. While the woman stirred about her kitchen, Stuart collapsed on a sofa in the parlor and fell sound asleep.

When supper was ready, Stuart at first refused to stir. McClellan had to take the general's arm, hoist him to his feet, and lead him to the table. Then Stuart merely pushed his food around his plate and hardly consumed a bite. When she noticed Stuart's apparent distaste, the hostess asked, "General, perhaps you would relish a hard-boiled egg?"

"I'll take *four* or *five*," Stuart blurted.

Because he was General Stuart, no one at the table remarked on his rudeness. In time the eggs appeared. Then Stuart ate one of them and abruptly left the table and the rest of his eggs.

Back in the parlor after supper, McClellan attempted to lighten the mood at the piano with a chorus of "If you want to have a good time, 'jine' the cavalry." Eventually Stuart roused himself and joined the singing. Later when informed of his boorish behavior at supper, Stuart was appropriately mortified and apologized profusely.

McClellan probably dismissed his general's performance at Hagerstown as an anomaly and nothing more. But a few days later Stuart drifted into an altered state of consciousness again. This time he and McClellan were riding through the Maryland countryside at night. Stuart dictated orders as they rode and then stopped at a turnpike tollhouse to permit McClellan to write down the instructions. While McClellan wrote, Stuart laid his head on the table and went to sleep.

When McClellan awakened the general to read his orders, Stuart appeared alert enough. But in the third of three dispatches he crossed out the names of the towns in Maryland he had dictated earlier and wrote "Aldie" and "Shepherdstown" in their place. In context, Aldie and Shepherdstown, two towns in Virginia, made no sense at all. McClellan had to awaken a man who was vertical with his eyes open and correct the General's corrections, before dispatching his dispatches.

"Harry" McClellan included the "eggs" and "Aldie/Shepherdstown" incidents in his memoir of service on J. E. B. Stuart's staff to illustrate McClellan's belief that "the mind can act and yet be unconscious of its actions." Historians and others who ponder Stuart's conduct during the Gettysburg campaign might well wish to extend McClellan's anecdotes and suggest that Stuart was in some sort of altered state throughout the entire period.[1]

Conventional wisdom and Douglas Southall Freeman begin an analysis of Stuart's actions in the Gettysburg campaign on June 9, 1863, at Brandy Station in Virginia. Stuart had his entire command, nearly 10,000 horsemen, north of Culpeper Court House ready to screen the passage of Robert E. Lee's army down the Shenandoah Valley, across the Potomac River, through Maryland, and into Pennsylvania. But before dawn on June 9, an equal number of Federal cavalry began forcing fords in the Rappahannock River and converging on Stuart's camps. Union cavalry commander Alfred Pleasonton intended no less than to "disperse and destroy" the Confederate cavalry, and the Federals came close to doing just that. Stuart and his subordinates recoiled from shock and surprise and rallied on Fleetwood Hill. In the largest cavalry battle ever in North America, the Southerners held their own and their ground, but just barely.

Brandy Station closely followed a series of grandiose reviews Stuart held to flaunt his strength and, some said, himself. In combination, Stuart's elaborate displays, then surprise and desperate fight with an enemy heretofore inferior might have inspired the "Knight of the Golden Spurs" to recoup his fame or at least to confirm his own vision of himself.[2]

Stuart was barely thirty years old in June 1863. He had been born into a prominent family in Patrick County, Virginia; but he knew from youth that he would have to make and earn his own way in the world. Stuart attended West Point (1850–54) and determined to become a "bold dragoon." He served in West Texas, Kansas, and Colorado, married Flora Cooke, the colonel's daughter, and happened to be in the right place at the right time to accompany Robert E. Lee to Harpers Ferry and participate in the capture of John Brown.

When Virginia seceded from the Union in April 1861, so did Stuart. He secured a colonel's commission and commanded a regiment of cavalry at First Manassas (Bull Run). Stuart achieved fame in June 1862 with his "Ride around McClellan" during the Peninsula Campaign and enhanced his reputation with raids on Catlett's Station (August 1862), Chambersburg (October 1862), and Dumfries (December 1862).

More important than forays behind enemy lines, however disrupting and daring they were, was Stuart's redefinition of the role of cavalry in concert with an army in the field. Stuart made the ground between friendly and enemy forces his arena of operations. He sought to "own" this space and in so doing to learn the disposition and probable intentions of the enemy while he denied such information about friendly forces to the enemy. Stuart's aggressive reconnaissance, the mounted equivalent of "air superiority" or "command of the sea," was his most significant contribution to Lee's army and a major ingredient in the successful Confederate campaigns in the eastern theater of the war thus far.

For all his "modern" understanding of the new mission of mounted troops and his appreciation of the futility of Napoleonic cavalry tactics, Stuart affected an antique facade. By turns he was cavalier, knight, and centaur. He enjoyed kissing pretty women, dancing in his spurs, singing en route to battle, and adorning his hat with a plume. Banjo and fiddle players were in his court, and he included freaks, jesters, and animals in his retinue.

With fame and success had come increased rank and responsibility. Stuart advanced to Brigadier General on September 24, 1861, and to Major General on July 25, 1862. At Chancellorsville, when Stonewall Jackson suffered wounds that became mortal, Stuart took command of Jackson's Corps and successfully directed infantry and artillery for the remainder of the campaign. Stuart had commanded all the cavalry in Lee's army from the fall of 1861. So although Stuart probably wanted to replace Jackson in corps command, Lee decided that Stuart was more valuable in charge of southern horsemen.[3]

Stuart heard his critics both within the army and in the larger populace following his embarrassment at Brandy Station. But he did not have long to brood. Very soon after the battle, Stuart's troopers rode north and began their screening operations just east of the Blue Ridge Mountains. Sharp fights ensued at Aldie on June 17, Middleburg on June 19, and Upperville on June 21. On June 22, Stuart moved his headquarters to the little village of Rector's Crossroads, perhaps four miles west of Middleburg, and opened correspondence with Lee, via James Longstreet, about what to do next.[4]

Lee envisioned an invasion of Pennsylvania that would provoke a showdown battle in the enemy's country. Indeed, he wrote the first of three letters to Jefferson Davis on June 23 earnestly asking the President to bring P. G. T. Beauregard and troops up from Charleston to assemble an army at Culpeper Court House, and so to threaten Washington from the south at the same time Lee and his army posed a threat from the north. Lee sought to raise already high stakes and win the war within weeks.[5]

In accord with Lee's plans, Stuart would continue his screen as long as necessary and then press forward into Pennsylvania on the right flank of Lee's axis of invasion (Richard S. Ewell's Corps). Specifically, Stuart was to "take position on General Ewell's right, place yourself in communication with him, guard his flank, keep him informed of the enemy's movements, and collect all the supplies you can for the use of the army." The question then arose as to what route Stuart would take on his ride northward. He favored circling behind Joseph Hooker's army, between Washington and Hooker, and so once again to "ride around" a Federal army.

On the night of June 23, Stuart elected to sleep under a tree in the rain instead of inside a house with the staff. Very late a courier brought Lee's orders to Stuart's headquarters, and McClellan assumed responsibility to read Lee's dispatch and awaken Stuart. Under his tree Stuart confirmed that he was to leave two of his five brigades to guard the gaps in the Blue Ridge Mountains and later to follow the infantry into Pennsylvania. Now with his other three brigades Stuart was to begin his march north as soon as possible. About the route Lee wrote, "You will . . . be able to judge whether you can pass around their army without hinderance, doing them all the damage you can, and cross the river [i.e., the Potomac] east of the mountains. In either case, after crossing the river, you must move on and feel the right of Ewell's troops, collecting information, provisions, etc." Stuart returned Lee's message to McClellan, gathered his blanket and oilcloth about him again, and went back to sleep.[6]

Next morning (June 24) Stuart made ready to execute Lee's instructions. He ordered his strongest brigades—those of Wade Hampton, Fitzhugh Lee, and W. H. F. "Rooney" Lee, now commanded by John Randolph Chambliss—to gather at Salem. Stuart left behind the brigades of William E. "Grumble" Jones and Beverly H. Robertson, to follow Lee's army after having screened the advance.

Hampton was forty-five, had served in both houses of the South Carolina legislature, and was one of the wealthiest people in the entire South. He had learned to command cavalry by doing so, and by now he was a self-taught success. Fitz Lee was a nephew of the commanding general and a graduate of West Point (1856). He was perhaps Stuart's most trusted subordinate. Chambliss, also a Virginian, had also graduated from West Point (1853). He had left the Old Army to become a planter, but volunteered for Confederate military service as soon as the war began. Stuart liked Chambliss, and, since he had served under Rooney Lee, Chambliss seemed his logical successor in brigade command when Lee suffered a wound at Brandy Station.

Stuart had reasons for leaving Jones and Robertson behind. "Grumble" lived out his unflattering nickname and doubtless believed Stuart was a flamboyant fool. Stuart returned the enmity. Robertson could drill and discipline troopers in his charge, but seemed to lose touch with reality in combat. At Brandy Station, for example, Robertson sat with his brigade in some woods and watched about half the Federal cavalry ride past his position. He never committed his men to battle during that long, desperate day.

At 1 A.M. on the morning of June 25, Stuart commenced his approach to the Potomac. About fifteen miles into the march, Stuart encountered Winfield Scott Hancock's U.S. Army Corps heading north. A detour around the Federals all but compelled Stuart to "ride around" Hooker's army. The Confederate cavalry rode for quite some time around northern Virginia and reached Rowser's Ford in the Potomac on the night of June 27. The river was wide and high there; only with heroic effort did Stuart's cavalry cross the Potomac, and by the time they did, it was 3 A.M. on June 28.[7]

After noon on June 28, Stuart rode into Rockville and paused to destroy a telegraph line and gather supplies. Then the troopers discovered women (girls who attended a school there) and wagons (a train of 150 wagons en route from Washington to Hooker's army). The horsemen chased the wagons, some of them almost back into Washington, and captured 125 of them. The girls flirted with the Southerners and made them reluctant to leave Rockville.

Now Stuart had to escort 125 wagons, as well as find Ewell's flank and the enemy. Those wagons impeded Stuart's movement at a time when he was already well behind schedule. The Confederates reached Union Mills on the night of June 29 and Hanover on June 30. Near Hanover Stuart encountered Federal cavalry; a running fight ensued, and Stuart ordered an all-night march to Dover to compensate for the time he had lost. Only on July 1 did Stuart begin to send scouts to try to locate Lee's army. The same day he ordered the march to bear northwest to Carlisle, where he hoped to find food and information about the whereabouts of his army.

At Carlisle Stuart found two brigades of Pennsylvania militia, and so he had to deploy for battle and shell the town. In the midst of all this, Andrew R. Venable, Stuart's scout, arrived with the news that Lee was at Gettysburg and the battle had already begun. Stuart disengaged from Carlisle and began his march to Gettysburg about 1 A.M. on July 2. The Southern cavalry rode thirty-three miles and arrived on the field behind the left flank of Ewell's corps on July 2.[8]

Stuart rode ahead of his men and found Lee on Seminary Ridge sometime in the afternoon. "Well, General Stuart, you are here at last," is the most credible account of Lee's greeting.[9] Coming from Lee, such words were reproof; but whether he said these words or others, Lee never after pursued the matter of Stuart's absence beyond noting in his formal report on the campaign, "The movements of the army preceding the battle of Gettysburg had been much embarrassed by the absence of the cavalry." Even then he followed this statement with a narrative of Stuart's march to explain why the cavalry had been absent.

If Robert E. Lee did not censor Stuart for his absence at Gettysburg, he was one of very few people, then and since. Lee's staff officer Charles Marshall supposedly wanted Stuart shot and did not seem to care very much whether Stuart's execution occurred before or after a court martial. After the war was over, Stuart's conduct in the Gettysburg campaign was often a factor in the interminable wrangling among aging veterans over who did what to win or lose the war. Confederate Gen. Jubal A. Early even switched sides in mid-controversy, retracting his criticism of Stuart in order to heap greater blame on James Longstreet for defeat at Gettysburg.[10]

Historians have been more even-handed than participants as a general rule. Douglas Southall Freeman, for example, asserted, "From the time the Army entered Pennsylvania, it was blinded by the absence of Stuart. Nothing was comparable to this in preparing the way for a tragedy." But Freeman also blamed Lee, Ewell, and Longstreet for ample contributions to the tragedy Stuart had prepared. Edwin B. Coddington in *The Gettysburg Campaign: A Study in Command,* still the best study of the battle, observed, "If, as Stuart's accusers insisted, the absence of cavalry permitted Lee to be surprised into an unfortunate encounter of major proportions at Gettysburg, they overlooked two important elements in the situation. Meade was just as surprised, and the initial advantage lay with Lee."[11]

Still, the indictment persists that Stuart rode off in search of glory leaving Lee helpless in the presence of his enemies. Michael Shaara won the Pulitzer Prize in 1975 for *The Killer Angels,* his novel about Gettysburg. To the degree that Shaara presented a villain, or perhaps better an anti-hero, that character was Stuart. Here is some of what Shaara wrote. "The cavalier, a beautiful man, was lounging against a white rail fence, in a circle of light, a circle of admirers." Marshall approaches Longstreet waving a sheaf of papers, "He was joyriding for the fun of it. He captured about a hundred enemy wagons. And left us blind in enemy country. Criminal, absolutely criminal. Several of us have agreed to ask for court-martial, but General Lee says he will not discuss it at this time." And finally Stuart confronts Lee. "Without your cavalry we are blind, and that has happened once but must never happen again." Stuart absorbs Lee's rebuke. "After a moment he reached down and unbuckled his sword, theatrically, and handed it over with high drama in his face. Lee grimaced, annoyed, put his hands behind his back, half turned his face. Stuart was saying that since he no longer held the General's trust, but Lee interrupted with acid vigor."

"I have told you that there is no time for that."

This scene from *The Killer Angels,* faithfully recreated, plays again in the feature film *Gettysburg* (1994), based on Shaara's novel. Of course the novel and film are fiction. Stuart in reality did not attempt to hand over his sword to Lee. But the novel-reader and the film-viewer believe he did, and, if not, he certainly should have done so.[12]

Stuart has not been devoid of defenders to justify his actions in the Gettysburg campaign. McClellan, his principle staff officer, entered the war of words after the war. John S. Mosby, the famous partisan and "Gray Ghost" who served Stuart as a scout, was rabid in his defense of his former commander. And most recently

Mark Nesbitt has published *Saber and Scapegoat: J. E. B. Stuart and the Gettysburg Controversy,* a thorough brief that exonerates Stuart from any blame on all counts ever raised against him. Nesbitt summons all of the criticisms made of Stuart's conduct before Gettysburg:

- Stuart's absence brought on the Battle of Gettysburg.
- Stuart left Lee with no cavalry to do the main army's reconnaissance.
- Stuart was "late" for the Battle of Gettysburg.
- Stuart was not following orders.
- Stuart was on a joyride around the Union army, wasting time seeking glory and fame.

He pronounces them all "patently false" and pretty well proves his points.[13]

Absolving Stuart of all these sins of commission, however, cannot relieve him of responsibility for "leaving undone some things that he ought to have done." Stuart in effect disappeared from the Army of Northern Virginia for six crucial days. Lee learned that Hooker had crossed the Potomac and that Meade was in command of the Army of the Potomac; but Lee did not learn these important facts from Stuart. Stuart had no idea where either army was and never seriously tried to find out until July 1. Of course, several circumstances mitigated Stuart's conduct. Stuart did not do anything wrong. But neither did Stuart make any meaningful contribution to Confederate success while he lurched through his private wilderness in south-central Pennsylvania.[14]

All of this angst and ink expended over Stuart's conduct before his arrival at Gettysburg on July 2 is interesting in an antiquarian sort of way. But the issue is only important to the extent that Stuart's actions did or did not affect the outcome of the Battle of Gettysburg. Jubal Early was hardly an objective witness; nor have many people accused Early of possessing monumental military genius. Yet Early, in the course of the campaigns waged well after the fact by feuding old warriors, may well have spoken an insightful verdict in the case:

> I have never thought that our failure at Gettysburg was due to the absence of Stuart's cavalry though I can well understand the perplexity and annoyance it caused General Lee before the enemy was found. He

was found, however, without the aid of cavalry, and when found, though by accident, he furnished us the opportunity to strike him a fatal blow.

In other words, Stuart's absence made little difference; with or without Stuart, Lee would have fought at Gettysburg more or less as he did.[15] Lee certainly had the option of not fighting at Gettysburg, yet he seemed to believe, with good reason, that this campaign might well be his last chance to win a battle of annihilation and thus the war. In fact, Lee said as much in several letters and conversations before and during the battle. In a letter to Jefferson Davis written June 10, 1863, Lee plainly stated his opinion on the relative strength of his own army and that of the enemy. "We should not . . . conceal from ourselves that our resources in men are constantly diminishing, and the disproportion in this respect between us and our enemies, if they continue united in their efforts to subjugate us, is steadily augmenting." Lee pointed out the dynamic of diminishing and augmenting strengths in the course of counseling encouragement to the peace faction in the United States.[16]

Perhaps Lee's clearest expression of his vision for the campaign occurred in a conversation with Isaac Trimble on June 27 or 28:

> Our army is in good spirits, not overfatigued, and can be concentrated on any one point in twenty-four hours or less. I have not yet heard that the enemy have crossed the Potomac and am waiting to hear from General Stuart. When they hear where we are, they will make forced marches to interpose their forces between us and Baltimore and Philadelphia. They will come up, probably through Frederick, broken down with hunger and hard marching, strung out on a long line, and much demoralized, when they come into Pennsylvania. I shall throw an overwhelming force on their advance, crush it, follow up the success, drive one corps back on another, and by successive repulses and surprises, before they can concentrate, create a panic and virtually destroy the army.

According to Trimble, Lee then pointed to the town of Gettysburg on his map and said, "Hereabout we shall probably meet the enemy and fight a great battle, and if God gives us the victory, the war will be over and we shall achieve the recognition of our independence."[17]

Soon after Lee spoke with Trimble, on the evening of June 28, came the news that the Army of the Potomac had already crossed its namesake and that George G. Meade had replaced Hooker in command. Lee heard all of this from James Longstreet's "scout" (i.e., spy) Harrison; certainly Lee should have learned it from Stuart. But he did know where the enemy was, and he was able to concentrate his army before Meade arrived in strength. Had Stuart been in constant contact, not much about the situation would likely have been different.[18]

On June 29, Lee ordered his concentration and reportedly said that afternoon, "Tomorrow, gentlemen, we will not move to Harrisburg, as we expected, but will go over to Gettysburg and see what General Meade is after." As it happened, Lee did not reach Gettysburg until July 1, and when he arrived the battle was in progress. After observing for a time, he proclaimed to Longstreet, "If the enemy is there, we must attack him."[19]

Some of these words that men remembered Lee speaking he may or may not have said. His listeners recalled conversations in some cases twenty years old. But Lee's actions spoke clearly to reinforce the vision he had for his march into Pennsylvania. Lee ordered attacks on July 2. He ordered attacks on July 3. Only after his assaults had failed and he had lost a third of his army did Lee elect to disengage and return south. It is difficult to imagine Lee doing anything differently if Stuart had been on hand and able to inform Lee of the strength and dispositions of Meade's army. Lee perceived Gettysburg as a "moment of truth," and Lee did not shrink from such moments. When it was over, Lee admitted that Southern failure was all his fault, and he was right.

If Stuart is guiltless in all the charges and countercharges about his actions before he reached the battlefield at Gettysburg and if Lee were going to have his showdown regardless of Stuart's absence as the two armies converged, then what remains to say about the "Flower of Cavaliers" and his horsemen? Contrary to conventional wisdom, the answer is "Plenty."

In all the emphasis and attention heaped on Stuart's role in the Gettysburg campaign before he reached the scene of the great battle, his contemporaries and historians alike all but ignore Stuart's significant cavalry battle on July 3. To be sure, reasons exist to overlook the mounted action on the battle's third day. George Pickett's charge on the center of the Federal line was the climactic moment in the conflict and maybe in the entire war. Indeed,

Pickett's charge is the most celebrated forty minutes in all of American military history.

Cavalry action on the third day calls first to mind the tragic dash of Union troopers led by Elon J. Farnsworth. Goaded into folly by Judson Kilpatrick, Farnsworth led a mounted attack on the Southern right flank about 5:30 in the afternoon. Farnsworth preserved his honor, but lost his life in the disaster.[20]

Stuart's participation in the events of July 3 usually rates no more than an afterthought, a meager mention, in accounts of Gettysburg. The cavalry battle that took place beyond the Confederate left flank about three miles east of Gettysburg does not even appear on most maps of the battle. Yet that battle was ferocious and for those who witnessed or participated, it must have seemed every bit as dramatic as Pickett's charge. Further, Stuart's cavalry fight generated one of the most fascinating might-have-been/what-ifs in all of American military history.[21]

Southern troopers spent some of the morning securing more ammunition, having expended almost all they had just getting to this battlefield. Then around noon Stuart led two of his brigades (those of Chambliss and Albert G. Jenkins, whose horsemen had accompanied the main army) up the York Pike. He ordered Hampton and Fitz Lee to follow his march.

Stuart posted his men on "a commanding [Cress's] ridge" that "completely controlled a wide plain of cultivated fields stretching toward Hanover, on the left, and reaching to the base of the mountain spurs, among which the enemy held position." He kept his troopers in the woods out of sight, but sent an artillery piece forward and directed fire randomly across his front; as though to announce his presence. Then Stuart sent dismounted troopers from Jenkins's brigade into the open to a barn and fence-line belonging to a family named Rummel.[22]

From the Federal side came similar actions—artillery fire and a line of dismounted cavalry as skirmishers. In command of Federal cavalry opposite Stuart's men was David M. Gregg. Approximately Stuart's age (thirty), Gregg, a native of Pennsylvania, graduated from West Point one year after Stuart. Gregg had come to this war from service on the western frontier and steadily advanced from command of a regiment (8th Pennsylvania Cavalry) to division command. Now he had about 3,000 horsemen confronting Stuart on the other side of the Rummel farm. Both sides reinforced their skirmish lines and the fight over Rummel's farm grew intense. Then Gregg sent mounted units forward into the fray. More men entered the conflict from both sides, both mounted and dismounted.

At last Stuart dispatched the greater portions of Hampton's and Fitz Lee's brigades, columns of squadrons with an axis of advance directed almost due south toward the Spangler house on the Hanover Road. Like Lee, Stuart had embraced a moment of truth.[23] A Federal officer at the scene recalled:

> A grander spectacle than their advance has rarely been beheld. They marched with well-alighted fronts and steady reins. Their polished saber-blades dazzled in the sun. All eyes turned upon them. . . . Shell, and shrapnel met the advancing Confederates and tore through their ranks. Closing gaps as though nothing had happened, on they came. As they drew nearer, canister was substituted . . . for shell, and horse after horse staggered and fell. Still they came on.

Then Gregg launched a charge of his own, also in column of squadrons. By this time the Southerners had lost much of their formation, but none of their spirit.

> As the two columns approached each other the pace of each increased, when suddenly a crash, like the falling of timber, betokened the crisis. So sudden and violent was the collision that many of the horses were turned end over end and crushed their riders beneath them. The clashing of sabers, the firing of pistols, the demands for surrender and cries of the combatants now filled air.

At the head of the Union stampede was a twenty-two-year-old general named George Armstrong Custer. He later claimed to have driven the Confederates from the field, but then the Ohioborn Custer usually boasted of more than he actually achieved. Only a few weeks previously, Custer had been a captain; now he was the youngest brigadier general in the United States army.

A Confederate officer in Jenkins's brigade was in a good position (near the Rummel barn) to describe the action:

> The charging of the mounted cavalry on both sides took place in front and to the left of the line of our dismounted men. Time and again the Confederates would charge the Federals driving them back to their

reserve dismounted men, and then the Federals would charge our men back to our reserve. Backward and forward the battle raged, and the fire of the dismounted lines and the artillery went on for hours.

The most effective actions taken on the Northern side were mounted thrusts against the flanks of the Southern column. These attacks broke whatever remained of the Confederate formation and reduced the fighting to bunches of men whirling about the field.

Stuart's horsemen withdrew, and the battle concluded on the Rummel farm where it had begun. In tactical terms the conflict ended in a draw; both Stuart and his foes claimed more for their efforts than they accomplished.[24]

Because Stuart had the greater opportunity, he had the most to lose. And lose he surely did. The Southerners apparently outnumbered their enemy in this place, in men actually engaged, by two to one—around 3,000 Federals against twenty regiments of Confederates, maybe 6,000 horsemen. Southerners could ill afford to squander such odds.[25]

Had Stuart been able to overwhelm his enemies, the direction of his advance would have carried his troopers into the rear of those Federal foot-soldiers on Cemetery Ridge. And had Pickett's charge succeeded in breaking the Union battle line, Stuart would have been in the right place at the right time to provoke a rout. Stuart might have become the hero of a climactic battle that destroyed Meade's army and quite possibly won the war. Even had Pickett failed as he did, Stuart still had the chance to thunder down on the Federal infantry posted on Cemetery Ridge and rescue the day for the Confederacy. It is doubtful that Lee tried to coordinate the attack upon Cemetery Ridge with Stuart's assault on the Federal rear. But what if it had worked that way? Pickett and Stuart would have shaken hands on Cemetery Ridge and prepared to destroy portions of Meade's army at their leisure.

But of course both Stuart and Pickett failed to drive their enemies. Given Stuart's supposed numerical superiority at the point of his attack, the question becomes why didn't Stuart prevail on that plain beneath Cress's Ridge? To answer that question and to understand Stuart's conduct in this campaign, it becomes necessary to reconsider the previous month in the experience of the Confederate cavalry and their commander.

One summary of the story of Stuart and his horsemen from Brandy Station until their arrival on the field at Gettysburg is above, told from the perspective of those who have analyzed the Gettysburg campaign in its entirety. In that story the emphasis is on Lee and the Army of Northern Virginia; Stuart and his cavalry are important because they were absent. Stuart's route and the detours, diversions, and delays that beset his ride are consequential only because they deprived Lee of his "eyes" until he and everyone else could see more of the Northern host than they wished.

Now it is appropriate to tell this story again, this time from the perspective of horses, horsemen, and J. E. B. Stuart. Now the focus is on those who endured this arduous odyssey. The point of this story, so obvious that it could easily be overlooked, is the exhaustion that routes, roads, detours, skirmishes, diversions, battles, delays, hunger, pace, and relentless stress inflicted on animals, men, and Stuart.

One month before the climactic conclusion of the Battle of Gettysburg (June 3, 1863), Stuart was just outside of Culpeper Court House preparing for his grandest review. The review occurred on June 5, and the Southern Troopers repeated their exertions for the commanding general on June 8. Next day Stuart and his men suffered surprise and desperate combat in the Battle of Brandy Station. Within a week after Brandy Station, Stuart rode north, and on June 17 at Aldie commenced five days of moving and fighting near Aldie, Middleburg, and Upperville.

During these running fights, Stuart became convinced that some of his enemies had singled him out as a target. "God saved me," he wrote to his wife Flora, "the First Dragoons tried to kill me." McClellan remembered:

> There was one feature of Stuart's conduct on this day [Upperville] which attracted my attention. Until the battle reached Upperville he personally participated in it but little, remaining, however, in close observation of the field. I asked the reason of this unusual proceeding, and he replied that he had given all necessary instructions to his brigade commanders, and he wished them to feel the responsibility resting upon them, and to gain whatever honor the field might bring.

This sounds lame. Was Stuart unsure of himself at this point, in the wake of Brandy Station, attempting to carry out a difficult assignment? For the first time in the war, did Stuart fear for his life? Was he suffering a failure of nerve? This is a very different Stuart from the cocksure cavalier seeking to recover his fame.[26]

After the engagement at Upperville (June 21), Stuart withdrew to Rector's Cross-Roads on June 22 and the next evening received orders to set out for Pennsylvania. With his three best brigades, Stuart embarked at one o'clock on the morning of June 25. In the past Stuart's forays into enemy country followed periods of rest and refreshment—indeed boredom. Stuart had planned his routes carefully, had arranged for guides to be available when needed, and had taken with him only fit troopers mounted on fresh horses. This time Stuart had none of these luxuries. The best he could do was to select veteran brigades commanded by men he trusted. And this time the ride/raid followed four major battles and nearly constant motion in the field for the previous sixteen days.

Almost as soon as the march began, Stuart fell well behind schedule. The detour around Federal infantry involved a ride of eighty miles to Rowser's Ford on the Potomac. Then the crossing through high water inspired McClellan to state, "No more difficult achievement was accomplished by the cavalry during the war."[27]

Soon after the crossing, the Confederates encountered the Union wagon train at Rockville. Capture cost more time and energy, and Stuart only made about twenty-two miles on June 28. On June 29, Stuart covered only twenty-five miles, from Cooksville to Union Mills. Coddington describes the mood that probably pervaded the march: "To those who participated, Stuart's expedition around the Army of the Potomac was a horrible experience with the nightmarish qualities of a bad dream. As they frantically went through the motions of hurrying, their appointed destination seemed to fade farther and farther in the distance."[28]

From Union Mills, the Southern march was still north toward Hanover. But about ten o'clock on the morning of June 30, the Confederate horsemen found enemy cavalry at Hanover. Stuart had to deploy his men and fight once more. And following the fight around Hanover, Stuart decided to ride all night to try to recover some of the time lost thus far.

During this forced march many men and horses reached the limits of their endurance. And within the captured wagon train,

"The mules were starving for food and water, and often became unmanageable. Not infrequently a large part of the train would halt in the road because a driver toward the front had fallen asleep and allowed his team to stop." Stuart observed, "Whole regiments slept in the saddle, their faithful animals keeping the road unguided. In some instances they fell from their horses, overcome with physical fatigue and sleepiness." Stuart permitted a brief rest at Dover on the morning of July 1 and then pressed on toward Carlisle. By this time, Stuart reported, "Our rations were entirely out." Yet enemy soldiers, albeit militia, occupied Carlisle, and Stuart had to halt, unlimber artillery, and engage in a skirmish of nerves, by turns demanding tribute and opening fire when the enemy refused his demands.[29]

Members of Stuart's staff recalled seeing one trooper sleeping while leaning against a fence not ten feet away from an artillery piece firing rapidly. Another man fell asleep while climbing a fence—one leg over the fence, fast asleep.[30]

Then came the summons to join the army at Gettysburg. The Confederates had to quit Carlisle before they had secured food, much less rest. The march to Gettysburg, one veteran declared, was "the most severe I ever experienced."[31]

Stuart's troopers must have been a sorry sight when they arrived at the battle zone near Gettysburg. With Pickett's Division, Stuart's three brigades were those rare Confederates who had not yet engaged the enemy in the great battle. However, these "fresh" troops would be less than worthless until they had had rest and food. One trooper understated:

> What a pleasing assurance to think that after so many days and nights of incessant toil, we were within our lines & there would be some prospect for rest, for at least one night!! . . . Men and horses very tired & hungry.

Men in the 4th Virginia looked forward to their first sleep in two and a half days. One of them remembered, "We laid down in a stubble field and were soon fast sleep."

Stuart initially ordered that his command "be kept in the saddle all night." Perhaps he was trying to compensate for his protracted absence and so wanted to demonstrate vigilance with a vengeance. Soon Stuart's motives became moot. Subordinate commanders informed him that his orders were out of the question. So Stuart rescinded them rather than confront mutiny by slumber.[32]

When he reached the battle lines at Gettysburg, Stuart had ridden at the very least 210 miles during a period of eight days. And of course those days and nights ran together as a consequence of marching all night and beginning "days" at 1 A.M. The cavalry had traveled about twenty-six miles per day; but this travel included excursions to destroy railroad tracks and cut telegraph wires, and beyond Rockville the Confederates had to shepherd mules, wagons, and prisoners, all of whom seemed to be in a conspiracy to impede the march.[33]

To place the march to Gettysburg in perspective, Stuart's Pamunkey Raid or "Ride Around McClellan" in June 1862 covered 100 miles in three days. The Catlett's Station Raid was essentially a two-day dash of seventy miles. Chambersburg was a three-day raid over 126 miles, and the Dumfries Raid covered 110 miles in four or five days. These previous missions had called forth maximum energy for relatively short periods. Gettysburg required nearly constant exertion throughout eight days. Those eight days followed more than two weeks of combat and hard riding. And never was there the prospect of completing the task and enjoying a respite from riding and fighting. Stuart and his men knew that even more intense combat awaited them when they overtook Lee's army.[34]

All of this energy expended took its toll on men and horses. An officer in the 9th Virginia Cavalry, for example, had to find another horse on July 6 because his mount had broken down. The new horse was the sixth he had ridden since embarking on this campaign. The 9th Virginia offers another index of the cost of so much action during a period of about a month. In May 1863, the regiment counted 713 officers and men; on July 3, the day of the cavalry clash at Gettysburg, an estimated 80 troopers were present for battle.

Circumstances in the 9th Virginia Cavalry were not anomalous. A captain in the 13th Virginia Cavalry wrote of his eighteen days and nights in the saddle, "No man can stand more, and I never wish to be called on to stand this much again. I had one horse killed under me and rode three others down." Then in the cavalry battle of Gettysburg, the same officer reported: "My Company lost four men killed, two men wounded, and my 1st Lt. Edwards received a sabre cut on the shoulder. My Company [supposedly at least sixty-four men] numbers for duty two officers & fifteen men. I have sixteen men without horses, most of the horses were killed in the different fights."

One careful estimate posed the strength of Chambliss's entire brigade on July 3 to have been 200. Of 320 men who composed the 2nd South Carolina Cavalry in mid-June, only 137 fought at Gettysburg. The rest were casualties of some sort between Aldie and Gettysburg. By the end of the battle on July 3 barely 100 men remained in their saddles.[35]

In the cavalry, not only the soldier, but his horse as well, had to be fit for duty for them to take part in combat, march, or anything else active. And in the Confederate cavalry, men, not the government, supplied the horses. So if a trooper found himself afoot, he usually remained afoot for some time.

Attrition on the march to Gettysburg may indeed have accounted for the performance of Stuart's cavalry on July 3. Stuart may have committed to battle twenty regiments; but if those regiments to any degree resembled the 9th Virginia, the 13th Virginia, or the 2nd South Carolina, the number of horsemen engaged was much smaller than the unit designations indicated. Did Stuart have at Gettysburg as many as 6,000 able horsemen?

And what about the toll exacted of Stuart? What effect did so many days and nights of activity, responsibility, and stress have on the cavalry commander? The best guess about the reason that "Stonewall" Jackson made camp instead of continuing his march to battle on June 26, 1862, is stress fatigue. Similar assumptions explain Jackson's determination to sit under a tree for five hours on June 30, 1862, at White Oak Swamp. "Fog of war," stress fatigue, whatever—Jackson's body told his mind to stop, and Jackson did nothing. The same sort of syndrome may have affected Stuart. But Stuart's body continued to function, even while his mind disfunctioned.[36]

For all his display and bravado, Stuart was at base a consummate professional soldier. Why did so careful a commander become careless? Why did he wait so long to dispatch scouts and staff to find Lee's army? What made him so obsessed with retaining his captured wagons, even though he should have realized that they slowed his pace and the obligation to protect them doomed his primary mission? Did Stuart's "fog of war" afflict him with "tunnel vision," such that he focused so intently on the next town or assumptions already invalid that he lost touch with the larger realities involved in this campaign? Did the combination of Brandy Station, Aldie, Middleburg, and Upperville shake his confidence to the extent that he became timid, more fearful of losing than he was eager to win? Practically everyone who knew Stuart made a point of saying or writing that he led by example; he was a "come on," rather than "go on" leader. Then why did he restrict himself to a "go on" posture during this campaign?

Why, having kept those 125 wagons hanging about his neck like a millstone, did Stuart permit his men and horses to be hungry or "out of rations?" Stuart's staff officer W. W. Blackford fed his horses Manassas and Magic all the oats they could eat from one of the wagons and slung a bag over his saddle for future feeds. Why were any horses ever hungry after Stuart's men captured those 125 wagons?[37]

These questions can have no definitive answers. But the fact was that Stuart did not seem himself during the Gettysburg Campaign. There should be some reason for his behavior. This was the same person who was able to lie down on the ground, arrange a rock for a pillow, and fall instantly asleep during the Second Manassas (Bull Run) Campaign. Yet the moment he heard Lee speak his name, Stuart came up from his nap, offered to deliver a message, and rode off saying "Jine the Cavalry" at the top of his lungs. Stuart took understandable pride in his capacity to come rapidly awake under all circumstances. If strain and fatigue impaired Stuart's judgment during the Gettysburg campaign, he would have been loath to admit any infirmity. Besides, Douglas Southall Freeman did not develop his theory of the "fog of war" regarding Stonewall Jackson until seventy-one years later.[38]

So Harry McClellan's stories about eggs and Aldie and Shepherdstown seem relevant indeed to understanding Stuart's behavior. As McClellan observed, "The mind can act and yet be unconscious of its actions." Stuart was functioning in a fog; if a somnambulist is a sleepwalker, then Stuart was a "somneques"—a sleeprider.

The best answer to the riddle of Stuart's aberrant performance in the Gettysburg Campaign is the simplest. He was long-term tired before the campaign even began. Stuart then became exhausted to the point of dysfunction as his exertions and stress only increased during the long march toward battle.

# 6

## "I Think the Union Army Had Something to Do with It": The Pickett's Charge Nobody Knows

CAROL REARDON

THE veterans of the 149th Pennsylvania Infantry who returned to Gettysburg to unveil their regimental monument had a bone to pick with history. "The battle of Gettysburg has served to magnify the glory of the rebels at the expense of the Union troops," the orator complained. Moreover, he continued, "The great event of the battle in the popular mind is the magnificent charge of Pickett's Division. . . . So much has been said of the courage of his men that the sublime sacrifices of the first day and the brilliant charges and stubborn resistance of the Union troops on the second and third days, on all parts of the field, are overlooked."[1]

The disgruntled Pennsylvanian's complaints open two vistas on "the uncertain, the undecided, the unknown" about the events of July 3 at Gettysburg. First, he reminds us that the Northern side of the story deserves greater attention. George Pickett knew that. Once, when asked why his assault failed, he answered, "I think the Union army had something to do with it."[2] Ever since the victors of Gettysburg lost the post-Appomattox literary war to the

South, however, history has paid far more attention to the Confederate search for scapegoats.

Second, the Pennsylvanian correctly understood that even by the 1880s Pickett's Charge had become the focal point of popular interest in Gettysburg. Many of his fellow veterans of the Army of the Potomac shared his frustration in knowing that when the Northern victors won any acclaim at all, the lion's share of praise went to the two divisions of Maj. Gen. Winfield Scott Hancock's II Corps that repulsed the grand assault. Forgotten now, but a vital part of the July 3 story, are the hundreds of discordant voices, such as that of this resentful "Bogus Bucktail," who refused to acknowledge the copse of trees as the "high water mark of the Confederacy."

There is considerable irony in this need to restore to history a proper appreciation of the Union Army's efforts on July 3. After all, it was the decisions and actions of Northern leaders that set the stage for the dramatic events that brought great fame to Southern arms that afternoon. Late on the night of July 2, Maj. Gen. George G. Meade, the new commander of the Army of the Potomac, called a council of war. He asked his senior commanders three questions: Should we stay or retreat? If we stay, should we attack or await attack? If we wait, how long? His critics viewed the council as certain evidence that Meade sought a face-saving way to leave the field. Most likely, however, Meade simply used this forum to assess his army's condition after two days of hard fighting. When the generals decided to stay, await attack, and wait at least one day, if not much longer, Meade did not balk or try to dissuade them.[3] He had learned what he needed to know. As the meeting broke up, Meade turned to Brig. Gen. John Gibbon, who commanded one division of Maj. Gen. Winfield Scott Hancock's II Corps on Cemetery Ridge, and warned him, "If the enemy attacks tomorrow, it will be on your front."[4] Meade even redeployed some Union units to close supporting distance of Gibbon's line. Still, he had only guessed at Lee's intentions. He could not afford to make radical changes in his dispositions. Nonetheless, Meade acted the role of army commander early on July 3 far more actively than many close students of the battle acknowledge.[5]

The decisions of the Union council of war limited Robert E.

Lee's operational alternatives on July 3. Unlike his Northern counterparts, he could not afford to watch and wait. The Army of Northern Virginia's supply needs demanded a quick resolution of the battle. Moreover, Lee could not bring himself to disengage from what so far had been a successful fight. He saw no other acceptable alternative but to fight. Had the Northern leaders chosen a different course—to leave, perhaps—Lee might have had other options, Pickett's Charge may not have occurred at all, and the Union might not have won a great victory. But when Meade decided to stay, Lee chose to fight him.

Complicating Lee's concerns, the Union army reclaimed the tactical initiative early on July 3. After two days on the defensive, Northern artillery and infantry at about 4:30 A.M. launched a counterattack on Confederate troops from Lt. Gen. Richard Ewell's Second Corps that had captured a portion of the Union trench line on Culp's Hill the night before. As the firing grew louder and more sustained, Lee reconsidered his initial plan for July 3. He had originally assumed that the previous day's fight had weakened both Union flanks and they would break if pressed. Therefore, the three divisions of Lt. Gen. James Longstreet's First Corps, including Maj. Gen. George E. Pickett's newly arrived division of three brigades of Virginia infantry, would attack the Union left, while, simultaneously, Ewell's men would assault Culp's Hill on the Union right.

The Union counteroffensive early on July 3 threw off Lee's timetable. Heavy, if sporadic, firing from Culp's Hill, lasting until perhaps 11 A.M., undermined his plan for a double blow at the Union flanks. The intense musketry further convinced Lee that the flanks of the Union line remained heavily defended. He decided, therefore, to attack where his foe must be weakest: the Union center on Cemetery Ridge.

For years, the story of Gettysburg has revolved around a myriad of contentious issues spawned by Lee's decisions, but this one remains the most controversial. Every issue related to the conduct of the assault—from the selection of the troops, to command problems in coordinating infantry and artillery from two different corps, to, of course, anything connected to James Longstreet's conduct that day—plays a prominent role in any story of "Pickett's Charge."

Since Union actions had pushed Lee to this decision, however, it is only right to restore to the Northern soldier his rightful place in the story of July 3. On Cemetery Ridge, two brigades of Brig. Gen. Alexander Hays's division of Hancock's corps enjoyed the protection of sturdy stone walls. To the south of Hays's position, a lower stone wall offered shelter to Brig. Gen. Alexander Webb's Philadelphia Brigade of Gibbon's division. The men of Col. Norman J. Hall's and Brig. Gen. William Harrow's brigades of Gibbon's division and detachments of the I Corps deployed on their left flank did not even enjoy that much concealment. Some fortunate soldiers found shade in a prominent clump of trees along the ridge line. About 1 P.M., a single cannon shot disturbed their lunch. The first act of Gettysburg's most dramatic moment had begun.

Few Union soldiers forgot that first shot. Their memories about the fate of that projectile, however, suggest just how much remains uncertain, undecided, and unknown about every event on July 3. No two soldiers seem to recall the incident the same way. One of Brig. Gen. George J. Stannard's Vermonters watched the shell explode behind his regiment. Col. Arthur Devereaux of the 19th Massachusetts saw it cut one of his lieutenants nearly in two, while another officer in the same unit, lying wounded in a hospital well behind Union lines, heard it whistle overhead. A captain in the 12th New Jersey remembered it as a dud that fell harmlessly behind his regiment.[6] A private in the same unit remembered, however, that the first shell exploded "in our midst; it fell on the rock we were sitting on, and bursted, scattering the little balls it was filled with all around us."[7] The major of the 16th Maine remembered "a huge Whitworth shell," which, "with lightning quickness, came crashing through the Union lines."[8] The men of the 106th Pennsylvania recalled an initial Whitworth round being followed by a series of signal shots "fired from different parts of their line" to open fire generally.[9]

This simple example warns against accepting as conclusive much of what is allegedly "known" about July 3 at Gettysburg. Most modern studies, for instance, concur that the bombardment after that first shot lasted about two hours. Contemporary sources reveal no such consistency, however. While some confusion about exact starting and ending times can be explained by the absence of standard times and the differing skills of hundreds of individual watchmakers, why did Color Sergeant Daniel Crotty of the 3rd Michigan recall a ten-minute bombardment while others remember a five-hour artillery preparation?[10] Maybe the parts of Pickett's Charge we seem most certain of are those that require the greatest reconsideration.

The alleged ineffectiveness of the Confederate cannonade usually ranks among the "knowns" of July 3. Capt. Charles A. Phillips of the 5th Massachusetts Battery, far down the line from the hottest fire, offered a colorful and often-quoted critique on the issue: "Viewed as a display of fireworks, the rebel practice was entirely successful, but as a military demonstration it was the biggest humbug of the season."[11] Objectively, the captain is probably correct. Most of the Southern rounds overshot the Union infantry line. He ignores important implications that have little to do with the technical proficiency of the Southern gunners, however. Artillery fire does not have to hit its target to wreak havoc. While most infantrymen considered rifle fire far more deadly than artillery, the Union soldiers on Cemetery Ridge that day found the prolonged cannonade especially unsettling. "It seemed as though, had a knitting-needle stood on end it would have been shot off a dozen times in so many minutes," wrote a survivor of the 19th Maine.[12] Veterans of the 1st Minnesota afterwards gave thanks that "the Lord of Battles put up His shield in front of many a man on the Union line and turned the deadly missiles aside."[13] Even a Massachusetts veteran far from the target area became so awed by the fury of the shelling that he wrote with some exaggeration that "the range of the rebel cannon was deadly exact; and different shells struck six men who occupied in succession the same place in the ranks."[14] For sure, "Malvern Hill did not compare with it."[15] Captain Phillips' colorful assessment of the ineffectiveness of Southern gunnery tells only one part of the story.

When the clouds of powder smoke lifted, even the dullest Union private knew what would follow. Thousands of Northern soldiers on Cemetery Ridge and nearby Cemetery Hill watched southern infantry emerge from the treeline on Seminary Ridge. Later, most of them remembered it as the beginning of "Pickett's Charge." Most likely, however, the troops whose advance they admired belonged to Brig. Gen. J. Johnston Pettigrew.[16] His four brigades—Col. B. D. Fry's Tennesseans and Alabamians, Col. J. K. Marshall's North Carolinians, Brig. Gen. J. R. Davis's North Carolinians and Mississippians, and the Virginians of Col. J. M. Brockenbrough—marched ahead of a second line, in which two additional North Carolina brigades under Brig. Gens. J. H. Lane and A. M. Scales advanced under the temporary command of Maj. Gen. Isaac Trimble. The Virginia brigades of Brig. Gens. James L. Kemper and Richard B. Garnett of Pickett's division, in a low swale by the Spangler barn more than 1,000 yards to the south, stayed out of sight of most Union troops on Cemetery Ridge during the initial stages of Pettigrew's advance.[17] One of Stannard's Vermonters remembered how "Two long and heavy lines *came over* the opposite ridge and advanced upon us," describing the Virginians coming out of the swale.[18] Sgt. Wyman S. White of the 2nd U.S. Sharpshooters heard Pickett's troops coming, but he saw them only when they came out of the swale and advanced "over the rise of ground just beyond the Emmitsburg Road."[19] Hundreds of Union soldiers wrote about the Confederate advance, but only these two and a very few others actually described the start of Pickett's part of the charge.

How many Confederates did Pickett, Pettigrew, and Trimble lead across that valley? James Longstreet's offhand opinion provides the most commonly cited number: "General, I have been a soldier all my life; I have been with soldiers engaged in fights by couples, by squads, companies, regiments, divisions, and armies, and should know as well as any one what soldiers can do. It is my opinion that no 15,000 men ever arrayed for battle can take that position."[20] Modern studies of unit rosters and the elimination of July 1 casualties from Pettigrew's and Trimble's commands reduce the numbers to a range from 10,500 to perhaps 13,500.[21] The question still belongs among the uncertainties of July 3 at Gettysburg.

Moreover, such exercises in raw numbers tell only one part of the story, and not necessarily the most important part. As Pickett and Pettigrew crossed the field, in whatever strength, the Union soldiers' *perception* of their opponents' numbers—not merely the reality—demands consideration. Northern soldiers had about twenty minutes to burn in their memories some lasting impressions of the power in the Southern advance. They believed they fended off far more than 10,500 or 13,000 or even 15,000 attackers. Stannard's Vermonters insisted that they were attacked "by an overwhelming force of seventeen thousand rebels, whose charge was gallantly repelled by this brigade alone."[22] A spate of Union regimental histories published in the 1870s and 1880s accepted a figure of 18,000. One of the first battlefield guidebooks described a "wonderful movement gallantly made by almost twenty thousand veterans."[23] A survivor of the 19th Maine impressed on an audience in his home state that they might be able to picture 18,000 to 25,000 attacking Confederates by looking at "every man, woman and child in this city of Bath" as "a strong, able-bodied man, fully armed, and then double that force and you would not reach the number engaged in that assault of our enemy."[24] At least one Northern writer suggested that the men on Cemetery Ridge took on nearly 40,000 Southerners.[25]

Such perceptions of overwhelming Southern numbers served Northerners well. The greater the odds they beat, the greater the glory they earned. They took no special pains to complete the numbers equation, the better to preserve that fiction. While Southern attackers unquestionably outnumbered the Northern troops waiting for them at the point of attack, we do not know how many Union soldiers actually contributed to the repulse of the Southern assault.[26] Estimated strengths for Gibbon or Hays may or may not include an accurate accounting for losses suffered on July 2. How many men still stood with Col. Theodore B. Gates' "demi-brigade" after July 1? Moreover, just who must be included in this count? Should those who arrived as the Confederate high tide receded—such as Meade himself—be counted? What about the XI Corps artillerymen whose guns pounded Pettigrew's left flank or gunners from Little Round Top who hit Pickett's right? What about units in close reserve who never fired a shot, but potentially canceled out the Confederates' initial numerical advantages? The question remains open.

A great victory, especially won against great odds, makes for exciting memories—and unreliable history. We easily recall the post-battle boast of Major Henry L. Abbott of the 20th Massachusetts, who wrote his father of the advancing Southerners, "The moment I saw them I knew we should give them Fredericksburg. So did everybody."[27] We find fundamental truth in the words of a Northern reporter who wrote from the battlefield that the charging Confederates "met those who were their equals in spirit and their superiors in tenacity."[28]

Unfortunately, both comments, penned in the first flush of victory, obscure as much as they reveal. They misshape reality. They hide the stark terror of most Union soldiers as they watched the enemy hosts arrayed before them. Corporal Christopher Mead of the 12th New Jersey thanked God for allowing the Union line to hold, a prayer inspired by the sight of advancing Southern infantry driving the Northern skirmish line before them "like so many frightened sheep."[29] After the attack ended, Charles Belknap of the 125th New York entrusted to his diary his fears that "our line would give way as I noticed the uneasiness of some of the men."[30] In battle, a soldier can know he is one of thousands defending that position, but deployed in a thin, single- or double-rank line, he can be overwhelmed with a sense of fearful isolation. Honest soldiers never forget that feeling. Even years later, Lieutenant Tully McCrae of Woodruff's Battery I, 1st U.S. Artillery, posted at Ziegler's Grove, still admitted that "knowing that we had but one thin line of Infantry to oppose them, I thought that our chances for Kingdom Come or Libby Prison were very good."[31]

What did this awe-inspiring host look like? Numerous postwar paintings and even contemporary woodcuts perpetuate a romanticized, far-too-neat image of soldiers marching "as if on dress parade." The rolling fields, numerous stout post-and-rail fences, and the Emmitsburg Road itself all disrupted the neatness of the Southern ranks even before Union artillery opened up on them, as thousands of witnesses—North and South—concur, but what perceptions survive the press of reality?

Many Union veterans recalled traditional battle lines. Most remember two fairly straight lines. But Sergeant Joseph Bishop of the 14th Connecticut remembered "those three lines of battle led by Pickett . . . as they came straight on across the plain fields,"[32] while one of his comrades recalled "three lines, and a portion of a fourth line, extending a mile or more."[33] The chaplain of the 125th New York added detail: "That magnificent line" was "a mile long, three lines deep, and each line a double line."[34] The 17th Maine's regimental history, published in 1866, stated that Pickett's Division advanced in seven lines, each led by a mounted officer.[35] Another Northerner noted a short "line of battle about one brigade front extended," but he was impressed nonetheless: "They mean business. You notice how few of their officers are mounted."[36] (Just how many Confederates rode their horses into the attack is one of the Southern "unknowns" of Pickett's Charge.)

Not all Union soldiers perceived distinct battle lines. Lt. Col. Franklin Sawyer of the 8th Ohio saw "the division of PICKET, followed by that of PETIGREW" advance "splendidly, deploying into column as they crossed the long sloping interval between the Second Corps and their base."[37] Others simply saw a shapeless mob or wedge. One of the Vermonters wrote six months later that "it looked to me like a column, and a very wide and deep one. Gen. Stannard also insists that it was a column and its depth was almost equal to the length of the line of battle of the 13th and 16th Vt. Regiment, which had about 500 men apiece, in the line."[38] After thirty years, another Vermonter recalled far greater tactical complexity that began with "a single brigade in our immediate front, marching by the front in line-of-battle and straight towards us. Less than a minute, probably, another brigade rose to the left of the first one and advanced in the same manner, and so on at intervals of a half minute or a minute five or six brigades advanced towards our lines."[39]

Despite such compelling evidence of the vagaries of perception and memory, this Vermonter's memoir, like many Northern accounts of the charge, concluded with a common sentiment: "It was a magnificent sight." The only thing remaining, as Sgt. James Wright of the 1st Minnesota explained, was to prepare to meet the "grand soldierly effort" and "face it, breast it, break it—or be broken by it."[40]

The details of the actual clash of arms on the slopes of Cemetery Ridge remain the most difficult part of the day to capture. Southern perspectives have dominated historical writing about the afternoon's fighting. For years Confederate veterans dissected the assault's maneuvers in minute detail, some to claim for one regiment or one brigade or one commander the greatest share of glory, others to place blame for the failure of the attack. Resting with amazing endurance on the shaky foundation of blatantly partisan Richmond press coverage—understandably more concerned with Virginia troops than with those from other Southern states—Pickett's men have carved out a place in the history books and won the war for popular memory.[41] The very durability of the name "Pickett's Charge" suggests just how completely Virginia interests won over the American imagination.

In the long term, Northern veterans became powerful—if unintentional—proponents of Virginia's version of events near the stone wall. If they recognized Pickett's men as the elite of Lee's army, and Virginians surely promoted that image, the repulse of such stalwart Southerners promoted their own fighting prowess as well. Stannard's Vermonters celebrated the defeat of "General George E. Pickett, the one of all the veteran officers of the great Army of Northern Virginia personally selected by General Lee to command and lead the flower of his army in whom was centered all his hopes on this field,—they were to him like Napoleon's body guard at Waterloo."[42]

Union men usually used Virginia's preferred name for the clash as well: "Pickett's Charge." This held true even for Hays's men, who actually had faced Pettigrew and Trimble. Major John L. Brady of the 1st Delaware wrote proudly of his men's contribution to the repulse of "the fairest of the chosen flower of the Confederacy under command of the redoubtable Pickett."[43] Colonel Clinton MacDougall told the survivors of the 111th New York: "When the smoke had cleared away, and the gallant Pickett and his heroic followers had vanished from your front, the great battle of Gettysburg had become history! the high tide of the Rebellion had been reached and the fate of the CONFEDERATE STATES OF AMERICA was sealed." An unknown editor later added a footnote to the published version of the speech: "It was Pettigrew's Division that attacked the position where the One hundred and eleventh New York stood. Pickett's Division struck the Union line to the left of the One hundred and eleventh."[44]

What did Union veterans preserve for posterity about their fight on Cemetery Ridge? Do their reports and memoirs reinforce traditionally accepted stories peddled by the Virginians? Do they unravel some of the uncertainties, undecideds, and unknowns of July 3 at Gettysburg? Or do they add even more?

Lieutenant Frank A. Haskell of Gibbon's staff understood how unlikely it was for a commander to recall much detail about any battle: "The official reports may give results as to losses, with statements of attacks and repulses; they may also note the means by which results were attained, which is a statement of the number and kind of the forces employed, but the connection between means and results, the mode, the battle proper, these reports touch lightly."[45] In the heat of combat, a tactical commander's battlefield shrinks to exclude all but his immediate and personal experiences. As adrenaline rushes and ebbs, the fighting most likely impresses on his memory as a series of vignettes, warping his understanding of the entire action. This same limitation—plus the added deterioration or exaggeration of detail that often accompanies the passage of time—affects personal memoirs of common soldiers as well. Victory adds another wrinkle to the question. Many soldiers gave in to the temptation to preserve the drama and color of the emotion-packed day at the expense of detailed deliberations about military art. As Haskell suggested, the results of the fight—and, in time, the realization of Gettysburg's implications for the success of the Union cause—proved sufficient to stifle any real need among Northern soldiers to dissect the day's military maneuvering.

What history preserves for us, then, are scenes frozen in time that, even when taken together, reveal much about men in combat but little about the military art and science that shaped the defensive effort against the last great Southern assault at Gettysburg. The veterans of the 8th Ohio reveled in the memories of the impact of their first volley against Pettigrew's left flank: "The distinct graceful lines of the rebels underwent an instantaneous transformation. They were at once enveloped in a dense cloud of smoke and dust. Arms, heads, blankets, guns and knapsacks were thrown and tossed into the clear air."[46] How did they discover their opportunity? How did they redeploy under fire to exploit it? How did Pettigrew's men respond to the threat? The Ohioans never tell us. Nor do they even admit they had help; survivors of the 125th New York demanded in vain that "distinct record should go into general history" of their "brave and skillful part at that important point of the battle."[47] From these kinds of insights, we can sense—but we cannot "know"—what happened on that part of the field.

Many Northern accounts—unlike Southern narratives that examine the progress of the Confederate advance in all its fine detail—downplay much of the preliminary fighting in favor of the actual clash of arms at the stone wall, especially where Pickett's Virginians broke through at the Angle. A lieutenant from the 1st Minnesota wrote little about his unit's initial brush with Kemper's men south of the high-water mark, gave scant attention to the movement of his regiment from its original battle line to the breach near the copse of trees, or how it helped to seal that gap. He recalled only: "If men ever become devils, that was one of the times. We were crazy with the excitement of the fight. We just rushed in like wild beasts. Men swore and cursed and struggled and fought, grappled in hand-to-hand fights, threw stones, clubbed their muskets, kicked, yelled, and hurrahed. But it was over in no time."[48]

Interest in the fight for the copse of trees ultimately blocked out many crucial details of the day's action. A nasty, running firefight that pitted Gates' I Corps command and Harrow's brigade against Kemper's Virginians before the Southerners' final oblique toward the copse of trees seldom gets more than a sentence in modern treatments of the fight.[49] Usually forgotten as well is a second, brief, Southern penetration of the Union line on Hall's front, just south of the copse. Lieutenant Hamilton of the 59th New York remembered how "both the Regts on our right and left gave way, leaving our Regiment" alone to contend with Pickett's men.[50] Colonel Macy of the 20th Massachusetts corroborated: "It was immediately on the right of the 59th that the enemy broke through."[51] It must have been a tough fight, surely too tough to surrender to obscurity. Among the timely reinforcements that sealed the gap was Captain Andrew Cowan's 1st New York Artillery and some of Harrow's infantrymen, one of whom admitted that "our shots affected them little more than to prevent their advance further."[52] Armistead's far more famous penetration of the Union line occurred several hundred yards farther north.

Union veterans could become interested in some specific element of the defense of Cemetery Ridge if a bit of controversy compelled their attention. As long as a quest to right the historical record did not include a demand for a larger share of credit than that to which the claimants were entitled, few Union veterans begrudged their comrades-in-arms an opportunity to boast a bit. Almost every regiment on Cemetery Ridge had a right to stake some claim to breaking the Confederate momentum, for instance. The commander of the 14th Connecticut, alluding to his men's use of breech-loading rifles, drew no criticism even when he claimed that "accounts seem to agree that the Confederate line broke quicker in the immediate front of the 14th than anywhere else."[53] Few dared to make stronger claims. Indeed, in the 1890s, when some of Stannard's veterans tried to make too much of their actions in crushing Pickett's right flank, one Union veteran put them in their place by poking fun at "the whole State of Vermont," which appeared "ready and willing, regardless of party, to rise and affirm that to the best of their knowledge and belief Gen. Stannard saved Gettysburg."[54]

A few Union controversies have left faint marks on the story of July 3. On senior command levels, Hancock and Brig. Gen. Henry J. Hunt, the Army of the Potomac's chief of artillery, never resolved their questions about command and control of the II Corps batteries during the pre-assault bombardment and the charge, even after they and their partisans fought a long literary war.[55] Friends of Hancock, Gibbon, and Stannard claimed for their general the responsibility for ordering the crushing attack that crumpled Pickett's right flank.[56]

Gibbon's men disagreed with each other about a number of annoying issues. The 72nd Pennsylvania compiled volumes of testimony to support their legal case against the Gettysburg Battlefield commissioners in an effort to erect their regimental monument near the stone wall and not on their initial line of deployment, fully one hundred yards farther back.[57] Even Webb, who earlier had expressed some dissatisfaction with the performance of the regiment, defended them in 1883 against some of Hall's and Harrow's men who "desire to wrest your laurels from you."[58] The entire Philadelphia Brigade rose up in arms against Lieutenant Frank A. Haskell's slanders about their conduct. As one Philadelphian snarled about the officer's self-serving observations,

"Haskell might, with equal truth and egotism, have written:—'To Dick and his rider belong the honor of meeting and repulsing Pickett's Division.'" The Pennsylvanian chided Pickett's Virginians, "You who killed or wounded 497 of our Comrades," wondering how those "who made such slaughter in OUR RANKS AT LONG RANGE could not even disable First Lieutenant Frank Aretas Haskell, or his horse."[59] When a Pennsylvanian asserted that the only dead Union soldiers near the stone wall came from Webb's Brigade or Cushing's battery, H. D. O'Brien, a veteran of the 1st Minnesota of Harrow's brigade, stormed back that "Capt. Farrell and a number of enlisted men . . . were killed within a few feet of the wall," adding that he did not "believe there was a regiment in either Harrow's or Hall's Brigades that escaped without the loss of killed and wounded at that point—'the high-water mark of the rebellion.'"[60]

Bad feelings occasionally turned Gibbon's and Hays's veterans against each other, too. Webb of the Philadelphia Brigade, for instance, expressed great distaste for Hays, who he considered "not capable of commanding a Brigade," calling him "nothing but a personally brave man. No head[,] no education & vulgar beyond measure."[61] For their part, Hays's men invariably perceived Gibbon's men as irredeemable blowhards. When the 111th New York dedicated its monument, its colonel reminded his men: "Many claims have been made as to who bore the brunt of Pickett's Charge. The Philadelphia Brigade laid claim to the most of the fighting and the greatest honor." Still, he did not think the 111th needed to indulge in such shameless self-promotion: "The most you have ever claimed was that you had assisted in repelling the greatest charge ever made upon a battlefield. In the language of the immortal Lincoln, you felt that 'there was glory enough at Gettysburg to go all around.'"[62] They especially liked to recount an alleged conversation between Webb and Hays as the fighting ended: "Hays, they got through my line," Webb had yelled, to which Hays retorted, "I'll be damned if they got through mine."[63]

To the units involved, these challenges demanded resolution. Yet, in the long term, not a single one of them evolved into much more than a short-lived tempest. Largely forgotten today, they never claimed a prominent place in the history books, nor do they erase or even challenge much of Virginia's image of Pickett's

Charge. Mostly, they help us "know" more about such larger questions as how Civil War soldiers felt about war and the obligations of citizenship. The sacrifice of Sgt. Albert Bunn of the 71st Pennsylvania, who left the safety of the stone wall to work and die at one of Cushing's guns, needed to be remembered, a comrade-in-arms wrote, if only because "Generals and Admirals win high renown for the military achievements of their men, but personal deeds of heroism by simple privates or subalterns are rarely recorded."[64]

Simply put, while we can learn some valuable lessons about war from Union soldiers who fought at Gettysburg on July 3, we cannot reconstruct the ebb and flow of the battle from their memoirs any easier or any more objectively than we can from the Confederate accounts with which we are more familiar. Honest soldiers understood that the entire story of Gettysburg would never be told. One of Stannard's Vermonters conceded that "Much history was made on this charge that can never be known, and much, though seen and realized that can never be adequately described!"[65] When his long military career came to an end at the turn of the century, Colonel Frederick Fuger, who served as first sergeant with Cushing's battery at the Angle, reflected that the passage of time had already irretrievably harmed the search for truth: "We may well hesitate before attempting to reconcile the many disputed questions which have arisen. Indeed, it is almost doubtful to the minds of many of the participants in the battle whether they were ever present,—so different from their recollections of the events do recent recollections appear."[66]

Indeed, memory can hardly recover those images that, in fact, never had time to set. To the much maligned Army of the Potomac, victory came as a heady tonic. They savored the results of battle, and even before the powder smoke cleared, they looked beyond combat to the broader implications of the day. A Boston journalist at Gettysburg wrote at sunset that day he "could discern the future—no longer an overcast sky, but the clear, unclouded starlight, a country redeemed, saved, baptized, consecrated anew to the coming ages.!"[67] Many of his fellow Northerners agreed. Even before Appomattox, veterans of Stannard's Vermont brigade avowed that the most important thing about their success on July 3 was simply knowing that "the nation's honor is being vindicated, and the fate of America is to be decided in the Union's favor."[68]

The strength of such sentiments among the survivors of the charge grew over time. Many Keystone Staters came to view Gettysburg as a special moment for them: "It was death or victory, and the soil was Pennsylvania."[69] The chaplain of the 14th Connecticut found a different kind of inspiration in knowing that when "the highest, mightiest surge of the slave-holders' rebellion was shattered and overcome at the stone front of the Second Army Corps," he and his comrades "were part of the living bulwark that broke it."[70] These became the most important memories of July 3 for the Northern soldiers who repulsed the great charge.

But that is not the entire story of the "uncertain, the undecided, and the unknown" about July 3 at Gettysburg. Not all Union veterans accepted the copse of trees as the symbolic "high water mark of the Confederacy." While they rejoiced in the success of Northern arms, substantial numbers of the veterans of the Army of the Potomac who had played no role in the repulse of Pickett's Charge feared that history would forget them. Their efforts to infuse some self-interested perspective into the history of July 3 also deserves to be a part of the story of Pickett's Charge.

Leading the assault against what he perceived to be false history was the redoubtable Dan Sickles, the III Corps commander at Gettysburg. In the mid-1880s, in a very public attack on the growing popular interest in Pickett's Charge, he invited other III Corps survivors to a reunion at Gettysburg in 1886. He announced his intention to "put on record the part taken by the Third Corps at Gettysburg, so that justice—tardy justice, perhaps—shall be done to the part we bore in contributing to the signal victory."[71] Nearly 2,000 of Sickles's men joined a sea of III Corps luminaries to hear "the man who made the victory of Gettysburg possible." At length, Sickles explained how his men bore the brunt of the fight on July 2, drained the fighting spirit out of Lee's army, and so demoralized the Confederate high command that they resorted to desperate measures—Pickett's Charge—in a futile effort to retrieve a battle already lost. More soldiers fell on July 2 than on the other two days combined, Sickles argued, and that simple reality should accord the efforts of the III Corps with greater significance. When Sickles finished, according to an eyewitness, "The Third Corps was wild with delight, and fairly worshipped their leader and vindicator."[72]

Sickles took so much pleasure in the response to his 1886 venture that he repeated his performance as often as he could. At the twenty-fifth anniversary of the battle in 1888, Sickles hosted James Longstreet, another senior commander interested in a fair shake from history. The two men went to Pitzer's Woods, where U.S. Sharpshooters from the III Corps first interrupted the deployment of the Confederate infantry on July 2. Sickles beamed and reporters wrote down every word when Longstreet said that "if Berdan had delayed him for only 35 minutes instead of 40 his army would not have been repulsed. That five minutes saved the day for the Army of the Potomac." As one correspondent recorded, "The spot where Berdan attacked Longstreet was the turning point of the war." The importance of Pickett's Charge paled by comparison.[73]

Sickles found partisans from all ranks of his old command Colonel Thomas Rafferty pointed to the broken ground, ravines, rocks, and woods on the III Corps front and asked those who persisted in believing that Hancock's men faced a tougher fight to consider. "What, in their judgment, would have been the result when our one thin line should have received the shock of that charge." The ground alone offered sufficient proof on which to "rest the vindication of the action of the Third Corps on the second day at Gettysburg."[74] One of Sickles's enlisted men took aim at Peter Frederick Rothermel's famous oil painting portraying "the charge of Pickett's Division and the stone angle guarded by the Second Corps under Hancock, as the dramatic point of the struggle." But neither this action, "nor Little Round Top, nor Culp's Hill, nor Buford's dismounted men, stood a shock like that hurled against Humphreys' Division of the III Corps."[75] Sickles's views found disciples throughout the Army of the Potomac, except in the II Corps, of course. A self-proclaimed veteran of the imaginary 107th Oshkosh Volunteers began his story of the "Battle of Podunksburg" with a disclaimer: "My views may not exactly dove-tail with history, but that's history's fault, not mine.

I was there, and history did not show up until after the trouble was over." The Union commander READE had two key subordinates, PICKLES and PEACOCK. Peacock's men always bragged far too loudly about the great losses they took in repulsing Pickett's Charge, so he explained how all TRUE soldiers felt about battle: "If victory didn't perch on our side of the fence we wanted to die, but we were in no great rush about it—we preferred to die of extreme old age."[76]

Veterans of the V Corps that bolstered Sickles's line on July 2 provided strong support for the III Corps argument. A veteran of the 22nd Massachusetts, one of the V Corps regiments that reinforced the III Corps in the Wheatfield, agreed that "the umbrella copse of trees" did not mark the "high water mark of the Confederacy." In his mind, the line marking the acme of Southern hopes "should run along the ground along the slopes and in the ravine of the Round Tops" in the III and V Corps's sector of the Union line.[77]

Many other veterans found something of substance in the III Corps crusade, too. Self-interest, however, prevented some from forging an alliance with proponents of Sickles's cause. No consensus could override some deeply felt grievances.

Survivors of the I Corps voiced several concerns about the usual history of July 3. Most galling, of course, I Corps troops had participated actively in repulsing Pickett's Charge, but they rarely received much credit for it. Capt. W. C. Dunton did not seek undue glory for Stannard's Vermonters since "nearly all the loyal states had their soldiers there, and they all did their duty faithfully." But, he continued, "by the fortunes of war, under the Providence of God, these three Regiments of the Second Vermont Brigade occupied the pivotal point at the most critical time of that great battle." Through their efforts, "the field of Gettysburg was won, and the nation saved. . . . It was the high water mark of the rebellion—a turning point of history and of human destiny."[78] Colonel Theodore Gates resented that history too often forgot that his two I Corps regiments on the left flank of Harrow's brigade first "met the onset of Pickett's attack—that they broke his line and killed and wounded a large number of his troops and that hundreds surrendered to them."[79] A "Bogus Bucktail" who had taken a few shots at Pickett's men complained that "it has been erroneously stated that the 143rd Pennsylvania played no part in repelling this famous charge, but every survivor here knows that Dana's brigade opened fire on Wilcox and upon the advancing column of Pickett."[80]

The I Corps's hurt went deeper, however. It had taken such huge losses that it was disbanded soon after Gettysburg. "Some would have us believe that Pickett's charge was the only event in the battle worthy of particular record," complained one man. "We of the I Corps have been entirely too modest, or if not too modest, have lacked spokesmen" to remind the nation of their service and their sacrifice.[81] A close connection with Sickles provided no solution; after all, he had dismissed July 1 as only "a preliminary skirmish." A disgruntled captain of the 147th New York retorted: "But for the heroism and staying qualities of Reynolds and his men the first day, General Sickles would never had the opportunity to make the handsome boast that the Third Corps fought the battle of Gettysburg."[82]

Veterans of the XII Corps, whose July 3 fight on the slopes of Culp's Hill also receded into the shadow of Pickett's Charge, joined the battle for the history books, too. A survivor of the 27th Indiana's charge at Spangler's Spring insisted that while Pickett's Charge "had about it certain theatrical, as well as tragical, features, well calculated to awaken popular interest and applause, . . . this was not the battle of Gettysburg, at least not all of it." When it came right down to it, the charge "was not even as conspicuous in actual blood-letting as is sometimes thought."[83] Still angry years later that Meade had slighted the XII Corps in his battle report, a veteran griped, "It is a curious fact that in popular estimation the whole thought of the Battle of Gettysburg seems to center about Pickett's Charge on the third day," overshadowing thousands of other Union soldiers, like those who fought equally hard on Culp's Hill to earn "a soldier's reward, the crown of immortal glory."[84]

In the long run, these complaints—like the internal II Corps squabbles—changed few minds. What Virginia first propounded and the II Corps validated as the truth of history required no further rewriting. Perhaps conceding this, ever so begrudgingly, even critics began to give in to the seductiveness of the imagery of

Pickett's Charge. Any connection to that great moment—even a remote one—provided a different kind of security to aging veterans: a guarantee that they would not be forgotten. Increasingly, units that only lay in reserve reconfirmed their willingness to answer duty's call. The 1st Pennsylvania Cavalry, deployed behind Hancock's line, had not fired a shot. Still, they swelled with pride as an orator reminded them of how they "waited, looking down on the maelstrom of death, dying yourselves each moment with those who were dying; that the circumstances did not arise that spared you from making that awful (and doubtless your last charge), was not your fault, you were here to do it."[85]

Even observing the charge from a distance placed old veterans close enough to the decisive field. From Cemetery Hill, the 136th New York of the XI Corps *may* have seen parts of the charge, but in their imaginations they *certainly* did. It was "awfully grand, magnificently sublime. The Rebels fall, as autumnal leaves fall from a forest tree, and cover the ground. In our mind's eye we see it now, as we saw it then. Memory vividly recalls it."[86]

Even veterans of the Army of the Potomac whose greatest moments came on fields other than Gettysburg found ways to measure their own accomplishments against Pickett's Charge and its repulse. Veterans of the VI Corps, perhaps because they played a comparatively small role at Gettysburg, became quite adept at such comparisons. "Every one who has read of Gettysburg seems to have their entire thoughts concentrated on Pickett's gallant charge," one wrote. Nonetheless, during the Chancellorsville campaign, "The simple facts are, a few of the Sixth Corps charged up Marye's Heights, over the same ground, in the same way Burnside did, in as gallant a manner as Pickett's men did and they got there, too; though one never hears of it."[87] Only veterans with no stake in such comparisons could write: "How gallant these Virginians are! As brave as our men that led the forlorn hope at Fredericksburg. The two charges should go down in history together."[88]

We have begun to understand how and why Southerners manufactured an event named Pickett's Charge and how and why whole parts of the South rejected it.[89] We know considerably less about how and why Northerners came to impose elaborate symbolic meanings on July 3 at Gettysburg, however. For some, the fight at the Angle represented the very essence of the sectional struggle itself, the arena where the best of both sides fought it out and where the cause of right finally won. Sickles might have cringed, but one of his New Hampshire veterans looked on "the spot where Armistead fell" as "not only the pivotal point of this battle and the war," and thus "the grave of slavery and the birthplace of universal freedom on Columbia's broad and beautiful domain," but also as "the real Itasca from which overflows and shall continue to flow for centuries to come, a stream that shall purify her cities and replenish her fields."[90] Colonel John A. Danks of the 53rd Pennsylvania, another III Corps unit, suggested: "When we think of humanity as being crushed by sin, and look for a remedy, we begin at the Garden, and find the conclusion at Calvary. When we think and speak of the government of England as threatened with dismemberment and ruin, and look for the remedy, we find it at Waterloo. So, when we think and speak of oppression, class and caste in America, and look for the remedy, we begin at Harper's Ferry, with old John Brown, and find the answer in Pickett's Charge at Gettysburg."[91]

Did Northerners ever embrace the tactical fine points of July 3 anything like their Southern counterparts did? No. In 1904, a Philadelphia congressman praised the bravery of the Union troops that defended the Angle and managed to insult many of his own constituents by identifying those heroes as the 69th *New York*.[92] One of the first movies to attempt a recreation of Pickett's Charge featured an actor of "the girth and height of the late Fitzhugh Lee" playing the role of Robert E. Lee, who, along with Longstreet and Pickett, were depicted after the charge as "weeping down the backs of each other's necks, and doing just exactly the thing that brave men would never think of doing." The Union repulse was included, too—briefly—in a segment mistitled "The Charge of Hancock's Brigade."[93]

Somehow, it is appropriate that the much-maligned Lieutenant Frank Haskell, one of the many Union heroes of July 3, should get the last word here. In that long letter in which he allegedly slandered the Philadelphia Brigade, he redeemed himself with this observation that warns us that what we seek—a resolution of some of the uncertainties, undecideds, and unknowns of July 3 at Gettysburg—most likely can never be found: "Of this battle, greater than that of Waterloo, a history, just, comprehensive, complete will never be written. By-and-by, out of the chaos of trash and falsehood that the newspapers hold, out of the disjointed mass of reports, out of the traditions and tales that come down from the field, some eye that never saw the battle will select, and some pen will write what will be named THE HISTORY. With that the world will be, and, if we are still alive, we must be, content."[94]

# 7

## Gettysburg's Gettysburg: What the Battle Did to the Borough

### J. MATTHEW GALLMAN
with SUSAN BAKER

HISTORY has an odd way of elevating relatively unknown locales into positions of prominence. The luck of geography or some strange twist of fate can suddenly turn a nation's eyes onto an unsuspecting community, forever linking its name with a single major episode. Gettysburg, Pennsylvania, in 1863 was hardly an obscure backwater. This bustling county seat of roughly 2,400 people boasted a vibrant commercial center, several hotels and taverns, a railroad depot, the county prison and a new courthouse, a Lutheran Theological Seminary, and a college. Nonetheless, few Americans were familiar with Gettysburg before the first days of July, when nearly 170,000 armed men converged upon the borough. By battle's end, the two armies had suffered over 51,000 casualties; Gettysburg would never be quite the same.

When we think of the Battle of Gettysburg, we do not imagine bloody street fighting. Indeed, the Union's famed fishhook stretched along the hills to the south of town. Still, the residents who opted to stay in Gettysburg saw the war firsthand, in a way that few Northern civilians would. At different points in the battle, both Yankee and Rebel troops occupied the streets. For years to come, the residents of the town would tell harrowing tales of terrifying escapes, hidden Union soldiers, suspicious Confederate patrols, and—most disturbing—thousands and thousands of the dead, dying, and wounded.

Historians who set out to reconstruct Civil War battles quickly learn that participants know little beyond the limited range of their own senses, obscured by clouds of smoke and deafening noise. To understand a battle's panoramic aspects, one must piece together dozens of small stories. Surely much of the enduring fascination with the battle of Gettysburg is in these smaller, personal stories. We never tire of the tales of heroic figures, such as Joshua Lawrence Chamberlain, or timeless relationships, such as that between Lewis Armistead and Winfield Scott Hancock.

Gettysburg's townspeople had their own array of battle tales, ranging from the highly celebrated to the barely documented. Even the casual observer of history has probably heard of Jennie Wade and John Burns. Virginia (Jennie) Wade became the town's only casualty when a stray bullet passed through two doors, mortally wounding her as she tended a kitchen fire. On July 1, John Burns—far too old to serve in uniform—grabbed a gun and went out to face the invaders, where he sustained three wounds. Most locals survived the battle in relative obscurity. Sarah Broadhead spent much of the three days in cellars, hidden from both stray bullets and hostile Confederates. Her terror did not subside until July 4, when she wrote in her diary: "For the first time for a week I shall go to bed feeling safe."[1] In the days after the battle, young schoolteacher Salome Myers threw herself into nursing the wounded soldiers, a passion she sustained into her later life. Neither woman enjoyed much fame either before or after the battle; we only have knowledge of their thoughts and actions because both kept diaries throughout the crisis.

For those in more public positions, the Confederate invasion brought particular difficulties. David Buehler, the town postmaster, watched Lee's progress north with special concern, fearing that his government post might result in his capture. When the Rebels approached Gettysburg, Buehler took several horses and fled the town, leaving his wife Fannie and their children to fend for themselves. Henry Stahle edited the *Gettysburg Compiler,* a vigorously Democratic weekly. During the battle, Stahle took in a wounded Union officer, Colonel William W. Dudley of Indiana. When the Colonel took a turn for the worse, Stahle left his home in search of a surgeon. Soon after the battle the controversial editor was arrested and incarcerated in Baltimore's Fort McHenry, charged with giving information to the enemy.[2]

Many Gettysburg citizens only reached the historic record indirectly, through the comments of other observers. For the town's African-American population, the Confederate invasion brought with it the specter of capture and forced enslavement, prompting many to abandon their homes and flee the neighborhood. Years after the battle, Albertus McCreary described the mass exodus of African Americans from the western portion of the town. McCreary particularly remembered the story of an African-American woman who apparently had worked for his family and fell into Rebel hands. "We never expected to see 'Old Liz' again," he wrote, "but the day after the battle ended she came walking in, exclaiming, 'Thank God, I's alive yet.'"[3]

Hundreds of individual stories such as these are embedded in Gettysburg's history. For the historian of the Northern home front, Gettysburg's experience is particularly compelling. On the one hand, most of its wartime experience was so "typical" that the town can nearly serve as the analytic proxy for towns across the North. On the other hand, neither the townspeople nor the historian can forget the thousands of men who fell in those three days. The task before us is to come to terms with Gettysburg, both as a perfectly normal Northern town that experienced the tremendous challenges of the American Civil War, and as a community that fate elevated to a special status. In the process, we must remain cognizant of the events that framed the town's wartime history and the narratives that defined its memory.

The Civil War's human costs still stagger the modern observer. The conflict's estimated 618,000 military deaths nearly equal America's combined losses in every other war before Vietnam. The death rate—more than 180 out of every 10,000 Americans— was more than six times as high as that of World War II and well beyond the 118 per 100,000 of the American Revolution.[4] It is only natural to assume that such tremendous casualties dramatically reshaped the United States. In some fundamental ways that assumption is correct: America after Appomattox was indeed a different place than it had been before Fort Sumter. Slavery had at long last been abolished. Following decades of debate and uncertainty, the nation had finally established the primacy of the Union against the constitutional claims of states' rights advocates. In the South, the economy and social structure faced years of acrimonious Reconstruction while the legacy of rebellion muted the region's political voice in national affairs for decades to come. And in dozens of ways—both large and small—the war fought on the battlefields of 1864 and 1865 would hardly have been recognized by military participants at the First Battle of Bull Run.

In other senses, the war's effects are less easily gauged, particularly insofar as they touched the North. Scholars have now agreed that the war had only a modest impact on long-term patterns of economic growth and development. The case for a rising centralized state driven by the war's unprecedented demands appears powerful on the surface when we consider the array of innovative war measures addressing conscription, banking, taxes, and civil liberties; but on deeper reflection the lasting effects no longer seem quite so compelling.

We may also measure the war's effect on the home front by considering the experiences of ordinary citizens. How did they mobilize to support, or resist, the war? What changes did the conflict force on their everyday lives? How, for instance, did they weave local and personal voluntaristic impulses into the emerging tapestry of state and national benevolent organizations? How did the war's new political and administrative challenges fit into established partisan conflicts? Wars commonly challenge, and occasionally recast, existing social hierarchies. What became of racial and gender hierarchies under the strain of war?

A survey of the Northern home front would reveal ample evidence of a world in flux, but the larger story is one of broad continuities. Citizens threw themselves into all manner of war-related activities, but they generally did so within the context of time-honored traditions and beliefs. Perhaps this should come as no surprise. After all, most communities north of the border states never saw an enemy soldier. And after a brief downturn during the secession crisis, the Northern wartime economy boomed. Since existing resources and traditions could meet the war's challenges, there was little reason for Northerners to pursue dramatic change. The contrast with the Confederacy is considerable. Southerners fought the war with far fewer men and materials, and most of the conflict's carnage fell on Southern soil. White Southerners on the home front lived in a world of invading armies, food shortages, and the gradual destruction of slavery. Confederate women faced new challenges—and opportunities—as the vast majority of military-aged white men were drawn into uniform. Slaves in the Confederate states experienced uncertainty and hardship as well as tremendous possibilities. For those and other reasons, Southerners felt the war's impact far more than their Northern counterparts.

As long as we paint with a broad brush, the contrast between the prosperous North and the embattled South is dramatic. In this context, Gettysburg becomes particularly interesting because the borough was distinctly Northern in all respects, *except* that it endured a moment of invasion and destruction akin to that experienced in the South. If the historian wants to find evidence of a Northern community transformed by war, Gettysburg is a logical place to look.

On the eve of the Civil War, Gettysburg was a thriving county seat with 2,391 residents, including 190 (8 percent) African Americans. While certainly not a major city, the borough was a substantial local center, with about 8 percent of the Adams County population. In fact, only about a quarter of Northerners lived in larger communities in 1860. Although only a short distance from Maryland, Gettysburg's population had a distinctly Northern character. More than four out of five residents were born in Pennsylvania (1,976) and an additional 44 were born in other Northern states. Only 185 (8 percent) came from Maryland and a mere 22 (1 percent) residents were born in states that would become part of the Confederacy (all but one of these came from Virginia). Nearly a third (59) of the 207 residents who were born south of Pennsylvania were African Americans. About one in fourteen (164) Gettysburg residents listed European birthplaces. This percentage of immigrants was roughly twice that for the Southern states (3.5 percent) although well below the aggregate

Northern figure of 20 percent, which included the major East Coast cities.[5]

Located in the midst of Adams County farmland, Gettysburg supported a variety of local businesses catering to agricultural and mercantile needs, reflecting its strategic position at the hub of several major roads and, more recently, as a stop on the Hanover and Gettysburg Railroad. The town had several tanneries and a thriving carriage manufacturing industry. Twenty-two shoemakers appear on the 1860 census; however, despite the rumors, there was no local shoe factory or storehouse of shoes awaiting the Rebel raiders in 1863. Roughly half of the residents with occupations listed in the 1860 census were in some sort of craft or artisanal position; nearly a quarter were professionals, merchants, or retailers. Most of the remaining employed citizens were unskilled laborers.

By most measures, Gettysburg's African Americans lived in a separate, and largely unequal, world. In the decades before the war, the town had been a stop on the "Underground Railroad," providing refuge for runaway slaves. Although roughly 8 percent of the population, the real estate owned by Gettysburg's blacks in 1860 was valued at only about 1 percent of the town's total. Only three African Americans held professional positions in 1860, seven more were craftspeople. The remaining thirty-eight blacks with occupations listed in the census worked as some type of laborer or servant. As was common in the North, the local African-American community supported separate churches, cemeteries, and other institutions. Black children attended a separate "colored" school.[6]

The hotly contested elections of 1860 proved to be important political litmus tests at the local, county, and state levels. The Republicans and Abraham Lincoln carried Pennsylvania with 57 percent of the vote, largely by stressing economic issues while playing down any discussion of slavery's future. In Adams County, Lincoln edged Illinois Democrat Stephen Douglas by a mere eighty votes. Gettysburg voters showed slightly more enthusiasm for the Republican ticket, giving Lincoln and Hannibal Hamlin 54 percent of the vote.

Local and national politics were the focus of spirited partisan debate in two weekly newspapers: the pro-Republican *Sentinel,* edited by Robert G. Harper, and Henry Stahle's staunchly Democratic *Compiler.* The debates over the 1860 election revealed both sharp political divisions and a shared distrust of abolitionism. Stahle's *Compiler* took every opportunity to paint Lincoln (and the *Sentinel)* as the voice of "Black Republicans" intent on forcing abolitionism down Americans' throats; the *Sentinel* denied such charges with equal vehemence.[7]

Abraham Lincoln's election triggered a series of events that would lead the United States into civil war. Between the firing on Fort Sumter in April 1861 and Robert E. Lee's invasion in the summer of 1863, the citizens of Gettysburg experienced the Civil War much like any other Northern community. The student of the home front is struck less by the borough's special characteristics than by the sense that this relatively small community was like the entire Union writ small.

Before the war began, Gettysburg, and most of the North, divided over how to treat the seceding states. All that ended with news of the firing on Fort Sumter. For at least a brief time, partisan disputes took a back seat to patriotism. In cities and towns across the North, flags flew, cannon roared, and local dignitaries delivered impassioned speeches at hastily assembled town gatherings. On April 16, the citizens of Gettysburg staged a "large and enthusiastic" Union Meeting "irrespective of party differences." The assembly attacked the treasonous South and resolved to set aside all party feeling to defend the Union.[8]

Immediately following the fall of Fort Sumter, Abraham Lincoln issued a call for ninety-day volunteers. For a time, fervent military recruiting seemed to absorb all attention. Gettysburg's patriotic young men flocked to emergency companies with exhilarating names and enticing uniforms: the Independent Blues, the Adams Rifles, and—most spectacular—the Gettysburg Zouaves. As these filled, new companies and regiments enlisted men from Gettysburg and across Adams County. Meanwhile, the town named a Committee of Safety to organize a Home Guard for local defense and a public gathering appointed seven men to raise money for the families of military volunteers. The rhetoric from these first few days is particularly telling. As the county mobilized to meet the state's quota, the *Compiler* declared: "Men of Adams

County, your country calls." At the time, no further inducements seemed necessary.[9]

After a few weeks of drilling, the emergency troops departed for the front, sent on their way with enthusiastic public displays. Gettysburg's volunteers often were escorted to the train station by the colorfully garbed Zouaves. Crowds lined the street and gathered at the station to see their loved ones off. Such carefully constructed rituals sealed the bonds between the regiments and the communities left behind. In the months and years to come, citizens on the home front followed the exploits of local regiments with particular care. In addition to personal letters from family and friends, Gettysburg's newspaper readers received a steady diet of stories following the local companies and published letters from soldiers in the field.

The initial enthusiasm for mustering volunteers into uniform was matched by a surge of benevolent voluntarism at home, particularly among the women of Gettysburg. On May 6 a group of women gathered at the Methodist Church "to organize a Union Relief Society." Before long, the Ladies' Union Relief Society was hard at work sewing flannel shirts, havelocks, and other military garments. The women of Gettysburg responded repeatedly to specific requests from neighboring towns or benevolent groups.[10]

By mid-summer of 1861, wartime Gettysburg had settled into a routine of sorts, much like the patterns established across the North. Near the end of July, the first ninety-day recruits began returning home, prompting more martial displays and another round of public celebration.[11] Even before the First Battle of Bull Run, the President issued calls for three-year recruits, leading many ninety-day volunteers to reorganize into three-year regiments. In these early days, the patriotic spirit was still generally sufficient to fill the ranks, but Gettysburg's recruiters were already experimenting with added incentives. Young men considering Captain Buehler's new company were promised a $100 bounty and were assured that "comfortable houses are to be erected" for winter quarters.[12] On April 20, Gettysburg's Town Council voted to contribute $500 to the fund for families of volunteers. That June the County Commissioners passed a modest property tax to fund more substantial assistance to the families of volunteers.[13]

In August, Gettysburg hosted a Grand Military Review of

Adams County troops, with several thousand citizens and roughly 350 soldiers in attendance.[14] Throughout the fall, local regiments departed for the front, and the two local newspapers continued to follow their exploits with care. As 1861 came to a close, the War Department ordered the Tenth New York Cavalry to winter quarters outside Gettysburg. The troops took up temporary quarters in several vacant buildings throughout the town. Gettysburg staged a reception in the New Yorkers' honor and their commander, Colonel James C. Lemmon, issued a statement requesting that any breaches of the peace by his men be reported directly to him.[15]

For several months, the 776 members of the 10th NY Cavalry, known as the Porter Guards, were the talk of the borough. Residents regularly attended the troop's afternoon parades and individual soldiers soon became part of the borough's social world. As the *Compiler* put it, "Our place is far more lively than usual, but good order prevails all the while." When new barracks were finally completed a mile east of town, the citizens staged a formal ceremony at which local women presented the Porter Guards with a banner. On their departure the *Sentinel* grew wistful: "We miss the lively Bugle in our Square. . . as well as the music of the Band, and the handsome military display." But even after the Porter Guards had left town, local citizens made regular sorties to the camp to watch the parade drilling. When the regiment finally left for the front, the *Compiler* noted that "many pleasant associations have been formed" during their stay."[16]

Diarist Salome Myers would certainly long remember the men from New York. From their first days in town Salome routinely attended gatherings with men from the Porter Guards. In fact, Ed Casey became such a consistent companion that Salome's ex-beau—an ailing local man named Snyder—charged that she had been the subject of town gossip. Salome never revealed a particular affection for Ed until mid-March, after the Porter Guards had left for Perryville. Then she wrote: "It is just a week since the Porter Guards left Gettysburg. i am beginning to miss them or rather Ed, for I knew him better than any other one in the Regiment. May God be with him *wherever* he goes." In the months to come, Salome's romantic plot thickened as she continued to alternatively see and reject Snyder while carrying on an intense correspondence with Ed Casey.[17]

Gettysburg's "adoption" of the Porter Guards is an interesting variation on the localistic theme that characterized Gettysburg's first few years of war. When the regiment departed, the *Sentinel* promised that "we shall follow the 'Porter Guards' as they go onwards." After their departure the local papers, like Salome Myers, followed their recent guests much as they traced the activities of Gettysburg's volunteers.[18] In this fashion, the local (and personal) became intermingled with the war's regional and national aspects.

The borough's wartime voluntarism also continued this combination of local sensibilities with an increasingly national perspective. The Ladies' Union Relief Society continued to orchestrate the borough's benevolent efforts. In October 1861, both newspapers published appeals from the U.S. Sanitary Commission to the "Loyal Women of America" calling on them to form local organizations of patriotic women. The *Sentinel* addressed these words to the women of Adams County:

> You are among the *loyal women of America*, who are called upon— while your sons, husbands and fathers are exposing themselves to great hardships, and death itself upon the battle-field—to come to the aid of the sick and wounded, and to do *what is in your power* to maintain our country—OUR EARTHLY ALL—against the traitorous hands that have been lifted up to destroy it!

The paper went on to make the Sanitary Commission's point more explicit:

> You have already done great service to those who have gone from our immediate neighborhood; and now you are urged to send as many of the articles mentioned in the Appeal of the Secretary of War, as you are able—that those who are SUFFERING, FAR FROM HOME, MAY BE MADE AS COMFORTABLE AS POSSIBLE."[19]

The *Sentinel* was joining the national umbrella organization in calling on Adams County women to look beyond their borders for objects of patriotic benevolence. In the next few weeks, "the Ladies of Gettysburg" answered this call by sending several boxes of food, clothing, and blankets to military hospitals in Baltimore, earning the profound thanks of the USSC's Washington branch.

Despite these highly publicized appeals from the Sanitary Commission, Gettysburg's Ladies' Union Relief Society seems to have carried on pretty much as it had before. Under the continuing leadership of Mrs. R. G. Harper (the wife of the *Sentinel*'s editor), the Relief Society moved from project to project. Throughout December 1861, they shipped packages to the wounded soldiers in Baltimore. The following June, they answered a new appeal from the female volunteers at the military hospital in York, Pennsylvania. When Lee invaded the North the next fall, the women of Gettysburg mailed bandages and food to Keedysville and Antietam. In February 1863, the Ladies' Relief Association issued a call for donations to the sick and wounded in Washington. In response to each of these special calls, the Relief Society published requests for donations of goods and money to be delivered to Mrs. Harper. If these periodic emergencies led the volunteers to look beyond their community borders, they never really had to look very far. In the meantime, the group apparently met regularly to prepare materials for local volunteers in the field.

This array of voluntary efforts suggest something about the public position of women in wartime Gettysburg. Nearly all the fairs, festivals, and voluntary societies active during these two years were formally designated as efforts by local "Ladies." Whereas male voices dominated the U.S. Sanitary Commission and U.S. Christian Commission at the national level, Gettysburg's Ladies' Relief Society—like many local bodies across the Union— had an entirely white female membership. The women and men of Gettysburg clearly viewed these war-related activities as the logical extension of women's proper sphere. Did these early efforts also extend the public position of women? Certainly their voluntaristic efforts received widespread recognition. Public calls for assistance were aimed at local women; announcements that packages were in the mail typically praised the efforts of "the ladies" of the town. In a particularly interesting public acknowledgment of women's warwork, the *Sentinel* took to publishing an extensive column of benevolent notices under the heading, "The Ladies."

The public role—and recognition—of Northern women extended beyond the philanthropic to the ceremonial. Departing troops routinely received hand-sewn banners or flags from local women's groups. At one gathering honoring the 10th New York Cavalry, Colonel Lemmon offered public thanks to the local women who had cared for the regiment's sick members and then the Porter Guards offered "three cheers for the Ladies of Gettysburg."[20] Such rituals suggest an appreciation for women, but largely in a symbolic context. The borough's 1861 Independence Day celebration was particularly telling. That afternoon a group of local women presented the Zouaves with a flag. This was followed by a military parade and a series of public toasts. Each toast—to the Union, the flag, leading public institutions, and major (male) figures both living and dead—was followed with a formal response. The final toast was offered to "Woman":

> The light of the world—God's noblest gift to man. The talisman of all our joys, and the sympathetic friend in all our distresses. Her beauty only excelled by her virtues and her devotion steadfast and pure as the Northern Star.

The official response was delivered by J. C. Neely, Esq., a leading male in the community.[21] On this grand public occasion, "Woman" was to be praised, but women were neither seen nor heard.

As the war entered its second year, the rising manpower demands put new strains on Northern communities. In July 1862, Lincoln called for 300,000 new three-year volunteers. Disheartened by the slow response to this latest appeal, Congress passed the 1862 Militia Act, laying the groundwork for state militia drafts. The following month the President asked for 300,000 nine-month recruits, to be conscripted if necessary. At the national level, this series of events, and the complex negotiations and calculations that followed, revealed a government inching toward federally controlled conscription. In the process, local communities faced new recruiting demands.

Gettysburg responded with several large "war meetings" to raise bounty funds. These voluntary contributions, which quickly amounted to over $1,400, were supplemented by appropriations from the County Commissioners.[22] Throughout August and early September, enrollers collected names and the people of Adams County braced for a draft. The Provost Marshal set the County quota at 1,645 men, including 157 for Gettysburg. Several weeks before draft day the newspapers announced that Gettysburg had been credited with 159 men in Pennsylvania service and another 18 who had volunteered in other states, giving the town an excess of 20 men beyond its quota. Therefore, while the county was still nearly a thousand men short of its quota, Gettysburg would be spared a draft. Nonetheless, the borough still remained in the thick of the conscription process. In early August, conscripted men from across the county converged on "Camp Gettysburg" where they were quartered awaiting medical inspection and official mustering into the army. In a sense, their presence was reminiscent of the Porter Guards. Local citizens ventured to the camp to watch the draftees drill; military officials asked Gettysburg's women to provide blankets, sheets, and even a flag for the new recruits. There were, however, important differences between these conscripted soldiers and the enthusiastic volunteers of the previous winter. Armed guards were posted around Camp Gettysburg to discourage deserters; $5 rewards were offered for help in capturing those who got away. And occasional newspaper stories suggest that these new visitors were not as universally orderly as their predecessors. Finally, in mid-December, the draftees boarded three railroad cars and departed for the seat of war.

Gettysburg's general enthusiasm for the war effort, reflected in both enlisting and voluntarism, masked deep political divisions. Whereas most Northerners claimed to support the Union, they split over crucial Republican policies. Once again, Gettysburg's experience during the first two years of war reflected larger national political patterns played out in a local arena.

From the outset, Stahle's *Compiler* served as a persistent critic of administration policies nationally and Republican sentiments closer to home. The *Sentinel* followed a more cautious path, emphatically supporting the Union while distancing itself from radical abolitionism. This approach was typical of Pennsylvania Republicans, who renamed themselves the "Union" party. In the fall of 1861, the *Sentinel* celebrated Union victories in the Adams County elections. The following March, the party triumphed in the borough elections, although the *Compiler* pointed out that the margins were smaller than customary. By the close of 1862, both parties were gearing up for a heated set of national, state, and local elections. The *Compiler* warned its readers of the dangers of imminent emancipation, claiming to unmask its opponents as closet abolitionists. When the votes were counted, the Democrats had swept to victory in Adams County, but Gettysburg voters continued to support the Union candidates in their losing efforts.

The following March the slate of local Republicans once again controlled the borough elections.

These political battles were fought in an atmosphere of rising partisan tension, amid acrimonious charges and countercharges. Soon after the Independent Blues returned from the field in August 1861, the company published a lengthy document beginning with the following preamble:

> Information having been communicated to us in regard to certain persons in the Borough of Gettysburg, and in different portions of the County, who by their words and actions have given indubitable evidence of *disloyalty*; and whereas, things have come under our observation, since our return, to satisfy us that such is the case.

These words were followed by a series of resolutions attacking treasonous talk and action and threatening ominous consequences for all those who persisted in such behavior. The Blues took particular care to include "those who *print* as well as those who speak and act—or in any other way give aid and comfort to the rebels."[23] The *Compiler*, perhaps feeling the sting of such threats, routinely insisted on its loyalty, going so far as to print warnings about the proliferation of treasonous "Dark Lantern Societies" in other parts of the country.[24] In August 1862, as political tensions were heating up and the county braced for the upcoming draft, the *Sentinel* warned: "It would, perhaps, be well for some individuals in this community to remember that there is a law on our statute books imposing heavy penalties on those who discourage enlistment." Editorials in the same issue chastised the *Compiler* editor for his insufficient patriotism and applauded government officials for political arrests in nearby Frederick, Maryland.[25]

By the following spring, the combined tensions of emancipation, conscription, and military failure had brought the North's political conflicts into the open. Partisans on both sides turned to new political organizations. On April 25, 1863, a gathering of Gettysburg men launched a chapter of the national Loyal Union League, an organization that they insisted was nonpartisan but which the *Compiler* dismissed as merely an abolitionist body. The previous month the *Compiler* described a "Festival of the 'Americans of African descent'" which was "largely and liberally patronized by 'black spirits and whites.'" The Democratic paper added that "it is supposed that the 'Union League' made it a point to have the Festival a more than ordinary success, because on the same night 'white folks' had a Promenade Concert at Sheads & Buehler's Hall."[26] This intriguing story indicates that local Republicans had an informal "Union League" in place before April.

In May several men from the surrounding towns were arrested as suspected members of the Knights of the Golden Circle, a secret organization with Confederate sympathies. When several Westminster men were arrested a few weeks later, Stahle's *Compiler* called the action the work of a "few low curs of the Abolition party."[27] One can only imagine what charges must have been made in more private settings.

In the first two years of the war, Gettysburg had evolved from fervent enthusiasm to a more organized, business-like approach to the conflict. Recruits responded to cash bounties as much as patriotic rhetoric. Voluntary societies had established regular routines to answer each new call for assistance. Nevertheless, the world had not changed very much. A few weeks in mid-summer would provide a new host of challenges.

In June 1863, Confederate General Robert E. Lee opted to head north for a second time. By this point, the citizens of Gettysburg had become accustomed to invasion scares and it was not until late June that most locals began taking the threat seriously and bracing for the worst. Farmers drove their animals to safety, merchants packed up their retail stock for shipment to more distant towns, and some citizens—including many local African Americans—fled the borough.

On June 19, Company A of the 26th Pennsylvania Emergency Volunteer Infantry, all men from Gettysburg, were mustered in for service. On June 22, a group of Gettysburg men—including Sarah Broadhead's husband—who had journeyed west of town to fell trees to impede the Rebels' progress rushed home to report that the Confederates were on their way. On June 26, the 26th Pennsylvania Emergency Troops made an unsuccessful stand against a Confederate contingent outside Gettysburg. That day, Confederate General Early arrived in town and demanded various supplies, including flour, meat, groceries, shoes, hats, and ten barrels of whiskey; he and his troops left the following morning. On June 28, Union cavalry were spotted just outside town, but they left the next day. By June 30, Gettysburg civilians could see Confederate pickets and officers on Seminary Ridge. That same day, Union cavalry leader Buford and his troops arrived in town to an enthusiastic greeting, and many soldiers were invited to dinner at Gettysburg homes. Finally, on the morning of the 1st, Buford's cavalry made contact with Confederate infantry on McPherson's Ridge to the west of the town. The battle had begun.

Although most of the battle was fought outside the town limits, Gettysburg civilians did come into repeated contact with soldiers from both armies. On the morning of July 1, people in the northwest section of town heard the first sounds of battle; a few young boys climbed up on the Seminary's cupola to watch the action while civilians gathered along Seminary Ridge or sought vantage points on rooftops in town. In late morning, the Union's 11th Corps marched up Washington Street to meet the enemy north of the College. But that afternoon the 11th Corps passed through again, this time in full retreat toward Cemetery Hill. Several civilians immediately began tending to the wounded, but soon Union officers rode through town warning everyone to take refuge in their cellars. From their hiding places, many reported hearing sounds of fighting between the retreating Union forces and the pursuing Confederate troops. By the evening, Confederate troops occupied the town.

On the evening of July 1 and throughout July 2, Gettysburg civilians faced the threat of Confederate vandals and stray bullets. Rebel soldiers searched houses for hidden Union soldiers and demanded food from civilians. Meanwhile, the occupying troops built barricades in the streets against possible Union attacks from Cemetery Hill to the south. In the southern part of town, sharpshooters targeted any vaguely suspicious people. Rebel marksmen commandeered homes with promising windows, drawing Union fire toward civilian targets. Mary McAllister was nearly shot when she ventured to the store to get whiskey for medicinal purposes. The town was literally split between Union and Confederate forces, the latter occupying much of it. At John Rupp's house, Confederates occupied the back of the house while Union men fought from the front porch.

By July 3, life inside the town had settled into a routine for most civilians: they stayed inside as much as possible. Loud cannonading continued through the late afternoon, and the danger from sharpshooters continued. Jennie Wade, the only civilian killed during the battle, was hit by an errant bullet. In a Confederate-controlled section of town, Agnes Barr left her house for the first time since the battle began. As she returned with supplies, she had to run to avoid Union sharpshooters. In the afternoon the tremendous artillery duel that preceded Pickett's charge seemed, to Sallie Broadhead, "as if heaven and earth were crashing together." That evening, citizens in their cellars could hear the creaking of Confederate wagons in retreat. It was the evening of July 4—Independence Day—that a relieved Sallie Broadhead wrote: "For the first time for a week I shall go to bed feeling safe." By the end of the day, many civilians correctly suspected that the Confederate forces would be defeated soon, but when the Confederates sent in a flag of truce the next day, some civilians feared it was a warning that they were going to shell the town.[28]

During the days of the battle, local citizens filled various roles. On the first day, many townspeople managed to observe some of the fighting from rooftops until the Confederates entered the town. During and immediately after the battle, Gettysburg civilians provided food, lodging, and care for the wounded of both sides. Citizens set up hospitals in public buildings and took wounded soldiers into their homes. Agnes Barr, for instance, aided wounded Union soldiers in her home and at a nearby church. Mary McAllister also helped with wounded soldiers, even venturing outside of the hospital to find doctors for them. Some Gettysburg civilians harbored Union soldiers despite threats of punishment from the Confederates. Catherine Foster managed to keep Confederate soldiers from discovering a Union soldier hidden in her home. The Forney family disguised a Union soldier in civilian clothes during the Confederate occupation. Some civilians found more direct ways to assist the Federal forces. John Burns, the aging veteran of the War of 1812, rushed to the battlefield to stand alongside the Union troops. Tillie Pierce Alleman recalled that two Gettysburg College professors "point[ed] out to the Union officers the impregnable positions of the locality"—that is, readily defendable positions.[29]

Black Gettysburg civilians experienced the battle differently from the white citizens. Although much of the battle was fought near the black section of town in the southwest, no black homes were used to house the wounded during or after the battle. Many African Americans had left Gettysburg before the battle. In her diary late that month, Salome Myers wrote that "[t]he town is pretty clear of darkies. . . . Darkies of both sexes are skedaddling and some white folks of the male sex." Some who stayed behind were hidden by their white employers. Jacob Taughenbaugh's mother hid her two African American servants in the cellar. "Old Liz," who had been captured by Confederate troops, managed to escape the Rebels on the first day of battle and hid in a church belfry for the next two days.[30]

The battle of Gettysburg and the invasion scares in June exacerbated previously existing local conflicts. Tillie Pierce Alleman described how tension between her family and their neighbors resulted in angry accusations in the tense days before the battle. Her father was described to a Confederate colonel as a "black Abolitionist" by a woman who blamed their family for her son's near capture. Shortly after the battle ended, Henry Stahle, the editor of the Democratic *Compiler,* was arrested for purportedly directing the Confederates toward hidden Union troops. That accusation, which stemmed from Stahle's efforts to find a doctor for a wounded Union soldier, likely reflected his controversial political stances.[31]

White citizens' experiences during the battle (and recollections after the fact) reflected continued assumptions about gender roles. Women were celebrated for being nurturers: nursing wounded soldiers, cooking, and providing lodging. Fannie Buehler wrote that after the battle started, "The wounded were brought in. Here was women's work, and they did it nobly." Agnes Barr and many other women remained busy providing food for the wounded soldiers they hosted in their homes. In one instance, Confederate soldiers killed Harriet Bayly's chickens, then brought the chickens to her to cook. Gettysburg's men were also engaged in tending to the wounded, but contemporary accounts consistently stressed

the contributions of women. Commenting on the praise lavish-
ed on Gettysburg women for their nursing efforts, the *Compiler*
was moved to add: "Some of our male citizens were active in ren-
dering all the aid in their power to alleviate the suffering wounded."[32]

The personal accounts emphasized that Gettysburg men were
responsible for protecting goods, home, and family, even when
these roles came into conflict. One week before the battle, Harriet Bayly's husband and son left town to remove their horses
and some valuables from the Confederates' reach. Harriet Bayly
stressed that her husband returned by the first day of the battle,
"being anxious about the welfare of his family." William Bayly,
thirteen years old during the battle, later wrote, "Our skedaddling
trips were entirely for the protection of our stock and not for personal safety, as my father was too old for military service and I
too young." Other men, such as Liberty Hollinger's father, attempted to keep Confederate soldiers out of their homes and tried
to retain their supply of food despite Confederate demands. Even
when men acted for their own protection, the published narratives stressed their heroic aspects. For example, Fannie Buehler
wrote that she persuaded her husband, David, "much against his
will, to prepare for flight should the enemy make an invasion into
Pennsylvania," as he was a staunch, outspoken Republican as
well as a postmaster.[33]

The most telling challenges to gender roles occurred when local
women were temporarily left alone to defend their families and
homes. Fannie Buehler's husband was unable to return through
the army lines until after the battle ended. As Sarah Broadhead
wrote, "I was left entirely alone, surrounded by thousands of
ugly, rude, hostile soldiers, from whom violence might be expected." Several narratives described local women brazenly confronting Confederate soldiers or demanding help for the wounded. In
other cases, women defied Confederate orders by helping to har-
bor Union soldiers. Although they cared for the wounded from
both sides, Gettysburg's women explicitly identified with the
Union soldiers. On July 11, Broadhead wrote, "[t]his day has
been spent in caring for OUR men."[34]

Any talk of historic "turning points" is almost inherently misleading: the past has few right angles. Nonetheless, the first few weeks

of July 1863 were certainly crucial in shaping the course of the Civil War. The day after Pickett's disastrous charge in the fields outside Gettysburg, Vicksburg fell to Federal forces, giving the Union control of the vital Mississippi. Nine days later, New York City erupted in bloody draft rioting, underscoring the North's conflicts about conscription, race, and the progress of the war. In hindsight, it is easy to argue that the South had little chance of achieving a purely military victory after the summer of 1863. For the next two years, Gettysburg had a strange dual identity. As the site of the Confederacy's "high water mark," the borough took a special place in the nation's consciousness. As a Northern community, Gettysburg continued to experience the war's evolutions much like the rest of the North. Our task is to sort out both how the battle affected Gettysburg and how the larger patterns of change touched this small Pennsylvania town.

For weeks after the battle, Gettysburg was dramatically different from all other Northern towns. Contemporary accounts decribe evidence of the "ravages of war" for miles in all directions. Fences and crops had been destroyed, animals were lost, and— above all—thousands of dead and wounded remained to be tended to. Scores of benevolent volunteers, including the famed Dorothea Dix, descended on the town. Both the USSC and the USCC established bases of operation, complementing the ongoing relief efforts by local citizens. Private homes became emergency hospitals, prompting the local papers to declare: "We feel satisfied that Gettysburg and its loyal citizens will not be forgotten when the history of this War is written by the future historian." As Sarah Broadhead noted ten days after the battle ended, "The old story of the inability of a village of twenty-five hundred inhabitants, overrun and eaten out by two large armies, to accommodate from ten to twelve thousand visitors, is repeated almost hourly."[35]

Soon calm returned to Gettysburg. Trains carried the many wounded soldiers to distant hospitals. Others were moved to a temporary General Hospital outside of town. Before long, the citizens began discussing how the battle should be commemorated, eventually settling on a proposal for a grand National Cemetery near the battlefield. After months of detailed planning, the cemetery's official consecration day was set for November 19. Once again, the nation's eyes turned to the Pennsylvania community as Abraham Lincoln and a huge assembly of dignitaries took the train to Gettysburg. Edward Everett, the leading American orator, delivered a lengthy address, which was followed by a few carefully chosen words by the President. The event, the *Sentinel* declared, "made Gettysburg famous for the second time."[36]

Throughout the weeks after the battle, the local voluntary organizations carried on their familiar routines, but the national benevolent societies began playing an expanded local role. In early August, a group of Gettysburg men, identifying themselves as the "Local Committee of the USCC," issued an appeal for food, clothing, and blankets for the wounded soldiers. The following month, several "ladies of the town," joined with USSC and USCC workers to entertain the soldiers at the General Hospital.

By early 1864, the local branch of the Christian Commission had taken on new prominence. In late March, the committee called for donations, suggesting "that our citizens collect and contribute relics and mementoes from our battlefield, by the sale of which in the city fairs, considerable sums can be realized." The Ladies' Aid Society for the Christian Commission formed a few weeks later. The Society's seventeen members included the wives of five of the six men on the local branch of the USCC. The Gettysburg branch of the USCC raised $1,132 in the town and the surrounding county.

In the final year of war, the two national benevolent societies grew in stature, often competing for limited resources. The Sanitary Commission responded by staging a series of fund-raising "sanitary fairs" across the North, with Philadelphia hosting the second largest in June 1864. Planning for the Philadelphia fair quickly became a statewide effort. In April, the Adams County subcommittee called on towns to form their own organizations to raise money and collect goods for the fair. Gettysburg's citizens were especially asked to collect trophies from the battlefield and local women were "earnestly solicited to prepare articles from the mosses, grass, ferns, pines, &c, taken from the Gettysburg battlefield." For the next several weeks, the local committee made repeated requests for assistance, often stressing the historic significance of battlefield memorabilia.

On one level it would seem that Gettysburg became a battleground between these two competing national agencies. In mid-April, local papers reprinted the following appeal from the Christian Commission: "In these days when 'Sanitary Fairs' are engrossing the public attention and absorbing immense sums of money, we ask the christian public to remember and aid the society whose unpaid delegates are upon the battle field." This request, which included a thinly veiled slap at the Sanitary Commission's *paid* agents, reflected the tensions between the two national agencies. Yet three of the ten Adams County women on the Sanitary Fair committee also served on Gettysburg's branch of the USCC's "Ladies' Aid Society," and a fourth was the daughter of a USCC committee member. The Fair Committee also included Mrs. R. G. Harper, who continued to direct Gettysburg's local Ladies' Union Relief Society.

In the summer after the battle, Gettysburg once again braced for a new Confederate invasion. In mid-July, the tension within the borough mounted as the streets filled with refugees and animals from farms and towns to the south. The initial scare turned out to be a false alarm and calm slowly returned. A few weeks later, word reached Gettysburg that Confederate raiders had entered Pennsylvania and burned Chambersburg. Following lessons learned the previous year, farmers fled with their animals, local merchants packed their goods off to distant towns, and a hundred armed volunteers stepped forward for home defense. When the immediate threat subsided, Gettysburg's philanthropic machinery eased into motion. A town meeting named a "Committee of Ladies" to assemble goods to ship to Chambersburg and an affiliated men's committee assembled to collect cash donations.

Neither the experiences following the battle nor the changing nature of benevolence in its aftermath seems to have had much of an effect on the perception or reality of Gettysburg's benevolent gender roles. Both the local and national societies separated men and women into different bodies, with men in positions of greater national authority and with appeals for assistance reflecting gendered assumptions. The committees named to assist the Chambersburg victims were quite typical: the women collected goods and packed boxes, whereas the men's group was charged with receiving cash donations. Other public roles reflected similarly persistent divisions. When patriotic occasions called for civic ritual, Gettysburg's "ladies" were still called on to present flags or serve similar ceremonial functions.

Recruiting practices, like voluntarism, took on new characteristics in the final years of the Civil War. By mid-1863, Northerners grew increasingly desperate to find volunteers to meet Federal quotas without holding drafts. The grim story of New York City's rioting only exacerbated such concerns. In August 1863, after months of recruiting and anticipation, the names of forty-nine Gettysburg men—including seven African Americans—were drawn to meet the borough's new quota.[37] That October, Abraham Lincoln called for another 500,000 men, with the draft to occur in March. As draft day approached, the town adopted newly aggressive measures. In January, the borough held a large meeting and named an official recruiting committee. The Town Council approved a motion to borrow $4,000 to fund $100 bounties for local recruits (to be grafted onto existing state and federal bounties). When draft day arrived, Gettysburg had already filled its quota.

The town had little opportunity to rest on its recruiting laurels. Lincoln issued three more major calls in 1864. On each occasion, communities were given ample opportunity to fill their quotas before draft day. These drafts are best viewed as recruiting incentives, rather than measures designed to put conscripts into uniform. Gettysburg responded to each call in typical fashion: with aggressive lobbying to reduce their assigned quotas and increasingly frenetic bounty-fund drives. By September, the town committee had raised $14,500 in voluntary subscriptions to go along with an $8,000 appropriation from the Town Council, providing recruits with sizeable $500 local bounties. These efforts enabled the town to escape each of the Union's remaining drafts. The three 1864 drafts yielded over 484,000 names drawn and 120,507 men "held to service." In contrast, Gettysburg met all its 1864 quotas without resorting to a draft.

Meanwhile, Gettysburg continued to link the Union's military successes with distinctly local concerns. Newspapers published letters from local soldiers and paid particular attention to the exploits of Gettysburg companies. The town celebrated the return of three-year regiments with familiar rituals, featuring parades, speeches, and receptions. Such celebrations mirrored rituals in communities throughout the North. The soldiers who returned home discovered that they had changed far more than the worlds they left behind.

The political tensions that festered through the first two years of war, and led to editor Stahle's arrest immediately following the battle, continued to divide Gettysburg for the rest of the war. Stahle's one week incarceration in Baltimore's Fort McHenry turned out to be only the first part of his ordeal. Immediately on returning to Gettysburg, he was arrested—and quickly released—a second time. The following week he returned to Fort McHenry to face new charges. Stahle insisted that he had acted innocently (and bravely) to assist the wounded Union colonel and that leading Republican lawyer David McConaughy was behind the charges.

Stahle's story suggests that political antagonisms persisted even in the midst of the fighting. In fact, he claimed that local "abolitionists" directed Union search parties toward Democratic homes and that his political enemies tore down the *Compiler*'s flag under cover of battle. The following year the issue resurfaced when the state House of Representatives debated a motion to limit reimbursements for military damage claims to those citizens who could "furnish positive proof of their loyalty." Democrats attacked this assault on their loyalty, insisting that they had been equally involved in assisting the Union troops.[38]

In 1863, Democrats had grown more open in their attacks on emancipation, conscription, and the suppression of civil liberties. After the battle, Gettysburg remained a Republican—or Union—Party stronghold in a largely Democratic Adams County. That fall the County supported the Democratic challenger to Governor Curtin, but Gettysburg backed the incumbent Republican 265 to 169. The following March the *Sentinel* celebrated as the Union ticket swept the Borough elections. Partisan political discourse heightened in the fall of 1864 when the Democrat George McClellan mounted a serious challenge to President Lincoln. The two parties staged large rallies in Gettysburg on consecutive September evenings. The language in speeches, letters, and editorials grew increasingly bitter as election day approached. Local Democrats delighted in playing the race card, accusing their adversaries of supporting Lincoln's most controversial abolitionist plans. Pennsylvania Democrats won victories in the crucial state elections, which preceded the national Presidential election, but Gettysburg continued to support Republican candidates for Congress and various local and county offices. A few weeks later,

Lincoln defeated McClellan with the support of Pennsylvania voters. Once again, Gettysburg supported the Republican candidate by a 259 to 178 margin. The following March, as the war was in its final stages, Gettysburg Democrats managed to win three local offices, including one of three positions on the Council. These modest victories led Stahle to declare that "The People [are] Getting Tired of Abolitionism."[39]

The wartime history of Gettysburg's African Americans, both before and after the battle, remains largely elusive. The March 1863 "Festival of the 'Americans of African descent'" reported in the *Compiler* indicates the continuation of separate civic rituals into the war years. As we have seen, many African Americans temporarily fled the town when Lee's troops advanced; others were captured and carried off by the Confederates. Those who returned after the battle often found property missing or destroyed. When the Union allowed African Americans to serve in uniform, several local men stepped forward and others appeared on the conscription lists. By one estimate, forty-three African Americans from the vicinity served in the Union Army. Despite such efforts, local whites clearly had little enthusiasm for racial equality, and both political parties were anxious to resist any taint of abolitionism.

In December 1864, Solomon Devan, a seventeen-year-old student at Gettysburg's "Colored School," drew a revolver and fired two shots at a teacher who had tried to "correct [him] . . . with a rod." Fortunately, Devan's shots missed their mark and thus he was only charged with assault and battery. The local court found the young man guilty, sentencing him to thirteen months in the state penitentiary. One can only guess at the untold story behind this episode. Perhaps Devan resisted because he saw his teacher's attitude as that of a master toward a slave. The two local papers reported the facts of the case, with the *Compiler* adding that "Abolitionism is costing more than it will come to."[40]

The Civil War's effect on Gettysburg's economy was generally quite modest. After a brief economic downturn during the secession crisis, the Northern economy prospered for the war years. Unemployment was extraordinarily low; demand for goods and services—partially stimulated by military need—was generally high. Whereas the Confederacy suffered from serious shortages and crippling inflation, most Northerners enjoyed the fruits of prosperity. The greatest exception were those unskilled or semiskilled workers who were hit hard by inflation and lacked the negotiating strength of their better organized brethren.

The anecdotal evidence from the local newspapers suggests that Gettysburg's businesses generally fared well during the war. Some local stores added military-related goods to their stock or used patriotic rhetoric in their advertising. A few individuals offered their services to citizens or veterans in search of pensions or bounties. Only a handful of local companies earned direct war-related profits. Two firms profited by building the barracks for the Porter Guards; the Gettysburg Railroad routinely reported modest profits from transporting military units; and, in October 1863, two local men won the contract to disinter bodies and move them to the new national cemetery. Periodically, Northern war contractors became embroiled in complex scandals involving shoddy equipment or illegal kickbacks. Adams County had its own small scandal during the war's first winter, when several farmers contracted with the War Department to board government horses. In the byzantine discussions that followed, it came to light that certain individuals were making exorbitant profits while subcontracting out the work to unsuspecting third parties.

The evidence from Adams County's Poor-House Accounts also tells a tale that is similar to the North as a whole. The auditor's annual report included a summary of residents in the almshouse as of the first of the year. Between 1858 and 1865, this population fluctuated between 107 and 118 people, suggesting that the almshouse probably ran at close to capacity. However, the number of transients assisted annually fluctuated dramatically. In 1860 and 1861—in the midst of the secession crisis—the county assisted 1,990 and 1,738 transients. By 1863 this figure had dropped to 814; the following year it fell to 430.[41]

In the war's final winter, the citizens of Gettysburg gathered for an emergency meeting "to adopt measures to relieve the wants of the destitute." The meeting named a "Relief Committee" composed of representatives from seven local church congregations and nine two-man "visiting committees" to visit the poor in their homes. They also named a parallel committee of "ladies of the Borough." Two months later, the Relief Committee called a public meeting to discuss their progress. But despite public announcements and bell ringing, only five committee members and no other citizens appeared.

What does the story of the Relief Committee indicate about wartime Gettysburg? Certainly it suggests unfamiliar demands for poor relief in the war's final months. The Committee's structure shared much in common with war-related philanthropies, with a steering committee of men and an auxiliary committee of women. Most of the members of the seven-man committee were drawn from the same pool of leaders that directed the town's benevolent and political organizations: three had been on the committee formed in April 1861 to assist the families of volunteers; three had run for local office (two Republicans and one Democrat); two had served on recruiting committees; and two served on the local branch of the USCC. Five of the eight members of the women's committee had served on at least one of the war-related benevolent committees and the remaining three were also from very active local families. Four years of war had done little to change the community's leadership structure.[42]

The events of April 1865 sent the Northern states through a bewildering series of emotional highs and lows. Early in the month, news arrived of the fall of Petersburg and Richmond, signaling the imminent end of the Confederacy. On April 4, the *Sentinel* reported: "Our town was quite jubilant last evening over the glorious intelligence. The flags, the ringing of bells, the firing of salutes, bonfires, and the cheering of the crowds, were evidences of the general rejoicing." With victory within reach, schools and public buildings closed and the town gathered for song, speeches, and celebration.[43] The revelry was to be short-lived. On the evening of April 14, Abraham Lincoln was shot while attending Ford's Theater. Newspapers across the North printed black-bordered accounts of the President's final hours. Gettysburg held a special town meeting that passed formal resolutions of sorrow and requested that citizens don black crepe armbands for the month to come. Before long, the Northern soldiers began filtering back home. In May, the returned Union troops staged a Grand Review in Washington. In early July, two years after the Battle of

Gettysburg, the town's surviving volunteers paraded through the flag-lined streets to enthusiastic cheers.

How had the Civil War and the Battle of Gettysburg altered the borough? By many measures Gettysburg, like the rest of the North, was surprisingly unchanged by four years of carnage. Whereas the South faced major physical damage, the destruction of slavery, and the concomitant demise of the plantation system, the North—and Gettysburg—experienced no comparable economic shocks (although of course some individuals suffered property losses from the invasion and battle). Certain local businesses profited from war contracts, but there was no need for substantial economic adjustments in response to the war's demands. In the long run, the town's notoriety as the site of the famous battle would dramatically alter its economic and cultural world. The evidence from the other end of the economic spectrum suggests a steady decline in the county's transient poor through most of the war, but a short-term increase in the demand for local poor relief during the war's final winter. One of the war's economic legacies that Gettysburg shared with many Northern communities was an expanded municipal debt. In 1869, the Town Council voted to implement a special Bounty Tax to repay subscribers who had invested in the town's 1864 bounty fund.

The best available demographic portrait comes from the census of 1870. In the decade of the 1860s Gettysburg's population climbed from 2,389 to 3,072, a rate of increase quite comparable to that of the national population. The military losses left some Southern states with a short-term "man shortage." Georgia, for instance had about 30,000 more women than men over the age of eighteen in 1870. No such shortage struck the more populous North. Gettysburg males made up roughly 51 percent of the population in 1870, a slight increase from 49 percent in 1860. The number of African Americans in Gettysburg increased from 190 to 223 over the decade, but the percentage of blacks in the population declined from 8 to 7 percent. One scholar has estimated that fewer than a third of the African Americans in the town in 1860 remained in 1870, perhaps owing to the dislocations accompanying the Rebel invasions. As in 1860, the vast majority of residents were born in Pennsylvania (82 percent) while an additional 271 (9 percent) were from Maryland. The African-American population included 63 (28 percent) people from Maryland and 24 (11 percent) from reconstructed Confederate states. The most substantial demographic shift was a decline in immigrants from 164 (7 percent of the total) to 127 (4 percent).

Of course, wars often have effects that resist quantitative measures. Some American conflicts, the American Revolution and World War II, for instance, affected the economic and social positions of women. The military experiences of African Americans have sometimes been connected to subsequent peacetime gains. Certainly both groups experienced important challenges during the Civil War. But the best evidence for concrete wartime changes—for blacks certainly, but for women as well—occurred in the Confederacy. The women of Gettysburg earned fame for their efforts after the battle, but such acclaim rarely challenged established gender norms.

Gettysburg's leadership structure seemed equally unaffected by four years of war. Periodically over the course of the conflict the borough selected men and women for special committees to address recruiting or philanthropic needs. A comparison of these committee lists reveals a handful of names appearing time and again. Moreover, these local leaders were drawn disproportionately from the town's economic elite. For instance, in the first days of the war, Joel B. Danner served on both the Central Relief Committee, to raise money for families of volunteers, and the Committee of Safety, which organized the Home Guard. In the next four years, the Gettysburg merchant, who had been listed with $6,000 in personal wealth in 1860, twice served on emergency recruiting committees and also on the local organizing committee for the Sanitary Commission's Great Central Fair. William A. Duncan, an attorney with $15,000 in real estate and another $8,000 in personal wealth, joined Danner on both April 1861 committees and later served on the 1864 recruiting committee and the 1865 Poor Relief Committee. Mary Carson served on the Ladies' Relief Society, on committees associated with both the USSC and the USCC and on the 1865 Poor Relief Committee. Her husband, T. D. Carson, was a local banker.

Another way to measure the war's impact is to consider the rising role of national institutions, both public and private, in everyday life. This was, after all, a war fought by national armies over the meaning of the Union. Gettysburg shared fully in many of the war's centralizing impulses, particularly after July 1863. In the war's final two years, the town threw itself into recruiting, stimulated by new federal conscription legislation. Both national benevolent societies played enlarged local roles after the battle, as did the patriotic Union League. And the wartime emphasis on national military and political affairs naturally drew the attention of citizens beyond their immediate surroundings. On the other hand, localism still prevailed in each of these areas: the Ladies' Relief Society maintained its autonomy; recruiting depended on local energies and fund-raising; and national political debates were viewed through the prism of local personalities and concerns.

We are left, then, with an almost troublesome conclusion. Although it was the scene of unimaginable carnage, Gettysburg survived the battle with surprisingly few effects. As traumatic as the events of July 1863 may have been, they did not last long, and when they were over the invading army had been vanquished. Communities across the South faced more serious challenges that were measured in months and years, rather than hours and days. In this sense, Gettysburg shared much more in common with the rest of the Northern home front than with the beleaguered Confederacy.

Perhaps the battle's true legacy is found less in the events than in their retelling. Immediately following the battle, the townspeople began seeing themselves as caretakers of an historically vital place. The creation of the National Cemetery in November 1863, spurred on by local citizens and sealed by Lincoln's famed visit, elevated Gettysburg into a new symbolic importance. The organizers of Philadelphia's Great Central Fair called on Gettysburg to provide battlefield "relics" rather than more routine donations. The town reflected its own shifting self-image in its annual celebration of Independence Day. The town celebrated July 4, 1862, in a traditional, highly localized fashion. In contrast, in preparing for the first Independence Day after the battle, the local organizers insisted on giving the celebration "a National character." Gettysburg's first postwar Independence Day featured a visit by President Andrew Johnson, who observed the laying of a cornerstone at the Soldiers' National Monument. The "great national celebration" that day included the President, the Cabinet, the Supreme Court, Ulysses S. Grant, and various other national dignitaries. Meanwhile, the town and the battlefield had already become a major tourist attraction, with visitors venturing from all over the North and South.

Gettysburg's civilians provided their own version of the battle's significance by telling their individual tales. Some citizens grew famous shortly after the battle concluded. Jennie Wade quickly became the subject of legend and controversy. John Burns survived his wounds to become a national hero. For other individuals, like editor Henry Stahle, the act of telling his story was part of his almost obsessive pursuit of vindication. In 1864, Sarah Broadhead printed her diary of the events between June 15 and July 15. In an almost apologetic preface Broadhead stressed that she was having her words "printed (not published) for distribution among [her] kindred and nearest friends" with seventy-five copies to be presented for sale at Philadelphia's Great Central Fair. She hoped that "these statements [would] disarm severe criticism" from those who objected to her rushing her "feeble efforts into print." As a woman, Broadhead felt the need for such disclaimers before placing her words in the public eye.

For a half-century and more, Gettysburg's citizens published diaries, memoirs, and interviews detailing the events during those three days in July 1863. By writing these personal "narratives," the civilian participants defined the battle as a momentous event in their individual lives. Their stories stressed the minutiae, not the grand themes. Perhaps this is because the North approached the battle, as it approached the Civil War, to protect what had previously been in place rather than to produce broad changes. For Gettysburg, victory ensured continuity. But in the process of remembering the battle, the borough helped shape inself into something quite new: a local community with a distinctive sense of its own national significance.

# 8

# The Pennsylvania Gambit and the Gettysburg Splash

## RICHARD M. McMURRY

Throughout the first three days of July in the year 1863, Union and Confederate troops fought a great battle at Gettysburg, Pennsylvania. This battle became the best-known engagement of the American Civil War. It may well be the best-known battle in the history of the United States and the subject of more historical studies than any other military engagement in which American troops have participated. Despite its prominence, and all the effort historians have devoted to studying it, and despite all the controversies it has engendered, Gettysburg is still a very much misunderstood battle. The more important the aspect of the battle, it seems, the greater the misunderstanding. This statement is especially relevant when it comes to the two most important facets of Gettysburg and the campaign of which it was a part—the battle's origins and its importance in the war's military history.

The soldiers who fought this great battle did not just drop from the Pennsylvania sky onto the hills and fields around the little town. Their arrival at Gettysburg was the end result of a long chain of events that began months earlier and at places far removed from southern Pennsylvania. Many of the men who played key roles in bringing about the battle, in fact, never set foot in Gettysburg and would never have heard of the town, had the battle not been fought there. Men with names such as Grant, Pemberton, Bragg, and Johnston are not usually associated with Gettysburg, but, in truth, they played important roles in bringing the war to Pennsylvania.

The campaign that led to Gettysburg grew out of the military situation that existed in the late spring of 1863. At that time, major Union and Confederate armies faced each other along a line of battle stretching from Central Virginia through Tennessee to the Mississippi River at Vicksburg, Mississippi, and on westward into Arkansas. Other contending forces stood along a second, less important line that curved from southeastern Virginia and eastern North Carolina down the South Atlantic Coast and westward along the Gulf of Mexico to Texas. Together these two lines formed a rough oval within which the embattled Confederate government of President Jefferson Davis, the Rebel armies, and the Southern people faced what the historians Thomas Lawrence Connelly and Archer Jones called "the crisis of April–May 1863."[1]

Rebel and Yankee troops glared at each other at hundreds of points along the circumference of this oval, but at only three of these places was there a real possibility of decisive action by one side or the other. One of these important points was in east-central Virginia, near Fredericksburg, where the Confederate Army of Northern Virginia, commanded by Gen. Robert E. Lee, confronted the Army of the Potomac under Maj. Gen. Joseph Hooker.

In the war's first two years, the Army of Northern Virginia had inflicted several crunching defeats on the Army of the Potomac, driving it away from the Rebel capital in Richmond and establishing itself as the Confederacy's premier military force and its commander as the South's best general. In the spring of 1863, the Army of Northern Virginia was a proud, veteran force, confident in itself and its generals and convinced of its ability to whip its adversary in any battle.

The second important point was in Middle Tennessee. There the Confederate Army of Tennessee under Gen. Braxton Bragg faced Maj. Gen. William S. Rosecrans and the Army of the Cumberland, which was based at Murfreesboro. Early in 1862, Bragg's army, then commanded by another general, had been driven out of Kentucky and the western part of Tennessee. Later that year Bragg had failed in an attempt to regain that area, and his army settled into its winter quarters about Tullahoma. Both Bragg and Rosecrans remained inactive throughout the first half of 1863—a veritable Tennessee *sitzkrieg*.

Unlike its sister army in Virginia, Bragg's force was internally weak. The rank and file was of excellent material, but the army's command structure was rotten at the top. Its generals squandered a great deal of their time and energy in unseemly squabbling and feuding with one another. Throughout the war, their intramural quarrels offset the bravery of their troops, hampered the efforts of their army, and made cooperation among themselves difficult and sometimes impossible.

Bragg himself was the worst offender. Indeed, the turmoil in the army's high command stemmed in large part directly from his spring 1863 efforts to place the blame for the failure of his recent campaign on some of his corps and division commanders and to purge the army of his personal enemies among the subordinate generals. Bragg's clumsy efforts, we must note, were fully justified by those generals' often lackluster performance and by their more-or-less open campaign to undermine his authority and bring about his removal from command.

This mutual vendetta between Bragg and his chief subordinates consumed their time and energy and ate away at the morale and fiber of their army. The psychological strains it produced played a major role in the rapid deterioration of Bragg's own physical and mental health in the first half of 1863.

The third crucial point was in western Mississippi, where the Confederate Army of Vicksburg, commanded by Lt. Gen. John C. Pemberton, sought to defend Rebel positions on the Mississippi River against Maj. Gen. Ulysses S. Grant's Army of the Tennessee. The Army of Vicksburg was a new and untried force, although many of its constituent units had been in service since the war's beginning. Pemberton's command had been created in late 1862 in an effort to bring some degree of order to the chaos that was then the secessionist military structure in Mississippi.[2]

Grant's army was a seasoned force that had won the North's

first important victories in February 1862. In the spring of 1863, Grant's objective was to capture Vicksburg. Achievement of that goal, along with the occupation of Port Hudson, Louisiana, by another Union column moving up the Mississippi from Yankee-held New Orleans and Baton Rouge, would reestablish Federal control along the entire length of the Great River and tear the Confederacy in half.

In the previous fall, Grant, based in Memphis, Tennessee, began his efforts to wrest the Mississippi from Pemberton. All during the winter of 1862–63, Grant tried first one stratagem and then another to get at Vicksburg. Each time his effort ended in failure. A column marching overland through northern Mississippi had to turn back when Confederate cavalry wrecked its supply bases. An assault on Walnut Hill (Chickasaw Bluffs) near Vicksburg was repulsed with heavy losses among the Northerners. Attempts to divert the Mississippi away from the Rebel fortifications at Vicksburg were thwarted by changing water levels in the river. Efforts to open an all-water route through the bayous north of the town were stymied by quickly constructed Confederate fortifications.

Finally, in mid-April, Grant managed to establish a land and water route along the west bank of the Mississippi so he could reach the river thirty miles below Vicksburg. Crossing to the east bank on April 30, Grant struck northeast toward Jackson, knocking aside ineffectual Confederate opposition as he went. His objective was to cut Vicksburg's ties to the rest of the Confederacy and isolate the river stronghold. Grant's appearance on the east bank of the Mississippi precipitated the crisis of April–May 1863.

Confederate response to Grant's threat to Vicksburg must be understood and evaluated within the parameters of the overall policies adopted by the Rebel government to offset the great numerical superiority of its enemy (see table); the command and administrative arrangements under which the southern forces were organized and controlled; and—most important—the abilities and personalities of, and the personal relationships among the Confederacy's political and military leaders.

From the beginning of the war, the Rebels insisted that they desired only to be let alone. At the opening of each year's cam-

**"Present for Duty" Strength of Opposing Forces March 31, 1863[3]**

| Location | Union | Confederate | Confederate as Percentage of Union |
|---|---|---|---|
| Virginia | 136,724 (Hooker) | 64,799 (Lee) | 47.4 |
| Tennessee | 81,923 (Rosecrans) | 54,305 (Bragg) | 66.3 |
| Mississippi | 105,151 (Grant) | 48,829 (Pemberton) | 46.4 |

paign, they stood passively on the defensive, waiting for the Federals to act.[4] At first such a policy led the secessionist government to post military units at virtually every point that might become the target of a Yankee attack. Once they ascertained the Unionists' objective, the Rebels would concentrate their forces at the point threatened by the Northerners. The telegraph and the railroad, which made possible instantaneous communication and rapid travel, would make such a policy feasible. This plan to shift troops from place to place was based on standard nineteenth-century military theories that stressed the use of "interior lines" of communication and defense to enable a weaker power threatened at several points on its borders to offset the numerical superiority of a stronger assailant.

In 1862, the pressure of events forced the Rebels to modify this policy. Confederate officials then realized that they could not hold every point. They, therefore, gave up many less important places to free troops for the defense of important ones. In the spring of 1862, for example, the Davis government more or less abandoned Florida to concentrate men in northern Mississippi. The basic concept, however, remained intact. Troops would move from one area to another to protect key points.

For military, administrative, technological, geographical, psychological, logistical, political, and diplomatic reasons, Confederate authorities sought to implement this policy and to hold as much Rebel territory as possible through a command and administrative system under which the Confederacy was divided into units called departments. Each department was commanded by a general officer who was responsible for its defense and the military forces stationed in it. Usually each department was independent and reported directly to and received orders directly from Richmond. On occasion, however, two or more departments would be placed under the temporary authority of one commander.

When several departments were under one commander, the crucial element in the system was his ability. When the departments were independent, the key to the system was to get the departmental commanders to work together to implement the President's scheme.

Except for a few weeks at the end of the war, the Confederacy had no commanding general or even a chief of staff to direct the operations of its field armies. For this reason the movement of troops across departmental boundaries normally would have to be coordinated by the civil authorities. Davis regarded himself as literally the commander-in-chief of the secessionist army, and he kept in his own hands control of all important, and numerous unimportant, military activities. In many cases, his secretary of war was little more than a clerk. One secretary of war, George W. Randolph, was, in November 1862, in effect driven from office because Davis refused to allow him any real responsibility and authority in military matters. In a very real sense, Davis's desk in Richmond was the headquarters of all Confederate military forces and therefore only the President could provide overall strategic direction for the Rebel war effort.

Davis's system of defending the Confederacy by shuttling troops from unthreatened areas to endangered points was based on six assumptions. For one thing, the President believed that the Yankees could mount but one major offensive at a time. To do so, he reasoned, they would have to transfer troops from other areas to strengthen their forces at the point they had chosen to attack. Davis also assumed that the Confederates would be able to ascertain the point at which the Unionists would make their major effort before the enemy campaign could get underway. Once he knew the objective of the Yankee offensive, Davis believed, he had but to advise Rebel commanders in unthreatened areas and they would rush reinforcements to the department menaced by the enemy. After the Northern advance had been defeated—that the Confederates would win was the fifth assumption—the reinforcements would return to their own department, where they would remain until another Unionist threat materialized. Then the whole process would be repeated. Eventually, Davis assumed, the Northerners would tire of the conflict and allow the South its independence.

Davis's system also had another side. It could be used to bring together troops from two or more departments for a quick offensive strike at the enemy.

Although in theory this system could be applied across the entire Confederacy, geography, politics, and the fragile condition of Rebel transportation conspired to place practical limits on it. The Appalachian Mountains and the Mississippi River divided the country into three militarily distinct regions—the East (Virginia, the Carolinas, and coastal Georgia), the West (between the Appalachians and the Mississippi), and the Trans-Mississippi. Owing to these geographical factors, Davis's system functioned most of the time as three distinct systems, one in each region.

By the spring of 1863, Davis's policy had proved brilliantly successful in providing for the defense of the eastern Confederacy. There the area of military operations was small and the Rebels enjoyed what was, by their standards, an excellent rail and road system that provided rapid transportation for the troops operating in the Old Dominion and along the coast of the Carolinas and Georgia. In the East, moreover, the nearby Rebel government was usually able to exercise a great deal of control over its military field commanders. In the East, also, the Confederates benefited from favorable terrain, enjoyed a real system of interior lines of communication, were to a large extent free from any danger from the Union navy which could not penetrate very far up the rivers, and were confronted by a collection of Federal generals who proved to be of less than mediocre ability. Most important, in the East the secessionists found a bold, daring, and skillful general who understood the importance of winning battles and often demonstrated his ability to do so. The system thus produced a stalemate in the East which allowed the Confederates to offset superior Yankee strength. So long as the Rebels could maintain such a balance, they would preserve their national independence. Unfortunately for them, the war was not limited to the East.[5]

As it turned out, there were nine fallacies in Davis's scheme of defense when it was applied to the West, and all of them came into play during the crisis of April–May 1863. First, Northern superiority in manpower and resources was so great that the Yankees were able simultaneously to undertake major efforts against many widely scattered parts of the Confederacy. On April 30, for example, as Grant was ferrying his army across the Mississippi below Vicksburg, Hooker was moving against Lee in the wilderness area around Chancellorsville west of Fredericksburg. At the same time, another large Federal force was active just to the north of Vicksburg, two long columns of Yankee cavalry—one in Mississippi; the other in northern Alabama and Georgia—were slashing through the western Confederacy, and reports and rumors abounded that the Unionists were about to advance from Kentucky into East Tennessee, to invade the North Carolina coast, to attack Charleston, South Carolina, and to move up the Red River into western Louisiana.

Even within the West itself, the Federals had the capability to undertake more than one operation at a time. The armies of Grant and Rosecrans could operate simultaneously and independently, and as they demonstrated in the late summer of 1863 the Yankees could also move a third western force into East Tennessee to capture Knoxville.[6]

A second problem arose because Davis in Richmond was unable to gather and interpret intelligence reports from all across the Confederacy. Many Rebel commanders in distant departments simply did not keep the government informed of what was transpiring in their areas or even of the strength and organization of their own forces. Indeed, in some cases, the local Confederate commanders were so confused that they did not know what was happening or they were distracted by the feints and demonstrations staged by the Unionists to divert attention from their real objectives. Sometimes Rebel generals were misled by inaccurate reports from their own scouts, spies, and subordinates who, in turn, might have been ignorant of or confused and bamboozled by Federal activities in their area. In two cases—those of Gens. Joseph E. Johnston and P. G. T. Beauregard—the personal relations between the general in the field and the President in Richmond were so bad that the generals had as little to do with the government as possible. Sometimes a Confederate field commander disliked his superior officer, or resented his own subordinate position, and therefore did not keep his commander informed of the situation in the local area. As a result of these conditions, the President was deluged with information about military operations in nearby Virginia while he often knew almost nothing about the situation in the far-distant West.

In early and mid-April, for example, the western Confederate commanders misinterpreted the movements of Federal steamboats on the Mississippi River. As a result, the Rebels concluded that Grant's army was moving to Middle Tennessee to reinforce Rosecrans for an attack on Bragg. In reality, Grant's troops were making their way south along the west bank of the Mississippi. Because of this intelligence failure the Rebels began to shift some of their own troops away from the endangered Vicksburg front to Tennessee where the Yankees were, and would remain, quiescent for two months.

"Much doubt it," Pemberton wrote on April 9 of a report that Grant was west of the Mississippi and moving south. As late as the fifteenth, he reported, "I am sending troops to [Tennessee], being satisfied that a large portion of Grant's army is reinforcing Rosecrans." Eleven days later, Maj. Gen. Dabney H. Maury, who had recently left Vicksburg, informed the Richmond authorities, "I believe that no immediate attack will be made there [Vicksburg]" and expressed the hope that a brigade might be transferred from Mississippi to reinforce his new command in East Tennessee. Because the information on which the Confederate decisions were based was often inaccurate, the decisions themselves were just as often wrong.[7]

Even when Davis's intelligence was accurate and his evaluation of it correct, he ran into a third problem. His whole system of defense depended on other Confederates concurring in his interpretation of the situation—or at least on their obeying Davis's orders whether or not they agreed with the President's view. Departmental commanders, however, had even less information about the enemy activities than did the Chief Executive. At best, each departmental commander was accurately informed only of the situation in his own front. He had no real knowledge of the threat to any other department, and his first concern was, naturally, to the defense of the area entrusted to him.

There is usually a tendency—called "localitis" in modern military jargon—for each commander to believe that he holds the most important point and that the greatest part of the enemy's military strength is being concentrated against him. Sad experience quickly teaches those in a military bureaucracy that men and materiel once released to another commander can be retrieved, if at all, only with great difficulty and delay. The new commander, believing his position to be in the greater danger, fights tenaciously to keep permanently the reinforcements sent to him on a temporary basis. As a general rule, the greater the distance between a Rebel general and Richmond, the less likelihood that he would accept the President's interpretation of reported enemy movements or hasten to obey orders from the distant capital to send some of his men to reinforce another department.[8]

Sometimes Davis's penchant for ignoring the chain of command and issuing orders directly to subordinate generals without going "through channels" constituted a fourth obstacle to the successful implementation of his system of defense. Such presidential interference with the normal workings of the chain of command could easily disrupt local efforts to compensate for some of the other weaknesses in the system.

In late 1862, Davis assigned Gen. Joseph E. Johnston to command all Confederate troops between the Appalachians and the Mississippi River and to exercise control over the armies of Bragg and Pemberton. Davis intended that Johnston would order troops from one to the other to meet whatever threat materialized.

The extent of Johnston's authority, his duties, the role expected of him as what amounted to a theater commander, and his official relationship to both the authorities in Richmond and the armies under his control were never made clear enough for the general to understand. To make matters worse for the Rebels, Johnston had convinced himself that Davis's plan to use the armies of Bragg and Pemberton to reinforce one another could not be made to work. Most important, Johnston was not of a temperament to use his own judgment and try to make something out of such an amorphous command situation. He hated Davis and believed that the President would do everything possible to humiliate him. Finally, Johnston resented being sent away from Virginia to what he regarded as a secondary area of operations.

On the other hand, Davis and many officials in Richmond were rapidly coming to the conclusion that they simply could not depend on Johnston. The general would not risk his great reputation by taking any bold action, and he refused to communicate with the government. For these reasons, Davis and the War Department often ignored Johnston, received some intelligence and administrative reports directly from Johnston's subordinates, and sometimes issued orders directly to units under Johnston's authority without consulting or even notifying that general. On March 27, 1863, an irritated Johnston, peeved at the Richmond authorities' habit of sending instructions directly to his subordinates, sarcastically telegraphed, "If the [War] Department will give me timely notice when it intends to exercise my command, I shall be able to avoid . . . interference with its orders." Doubtless, many officials in Richmond would liked to have replied that, if Johnston would exercise his command, it would not be necessary for them to do so from the capital.

As a result of this ambiguous command arrangement, these confusing administrative practices, and the bad personal relations between the two men, neither Davis nor Johnston had all the intelligence available on the situation in the West. Each could find his plans disrupted by schemes being implemented by the other, and subordinate commanders sometimes found themselves with conflicting orders.

In mid-May, Maj. Gen. Simon B. Buckner complained that troops in the Department of the Gulf were subject to the sometimes conflicting orders of four different superior officers—their own commander; Bragg, to whose area of responsibility the Mobile forces had long been assigned; Johnston, who at least nominally directed all Rebel troops in the West; and the War Department in Richmond. At about the same time, Pemberton, in Mississippi, had to decide whether to obey Johnston's order to abandon Vicksburg and thereby save his army or what he understood to be Davis's instructions to hold the city at all hazards, even if doing so meant that his troops would be trapped in the town and have to undergo a siege.

Such a command arrangement meant that any Confederate effort in the West would proceed in a chaotic, jerky fashion at best. This result, in turn, greatly exacerbated the existing personal animosities—especially that between Davis and Johnston—that did so much to hamper the Southerners. In summary, the situation was a disaster waiting to happen. In the crisis of April–May 1863 it did.[9]

A fifth problem with the President's plan to defend the West arose from his habit of giving equivocal orders. Davis would frequently conclude that some point was in danger, and he would telegraph the commander of another department to send "any available reinforcements" or to "send reinforcements if practicable" to the endangered point. Whether transmitted through normal channels or issued outside them directly to a local commander, such weakly worded instructions often made a bad situation worse.

The President had a long history of being unwilling to make up his mind and leaving crucial decisions to others. In the spring of 1863, he may, however, have realized that he did not know fully the situation in the department from which the reinforcements were to come and desired to preserve some degree of flexibility for local commanders.

Whatever the motive behind Davis's actions, such orders were open invitations to provincial commanders to conclude that no reinforcements were available or that it was not practicable to send them. An enterprising general could always find some excuse to disregard the President's telegram. Perhaps a recently captured newspaper contained a report that the Yankees were organizing a naval expedition for some purpose. In such a case, the general had little difficulty convincing himself that he best not send away any of his troops until he had ascertained the expedition's objective. In other cases, a commander could base his refusal to obey the President on the grounds that the distance to the threatened point was too great for the reinforcements to arrive in time or that adequate transportation for them was not available.

In many cases, a message from Richmond for one commander to reinforce another was followed by a lengthy telegraphic debate over the wisdom or practicality of the order. Eventually the Richmond authorities either acquiesced in the general's refusal to part with any of his troops or they overruled him and issued a peremptory order to send the reinforcements. In either case, valuable time had been squandered and much ill will had been created.

In November 1862, when Vicksburg was threatened by an enemy force, the brigade of Brig. Gen. Henry H. Sibley was ordered from Texas to the Mississippi River. While *en route* it was diverted to the Gulf Coast by Maj. Gen. John B. Magruder, commanding the District of Texas, New Mexico, and Arizona, who had concluded from newspaper reports that the Yankees would soon invade the Lone Star State. In January 1863, after the brigade had been pried loose from Magruder, it resumed its march. Soon, however, it was ordered to join Maj. Gen. Richard Taylor, whose western Louisiana command was thought to be in danger.

In late 1862, the Richmond authorities sent a request to Lt. Gen. Theophilus H. Holmes, commanding the Trans-Mississippi, to dispatch 10,000 men from northern Arkansas to help defend Vicksburg. This message read, "Can you send troops . . . say 10,000 . . . ?" It is indicative of the administrative confusion among the Rebels that in correspondence with Pemberton the authorities described this message as an order ("Holmes has been ordered"; "peremptorily ordered").

In his first reply, Holmes claimed that it would take at least two weeks for him to get troops to Vicksburg. Several weeks later, he reported to the authorities from his Little Rock headquarters that he had had to send most of his command to meet a Federal column advancing from Missouri into northwestern Arkansas. Withdrawal of his remaining force, he argued, would lead to the loss of the Arkansas River Valley. Besides, he pointed out, reinforcement of Vicksburg by his army would involve a march of three hundred miles across a barren area and take twenty-five days. In later communications, he put the time at thirty days.

Soon afterward, the Richmond authorities threw up their hands and telegraphed Holmes that he must use his own discretion since "It is impossible at this distance to judge of your necessities." The authorities did, however, express the hope that Holmes would reinforce Pemberton if it were possible for him to do so. Needless to say, the Rebels at Vicksburg did not see any of Holmes's men until the postwar veterans' reunions.[10]

Once Davis finally pried reinforcements loose and put them in motion, his plan ran into a sixth problem. The important points in the western Confederacy were so far apart and the rail routes so roundabout that it required a great deal of time to transport military units with their baggage and equipment from one place to another. In December 1862, a single infantry division took more than three weeks to move by rail from Bragg's army in Tennessee to join Pemberton's troops in Mississippi. The only rail route between the two armies—and it was not continuous—involved travel via an exterior line by way of Chattanooga, Atlanta, Montgomery, Mobile, and Meridian. The division's wagons, which went overland, were on the road for an additional week. Four months later, Gen. Joseph E. Johnston, who in theory exercised supervision over both Bragg and Pemberton, estimated that Confederate railroads had deteriorated so rapidly that the same movement would then require six weeks.[11]

The basis for some of Davis's policies had changed drastically in the early months of 1862 when the Confederates were driven from much of West and Middle Tennessee and parts of northern Mississippi and Alabama. Loss of those areas deprived the Rebels of some key railroads and changed the whole strategic picture in the West. If distance was measured in real terms of time and rail mileage—not straight line miles—the Rebels had to use an exterior line in the West after early 1862. The Federals who could transport men on the rivers could shift troops around in the West at least as quickly as the secessionists could. Davis seems not really to have understood this fact. At any rate, he did not adjust his strategic thinking to take it into consideration.

Overall Yankee numerical superiority constituted a seventh major impediment to the success of Davis's scheme. Even if the President could get reinforcements to an endangered point in time, there might well not be enough of them to offset the great numerical strength of the North. When the Chief Executive's order was to send whatever troops could be spared, the commander from whom they were to come often had no great difficulty convincing himself that he could spare only a few men. Sometimes local commanders simply ignored or unilaterally modified the instructions they received from the distant Rebel capital.

On May 2, 1863, for example, as Pemberton was trying to scrape together a force to oppose Grant south of Vicksburg, the

Confederate government ordered Gen. P. G. T. Beauregard, commanding the Department of South Carolina, Georgia, and Florida, to send 8,000 to 10,000 troops to Mississippi. Beauregard reported the following day that he had ordered two infantry brigades, in all about 5,200 men, to Pemberton. "To reduce this command further," he added, "might become disastrous." A week later, after the exchange of additional messages, he pleaded, "Don't strip us of troops. . . . There are evidences of impending attack [on Charleston]; don't invite it. I beg you to reconsider last order, and leave here what few troops [are] left." More positive orders followed, and a few days later Beauregard announced that "contrary to my opinion" additional troops had left for Mississippi.[12]

Unfortunately for the Confederates, even if all the reinforcements called for were sent, the Yankees were still likely to outnumber the Southerners. New York, Massachusetts, and Vermont alone could have fielded an army of eighteen- to forty-five-year-old white males that outnumbered the military age population of the entire Confederacy by more than 50,000 men. This great overall numerical superiority enabled the Northern armies simultaneously to undertake two or more major operations.

The simple fact was that the Federals would almost always outnumber any force that the Rebels could bring together. Even when Davis and his generals managed to concentrate a numerically superior army at some point, that superiority was likely to be short-lived, since the Federals could also quickly rush reinforcements to the crucial area. Meanwhile, the Confederates at the points from which their reinforcements had been taken would be even more outnumbered than before and even more vulnerable to the Yankees in their front. A Southern general who received reinforcements had to use them quickly or the secessionists would be worse off than they had been before the additional troops arrived.

Northern numerical superiority was so great that only an egregious blunder by the Federals, pure luck, brilliant strategy and tactics by Southern field commanders, and hard marching and fighting by Rebel troops would permit the Confederates to win a victory in any battle. In the West the secessionists could count on only the last of these factors.

For all these reasons, it was most unlikely that the Confederates could or would get enough reinforcements to the endangered point in time to wage a successful battle of the kind envisioned by Davis. In the crisis of April–May 1863, the time available to the Southerners was very limited. It was not until April 15 that Pemberton began to suspect that Grant might be maneuvering against Vicksburg, and it was a day or so after that that he began to try to accumulate troops with whom to meet the threat. As late as April 28, Maj. Gen. Carter L. Stevenson, commanding at Vicksburg itself, still believed that Grant's troops on the west bank of the Mississippi were there to "lay waste the country on that side" of the river and to distract attention from efforts being made against Stevenson's position. Not until Grant crossed the river on April 30 did it become clear where the danger lay.

At the same time, a major battle was raging in Virginia, where Hooker had moved across the Rappahannock and sought to defeat Lee or force him back to Richmond. Indeed, as early as April 14—when Pemberton still believed Grant to be *en route* to Tennessee—Lee detected signs that the main Federal army in Virginia would soon become active. By May 5, Lee had defeated Hooker and forced him back over the river. Lee's army, however, had suffered some 13,000 casualties, and its organization had been disrupted by the death on May 10 (he had been wounded a week earlier) of Lee's greatest lieutenant, Thomas J. "Stonewall" Jackson.[13]

Things did not settle down in Virginia until mid-May. By then the Confederate situation in Mississippi was hopeless. After a few efforts to stop Grant, a thoroughly befuddled Pemberton shut his army up in the Vicksburg fortifications to await succor from a then nonexistent Confederate relief column. Grant destroyed the railroads in East-Central Mississippi, brushed back the handful of Rebels gathered at Jackson, and turned west, trapping the hapless Pemberton against the river in the Vicksburg trenches.

With his own position at Vicksburg strongly fortified against both Pemberton within the city and any Confederate relief column that might approach from the east, with his own army reinforced, with both of his flanks resting securely on the river where they were protected by the Federal navy, and with the Great River itself serving as his indestructible line of supply, Grant by May 20 had put his army into an invulnerable position from which it could not have been driven by any force that the secessionists could possibly have concentrated against it.

Even if the Rebels had been able to assemble in Mississippi an army large enough to break Grant's grip on Vicksburg, they would have faced the enormous—and probably insurmountable—eighth obstacle to applying Davis's scheme to the military situation that then existed: the task of supplying and feeding the troops in the state. The destruction of Jackson and the railroads radiating from that city would almost certainly have made a lengthy campaign by a large Confederate army in Central and western Mississippi in May and June 1863 a logistical impossibility. In early May, during a conversation with Lt. Gen. James Longstreet, Secretary of War James A. Seddon mentioned the difficulty that the government was experiencing feeding the very small Rebel force then in the Jackson area.[14]

If Davis had been able to overcome all eight of these difficulties and to get an adequate number of reinforcements to a beleaguered point in time and to feed and supply them once they were there, his scheme would then have run directly up against the greatest obstacle to its successful implementation. The Confederates had only one army commander (full general) who ever exhibited an ability to devise and execute the bold and daring yet rational plans that were necessary if the smaller Rebel armies were to defeat their more numerous opponents. That general was Lee.

Gen. Joseph E. Johnston, who was ordered to Mississippi on May 9 to organize the relief of Vicksburg, was an extremely cautious, pessimistic officer, who was simply not psychologically, mentally, or morally capable of taking the risks essential for a weaker army operating aggressively against a much stronger opponent. As previously mentioned, Johnston disagreed with Davis's whole defense scheme for the West and believed from the first that it was doomed to fail. More serious still, Johnston was not capable of cooperating with the Confederate government because of the paralyzing quarrel that had erupted in 1861 between himself and President Davis.

By the spring of 1863, Johnston was becoming convinced that the President was conspiring to disgrace him by bringing about his defeat on the battlefield. Owing to this conviction, Johnston viewed with a suspicion bordering on paranoia every action by the government that affected him and his army. Consequently, he both complained of government meddling whenever he received detailed instructions from Richmond and refused to take any meaningful action without specific orders from the authorities. Like many Rebel commanders, he often did not comply fully with the orders he did receive.

By early July, the Confederates had scraped together in eastern Mississippi a motley force of some 30,000 men. At that time the rebels estimated Grant's army at Vicksburg to number from 60,000 to 100,000 men, and the consensus was that it was closer to the second figure.[15] No one familiar with the career of Joseph E. Johnston can believe that he, with a force of only 30,000 men, could have overcome Grant. On July 4, as Johnston with his tiny army maneuvered cautiously, hoping to open a route by which the trapped garrison might escape the doomed city, Pemberton surrendered Vicksburg and its defending army to Grant.

The gloomy situation in Mississippi and the collapse of President Davis's defensive scheme in the West led some high-placed Confederates to put forth two other possible solutions for the dilemma posed by the crisis of April–May 1863. Several of these men believed that the Rebels should use their departmental system for offensive purposes—to draw together troops from three or four departments for a quick strike against some vulnerable point. The most prominent of these leaders made up a political–military faction that has been identified as the "Western concentration bloc." Whereas Davis focused on defeating Grant in Mississippi by moving troops from other departments to the Magnolia State, members of the Western concentration bloc advocated offensive action on Bragg's front in Tennessee by troops taken from all over the Cis-Mississippi Confederacy. Such an offensive, they argued, would enable the Rebels not only to recover the area they had lost in the West in the war's first two years but also to sweep into Northern territory.

The most prominent member of the Western concentration bloc was Gen. P. G. T. Beauregard, commanding Confederate forces on the South Atlantic Coast. Beauregard had long urged the Rebels to effect a quick concentration against some isolated portion of the Federals. Observing events from his perch in Charleston in the spring of 1863, Beauregard came to the conclusion that the time for such action had arrived. On May 15, he wrote to Bragg, Johnston, and his friend Senator Louis T. Wigfall of

Texas explaining his plan. (Note that he did not communicate with anybody who had the authority to put his plan into effect.) "Suddenly and boldly," he urged, the Confederates were "to take the offensive in Tennessee and Kentucky." Forces in other areas were to be held "strictly on the defensive," and 25,000 to 30,000 troops were to be rushed to Middle Tennessee. They and Bragg's army, all commanded by Johnston, would crush Rosecrans. The increased prestige resulting from this victory would lead an additional 30,000 Tennesseans and Kentuckians to volunteer for the Rebel army. Johnston would then sweep west to the Mississippi River, cutting Grant's communications with the North and forcing him to fight his way upstream. "The result could not be doubtful for an instant." Once Grant had been disposed of, the mighty Confederate juggernaut could move into Louisiana and Missouri or it could turn eastward and hurl itself on the Yankees in Virginia. Meanwhile, a fleet of "torpedo rams" would be built in England and brought across the Atlantic. These vessels would enable the Confederates to dominate the lower Mississippi River, regain New Orleans, and capture a large part of the Federal army on the Gulf Coast. All of this, Beauregard believed, could be accomplished in about six weeks.

Eleven days later Beauregard wrote to Charles J. Villeré, his former brother-in-law and a Louisiana representative in the Confederate Congress, elaborating his ideas about what course the Southerners should follow. "We must take the offensive," Beauregard pontificated. Thirty thousand men should be detached from Lee's army and rushed to reinforce Bragg. Then Bragg ("or whoever is put in his place") would overwhelm Rosecrans and move into Ohio, where he could entice Indiana, Illinois, and Missouri "to throw off the yoke of the accursed Yankee nation" and persuade the entire Northwest to enter an alliance with the Confederacy.

Beauregard's personal relations with Davis were so bad that he urged Wigfall to present the May 15 plan to the government, but not reveal the name of its author. It is not known if Wigfall ever brought Beauregard's fantasy to the attention of officials in Richmond. If he did, perhaps President Davis had a much-needed laugh.[16]

It will be observed that if Beauregard's plan had been implemented on the day his first letter was written and had worked exactly as he envisioned it, it would not have achieved success until June 26, only eight days before Pemberton surrendered— and this assumes that the Rebel postal service should have delivered the letter the day it was written and that the government would have approved the plan immediately and implemented it without delay.

Lt. Gen. James Longstreet, commander of the I Corps of the Army of Northern Virginia, was another and slightly more realistic advocate of a concentration in Tennessee. As early as January 1863, long before the crisis of the spring, he suggested that one half of the Rebel army in Virginia be sent to reinforce Bragg while the other half stood on the defensive in the Old Dominion. Four months later, as he was passing through Richmond on May 6, Longstreet conferred with Secretary of War James A. Seddon. At that time, Confederate authorities were trying to assemble a force in Mississippi to save Vicksburg. Seddon mentioned the possibility that all or part of Longstreet's Corps might be sent to join Joseph E. Johnston's army in Mississippi. Longstreet, assuming that the Rebel army in Virginia would remain idle throughout the summer, countered with the suggestion that both he and Johnston join Bragg in Middle Tennessee. The combined Confederate forces could then sweep northward to capture Cincinnati. Such a Rebel offensive, he maintained, would force the Federal government to recall Grant and thus Vicksburg would be saved. (Some cynical historians have suggested that the ambitious Longstreet saw in such a proposal the opportunity to supersede Bragg and thereby win fame and promotion for himself.)[17]

The second alternative to Davis's system came from Lee who, one senses, had begun to realize that in 1863 time was not on the side of the Rebels and that if they were going to win they had to do so quickly. He, therefore, wanted to move north with his army and fight a great battle to settle the issue. When the crisis of April–May 1863 erupted, some Rebel officials had considered sending part of Lee's army to the West. Lee then expressed a willingness to do so as soon as the situation in the Old Dominion permitted. The early April intelligence from the West that Grant's army was moving to Tennessee and that other Federal troops were being sent west from Virginia gave a new urgency to the Confederates' deliberations and prompted Seddon on April 9 to make a specific request to Lee that two divisions from the Army of Northern Virginia go to the West.

By that time Lee had developed some other ideas about overall Rebel strategy and saw an opportunity both to pursue his long-standing desire to invade the North and help the Southerners deal with the April–May crisis. "The most natural way to reinforce" the Western Confederates, he wrote, "would seem to be to transfer a portion of the troops from this department to oppose those [Yankees] sent west, but it is not as easy for us to change troops from one department to another as it is for the enemy, and if we rely on that method we may always be too late." The Confederate transportation system, Lee realized, simply could not move large numbers of troops to Mississippi or Tennessee in time, even if such bodies of reinforcements were available.

On the day after Lee penned his reply to Seddon, Johnston wrote to President Davis expressing his view that "our disadvantage in this war is, that the enemy can transfer an army from Mississippi to . . . [Middle Tennessee] before we can learn that it is in motion, while an equal body of our troops could not make the same movement (the corresponding one, rather) in less than six weeks."

Johnston, who had long argued that the Rebels could not shift troops between Mississippi and Tennessee rapidly enough to meet Federal threats, saw the problem in terms of his command in the West; Lee saw it for the entire Confederacy. No matter what the range of their vision, however, both the major Southern field commanders went on record—before the crisis of April–May 1863 erupted—with the opinion that the President's cherished scheme of interdepartmental movements of troops to meet enemy offensives simply would not work across the vast distances of the Confederacy.[18]

Lee also put forth two other objections specifically to the transfer of any of his troops to Mississippi. In common with virtually all informed people of the time, Lee believed that the unhealthful mid-summer climate of the Deep South would make it impossible for white men to labor and fight in that region at that time of the year. He therefore thought that what he sometimes called "the season" would soon compel the Yankees to abandon their campaign against Vicksburg. It would be especially bad, he argued on May 10, to send troops acclimated to Virginia to Mississippi in the middle and late parts of the summer. Finally, Lee expressed worry about what he tactfully called "the uncertainty of the employment of the troops"—by which he seems to have meant the strong possibility that none of the Confederate generals in the West was likely to use reinforcements intelligently.[19]

With these factors influencing his thinking, Lee now offered his alternative to the ideas of Davis and the Western concentration bloc. Whenever the Federals began to assemble troops for an offensive, he suggested, the Confederates in the areas from which the Yankees were moving should "take the aggressive & call them back."

An example of how Lee would apply this strategy occurred in early April. The secessionists learned then that the Yankees were sending reinforcements from western Virginia to Tennessee, and several Rebels suggested that their government should make a corresponding transfer of troops. Lee, on the other hand, argued that the Confederates from whose front the Federals had gone could "by judicious operations in their areas" render more help to Southern troops in Tennessee than they would if they were sent to reinforce Bragg's army in the Volunteer State. Lee, in summary, believed that a policy of offensive activity on the part of local Confederate forces would keep the Yankees off balance, prevent them from concentrating for an offensive of their own, and disrupt their plans by forcing them to protect their own bases and lines of supply.[20]

The Rebels thus had three proposals about how they should deal with the crisis of April–May 1863: the President's plan to send reinforcements to Mississippi to drive Grant away from Vicksburg; the western concentration bloc's strategy of reinforcing Bragg for an offensive in Tennessee; and Lee's concept of having local Confederate forces assume the offensive in their areas to disrupt the Yankees' plans. As applied on a national scale, Lee's idea meant that the Army of Northern Virginia could best help relieve pressure on Rebel forces in Mississippi and Tennessee by moving into Maryland. Lee, with good reason, had no doubt that he could outmaneuver and defeat Joseph Hooker.

In mid-May Confederate authorities had to decide how they

would meet the crisis then facing their country. Although a few others were peripherally involved, the decision was made by two men—Lee and Davis—at a conference in Richmond on May 14 to 17. At that meeting, Lee urged his policy on Davis. The President, faced with the collapse of his western defense system, accepted Lee's plan; the cabinet voiced its approval with but one dissenting vote (that of Postmaster General John H. Reagan of Texas—the group's only Trans-Mississippi member); and what became the Gettysburg Campaign was launched.

Any just evaluation of the Gettysburg decision—what Confederate Gen. E. Porter Alexander called "the Pennsylvania gambit"—must focus on two central questions and one crucial fact. First, was there any feasible alternative? Would either Davis's policy or the strategy of the Western concentration bloc have offered a better chance for the South? Such questions cannot be answered definitively, but a brief examination of the other Rebel options can give us some clues.[21]

Could the Confederates have assembled in either Mississippi or Tennessee a large enough army in the short eight-week period between the end of the Chancellorsville Campaign and the surrender of Vicksburg? This oft-ignored time factor is crucial. Johnston, it will be recalled, had estimated that it would take six weeks to transfer a single infantry division from Mississippi to Tennessee. The pressure of time, let us note, would have forced the Rebel commander in Mississippi or Tennessee to act on the tactical offensive. In Tennessee, he would also have been on the strategic offensive. Lee's plan offered at least the possibility of acting on the tactical defensive with all the advantages that would have given the Rebels.[22]

Could such a force have been fed and supplied if it had been assembled? Grant had wrecked much of the transportation system in western and Central Mississippi. In mid-April, an inspector reported a serious supply problem in Tennessee and noted that Bragg's army "is living from hand to mouth." "By the spring of 1863," wrote historian Connelly, Bragg was "almost immobilized because of the strain imposed on his wagon transportation in obtaining forage from as far away as 250 miles." Doubtless had the Rebels sent 20,000 to 30,000 reinforcements to Bragg, they would have revamped the logistical support system of the Army of Tennessee, but they almost certainly could not have gotten such a new system functioning in time to support an offensive before Vicksburg fell.[23]

How large a force was necessary in Mississippi? In Tennessee? Had it been possible to double the size of Johnston's army in Mississippi, it would still have been smaller than Grant's force and would have had to operate against Grant's strong lines about Vicksburg. Even counting Pemberton's trapped Army of Vicksburg as part of Johnston's force, the Rebels would almost certainly have been unable to concentrate enough men in Mississippi to raise the siege.

How were the Federals to be prevented from making a corresponding transfer of troops that would have more than offset the Rebel effort? On May 20, Bragg reported 54,951 troops present for duty. Rosecrans's strength report for May showed 79,977 present for duty, and the adjacent Federal Department of Kentucky carried another 37,992 soldiers on its present for duty rolls. Thirty thousand reinforcements from Lee would have given Bragg only a slight numerical advantage over Rosecrans, and it would not have lasted long.[24]

What would have stopped the Yankees from reversing Lee's strategy, standing on the defensive in the West, and assuming the offensive in the areas from which the Rebels had stripped troops to reinforce their armies in Mississippi or Tennessee? Which Confederate commanders would have been willing to release large numbers of troops to Rebel forces in Mississippi or Tennessee? Certainly not Beauregard, the great advocate of western concentration, who howled so loudly about sending some of his men west in the spring of 1863.

The second question is even more crucial. Did the Confederates have in the West a general who would have been likely to win a victory? Is there *anything* in the record of either Joseph E. Johnston or Braxton Bragg to justify even a slight hope that either of them would or could have brought about success, no matter how many reinforcements he received or how ample his supplies? Was Bragg more likely to outwit Rosecrans or Johnston to best Grant than Lee was to defeat Hooker?

In addition to his oft-demonstrated incompetence as a field commander, Bragg was also in wretched health in the spring of 1863. He described his own condition then as "well nigh prostrated," and he was, as Thomas Connelly noted, "suffering from the beginnings of a nervous and physical breakdown." In early July, he admitted that he was "utterly broken down."

Johnston, although in better health than Bragg, wrote on May 9 that he was "unfit for field service." Even if Johnston had been in excellent health, one cannot help wondering how eagerly and successfully he would have taken the offensive against Grant given his aversion to aggressive action and how well he would have cooperated with his government. Would he have acted decisively no matter how strong his force?[25]

On the other hand, was there anything in Lee's record to suggest that the Confederacy's only realistic hope might well lie in the possibility that he could again defeat Hooker and win on Northern soil a great victory that would lead to Confederate independence or at least offset the loss of Vicksburg should that citadel fall. Lee had won seemingly miraculous victories before. Could he do so again? Could he do so without Jackson?

Finally, we must not forget the fact that Davis and Lee almost achieved success—at least to the extent of winning a victory on Northern soil. Even Porter Alexander, perhaps Lee's most astute critic among his fellow Confederates, admitted that the Rebels won a smashing success at Gettysburg on July 1 and that they came very close to breaking the Federal army there on July 2.[26]

In reality, Davis's choice in dealing with the crisis of April–May 1863 was not between "the line of Virginia" and "the line of the Mississippi," as Lee once put it. Nor was it between Tennessee and Mississippi, as Joseph E. Johnston and some others suggested.[27] Davis's only real choice was between Robert E. Lee on the one hand and either Joseph E. Johnston or Braxton Bragg on the other.

Can we doubt that Davis made the best decision? When he sent Lee and the Army of Northern Virginia across the Potomac in June 1863, Davis played his and the Confederacy's strongest possible hand, and a very strong hand it was. Very strong hands, however, do not always win—as I once discovered to my chagrin when I held four jacks in a game with someone who held four queens.[28]

More than 130 years have now elapsed since the guns fell silent at Gettysburg and Lee's beaten army limped away to the south. Over the course of more than thirteen decades, the three-day battle fought around the little Pennsylvania town has come to possess a great mystique both in the popular mind and the literature of the war. The Battle of Gettysburg is often called "the high watermark" or the "high tide" of the Confederacy. It is frequently described as "the turning point," the pivotal battle," or "the decisive battle" of the war.

In truth, the Battle of Gettysburg was none of these things. It was, in fact, an engagement that had no impact on the outcome of the war. The battle owes its vastly inflated notoriety to six factors, none of which had anything to do with its place in the military history of the war.

For one thing, the armies that clashed at Gettysburg were the two best-known and most studied military forces that took part in the war. Measured by its duration and its total of about 51,000 casualties Gettysburg was the biggest battle of the war. (On a casualties per day basis, however, it was equalled by Chickamauga and exceeded by Antietam.) Gettysburg was the only major Civil War engagement fought on the soil of a free state. It took place fairly close to the population and news media centers of the North. The battle provided the occasion for the most famous speech in American history—one in which the nature and purpose of the war were made clear in language that has rarely been equalled by that of any public figure. Finally, and perhaps most important, the Gettysburg mystique can be traced to the fact that students of the Civil War have long misunderstood the basic military history of the conflict. For well over a century after the war's end writers focused the greater part of their effort on the campaigns in the East. This myopic view produced a false and misleading interpretation of the war. To one who studied only the eastern operations, it appeared that the Confederates enjoyed a great deal of military success in the war's first two years—up to the Battle of Gettysburg—and that their cause went rapidly downhill after the summer of 1863.

None of the six factors that make Gettysburg loom so large in the writings about the war has anything to do with the battle's military importance, and the last gives a very distorted view of both the war in general and of Gettysburg's place in it in particular.

The true highwater mark of the Confederacy, most students of the war now realize, came in the fall of 1862. Then Lee's army first crossed the Potomac and Bragg's Army of Tennessee was in Kentucky in an effort to impose Rebel rule on the Bluegrass State. At the same time, other secessionist forces were pushing forward in Mississippi. These offensive movements were turned back in the Battles of Antietam, Perryville, Iuka, and Corinth. An offensive across such a broad front, however, was clearly more of a high tide than was the Gettysburg Campaign. In the summer of 1863, by contrast, the Confederate cause was foundering almost everywhere outside Virginia. Since water seeks its own level, the Rebel cause could not be at high tide in the East even as it ebbed in the West. Rather than high tide or high watermark, Gettysburg was—to continue with the aquatic metaphor—a simple splash on the eastern side of a very shallow pond that was rapidly draining away on the west.

To call Gettysburg the "turning point" implies that the course of the war was somehow different after that battle than it had been before July 1863. It was not. In fact, the pattern of military operations on both major fronts of the war remained constant from 1861 until the Confederacy disintegrated in the spring of 1865. In the West, the Yankee armies advanced from victory to victory, chipping away the Confederacy and reestablishing the authority of the national government as they went. In the East, by contrast, the opposing armies were locked in a bloody stalemate that lasted throughout the entire war (except for the last few days). Gettysburg did not change the eastern equilibrium. At most, Gettysburg restored a balance in the East that was threatening to tilt toward the Rebels after their great victories at Fredericksburg and Chancellorsville. There was in fact, no "turning point" in the war.

If the word "decisive" has any meaning when applied to a military engagement, it must denote a battle that determined the outcome of a war—or a battle that at least put the conflict irrevocably on the path to its final outcome. The Battle of Gettysburg did neither. Indeed, no eastern battle can be said to have led to final Federal victory.

The Fort Henry–Fort Donelson–Shiloh Campaign of early 1862, the Vicksburg Campaign of mid-1863, the Tullahoma–Chickamauga–Chattanooga Campaign in the fall of 1863, and the Atlanta Campaign of 1864 all have far stronger claims to having been "decisive" than does the Gettysburg Campaign of June–July 1863. If one seeks a single "decisive" battle, the engagement at Champion Hill, fought May 16, 1863, in West-Central Mississippi, came far closer to having determined the war's outcome than did Gettysburg.

Gettysburg was a great defensive victory for the North. Like a defensive stand by a football team, however, it did not—and could not—bring victory to one side or defeat to the other.[29] Even had the Confederates won at Gettysburg (as the battle was fought), it almost certainly would have made no difference even in the outcome of the campaign. Lee lost about one-third of his army and by the evening of July 3 was running short of munitions and supplies. Would his logistical situation have allowed him to take advantage of a tactical success at Gettysburg that afternoon? Could not the Federals simply have pulled back to another strong position a few miles to the rear?

As the battle at Gettysburg developed, it could not have been the great, crushing victory Lee was seeking. Nor did it hasten the ultimate Northern triumph. Indeed, to the extent that their failure at Gettysburg prompted the Rebels to send reinforcements from Lee's army to the West in September 1863 and those reinforcements helped win the victory at Chickamauga, the battle in Pennsylvania may well have prolonged the life of the Confederacy.

Those who would understand the military history of the Civil War—the campaigns and battles that sealed the fate of the Confederacy and preserved the Union—must look elsewhere than to southern Pennsylvania. They must go to the Peach Orchard—at Shiloh, not Gettysburg; to the railroad cut—at Atlanta, not Gettysburg; to Missionary Ridge, not Cemetery Ridge; to the Carter House, not the Codori House. At these points, and at hundreds of others on the great battlefields of the West, the war was won and lost.

# 9

# *From Turning Point to Peace Memorial: A Cultural Legacy*

AMY J. KINSEL

**"T**HE great battle of the war has been fought and thanks be to God the Army of the Potomac has been victorious at last." Elisha Hunt Rhodes of the Second Rhode Island Volunteer Infantry wrote those words in Middletown, Maryland, on July 8, 1863. His regiment, part of the Union Sixth Corps, had witnessed the climactic third day of fighting at Gettysburg from a reserve position on Cemetery Ridge. Rhodes, noting that his brigade had come under artillery fire during the two-hour barrage that preceded the Confederate army's final infantry assault, described in his diary what he had observed:

> We could not see the enemy, and we could only cover ourselves the best we could behind the rocks and trees. About 30 men of our Brigade were killed or wounded by this fire. Soon the Rebel yell was heard, and we have found since that the Rebel General Pickett made a charge with his Division and was repulsed after reaching some of our batteries. Our lines of Infantry in front of us rose up and poured in a terrible fire. As we were only a few yards in rear of our lines we saw all the fight. The firing gradually died away, and but for an occasional shot all was still. But what a scene it was. Oh the dead and the dying on this bloody field.[1]

Despite the loss of life sustained on all sides, Rhodes was jubilant about the Federal victory. On July 4 he asked, "Was ever
the Nation's Birthday celebrated in such a way before[?]" July 5
brought more "Glorious news!" Lee's forces were retreating toward Virginia, and Vicksburg had fallen. On July 9 Rhodes was
still overjoyed by the Union army's success. "Again I thank God
that the Army of the Potomac has at last gained a victory. I wonder what the South thinks of us Yankees now. I think Gettysburg
will cure the Rebels of any desire to invade the North again."[2] As
the Sixth Corps pursued the "Rebel Army" south, Rhodes hoped
the Federal forces would prevent it from crossing the Potomac
River and returning to Virginia.

Meanwhile, J. Paxton Lloyd of the Sixth U.S. Cavalry was already in Virginia with part of that very "Rebel Army." Lloyd had
been captured by the Confederates on July 7, 1863, during a cavalry skirmish near Hagerstown, Maryland. Escorted by members
of Gen. John D. Imboden's Virginia Cavalry Brigade, Lloyd and
a group of Union prisoners of war had crossed the Potomac on
July 9. In a letter to his family sent at the end of the month, Lloyd
described the forced march through Virginia that he and the other
prisoners had endured. He complained of harsh treatment and
lack of food. In Martinsburg, Virginia, he wrote, local women
had wanted to feed the hungry prisoners, but, as Lloyd put it,
"That cursed old hog Imboden," would not allow it: "If one of
our men would run to the sidewalk to get a loaf of bread they
[the Confederates] would knock him down with a musket. They
treated us inhumanly [sic] takeing [sic] it all together[;] they stole
everything we had."[3]

With no rations, the Union cavalrymen marched on foot for
over 150 miles to Staunton, Virginia. To complete the journey,
Lloyd had to tie his broken-down boots together with his sus-
penders. From Staunton, the prisoners were taken by train to
Richmond, and from there to Annapolis, Maryland, to await
"parole" in a prisoner-of-war exchange. Despite the poor treatment he described in his letter, Lloyd declared that he would
always "remember kindly" two Confederate officers who through
unspecified displays of good will had behaved like "Gentlemen."[4]

The testimony of wartime observers like Elisha Hunt Rhodes
and J. Paxton Lloyd represents a mere fraction of the information

that has contributed during the past 134 years to popular perceptions about the Battle of Gettysburg and its aftermath. For most Americans, Gettysburg's legacy has been unavoidably shaped by a host of important events that occurred after July 1863, and it includes many more elements than the participants in the battle could ever have imagined. Rhodes and Lloyd, and thousands like them, experienced, after all, only a small portion of what those of us who view the battle from a distance of years think we know about what happened.

Rhodes, for example, witnessed the repulse of Pickett's Charge, but he realized only from hindsight that Pickett's Division led the assault. Lloyd, trying to make sense of his journey through Virginia as a prisoner of war and not knowing for certain whose side would ultimately prevail, recorded both the cruelty and the kindness of his captors. Neither man could have recognized in 1863 what the Battle of Gettysburg would eventually represent for many Americans, for it was during the postwar period that most Americans—aware of both the extent of the Union victory and the nature of the Confederate defeat—came to regard Gettysburg as the preeminent battle of the Civil War and to invest it with a complex set of meanings that went far beyond its strictly military ramifications. The reasons for Gettysburg's lasting renown cannot be fully understood, therefore, without peeling back and examining the layers of interpretation that generations of Americans eventually imposed on it.

Writing in July 1863, Rhodes and Lloyd were not, of course, influenced by postwar opinion. Elisha Hunt Rhodes did not need the verdict of history to recognize that the Union army had done well at Gettysburg. He was clearly impressed by the battle's significance even as it occurred. Meade's Federal forces had, he knew, pursued the Army of Northern Virginia and sought a decisive victory. Given its many disappointing engagements, success at Gettysburg represented an important milestone in the life of the Army of the Potomac, an achievement in which Rhodes and other Union observers rejoiced. Just when the battle became more than an important Federal victory, however, is somewhat harder to discern. Many contemporary witnesses did not mark Gettysburg as a critical turning point of the war until much later. And only in retrospect did Gettysburg assume the legendary role of the "High

Water Mark of the Confederacy," the time and place after which ultimate Union victory seemed assured and the hopes of Lee and the Confederates dashed.

J. Paxton Lloyd, waiting in 1863 for his return to the Union army, must for his part have been thankful that he had survived the ordeal of his brief confinement at Libby Prison. If Lloyd's reaction to his capture during the Gettysburg campaign is of more than passing interest to us, however, it is because such reminiscences of wartime experiences influenced the manner in which Americans interpreted the conflict in later years. As a prisoner of war, Lloyd had feared death and suffered hardships at the hands of men he wrote of with contempt. Yet Lloyd's complicated sentiments about his captors presaged one of the difficult dilemmas that Americans wrestled with in the postwar period. The war had fostered large-scale killing, but the enemy had not been entirely despised. As Lloyd saw it, for example, the women of Virginia had acted generously in offering bread to Union prisoners, and, in addition to hunger and other privations, Lloyd seemed likely to remember the kindnesses shown him by at least two Confederate officers. After the war, Americans had to decide which collective memories resulting from an accumulation of similarly complex individual experiences would endure and would thereby contribute to the reunited nation's understanding of its recent past.

The struggle to interpret the Battle of Gettysburg and determine which perspectives on the past would prevail began shortly after the fighting ended, and it ultimately engaged the energies of literally hundreds of people. These people—who were for the most part white Americans—produced histories, memoirs, novels, photographs, poems, anecdotes, and songs, and created paintings, sculptures, souvenirs, memorials, monuments, a cemetery, and a park that together served to define the significance of the Gettysburg campaign for millions of their countrymen. Through this overlapping process of both privately and publicly generated interpretation, the Battle of Gettysburg became by the late nineteenth century a major touchstone of the war. It would not be overstating the case to argue that before the fiftieth anniversary of the battle, Gettysburg entered the American imagination as an essential symbol of what the war had been about.

By thinking of the Gettysburg battle and the place where it occurred as representative of important aspects of the Civil War, Americans attempted to make the past meaningful rather than senseless. They tried, in effect, to discover order in the inherent chaos of human experience, and of necessity imposed on the past their own postwar values and interpretations. Thus, the memory of the battle as expressed in a variety of written, pictorial, narrative, and commemorative forms became more than merely the reflected image of an ever-receding historical reality. Indeed, the manner in which most Americans recalled the Gettysburg battle decades after the fact took on as much significance for the national culture as did the events of 1863.

Through their efforts to understand and commemorate Gettysburg, moreover, Americans sought to describe accurately and define precisely a past that they could not really know with certainty. Naturally, there were disagreements about points of fact and analysis both in print and memorial activities. Paradoxically, however, the oft-stated goal of preserving the battleground and definitively marking the lines of battle on the field served to mask the confusion normally caused by the inconsistencies of historical memory and made visitors to Gettysburg believe that many still-contentious points had been settled. By the 1890s, Americans who traveled to Gettysburg found scores of monuments and markers on the field confirming the idea that what was known about the battle could indeed be collected and set down in stone.

Thus, even as Americans—both Northerners and Southerners—examined their sometimes contradictory historical opinions, they nonetheless developed shared traditions about the Battle of Gettysburg. They increasingly viewed the site of the battle, preserved first under the auspices of the private Gettysburg Battlefield Memorial Association and later by the U.S. government, as a concrete and somehow unassailably true link with the past. Especially during the late nineteenth century when there was an upswing in memorial activities at Gettysburg, popular symbols, images, and interpretations of the battle both emerged from and were reflected in battlefield commemoration. And by the early twentieth century, nearly a million Americans visited the field annually, perhaps hoping to find there a personal connection with their national heritage.[5] The battlefield became not just a historic site but a sacred landscape, a memorial park which itself presented to Americans the basic elements of their historical and cultural interpretation of the Battle of Gettysburg.

That interpretation contained three main parts. First, Americans embraced the idea that the Battle of Gettysburg represented nothing less than the turning point of the Civil War. Both men who had defended the Union and men who had fought for the Confederacy agreed that the Gettysburg battle had been an especially dangerous encounter, a dramatic contest that they were convinced had decided the fate of the nation. For the North, this battle seemed to have secured eventual victory, and, looking back, guaranteed the Union's survival. For the South, by contrast, July 1863 appeared to have been a time of missed opportunity, and after Gettysburg the Confederate cause, it seemed, had been lost. Ultimately, Gettysburg became for many Americans the crucial "what-if" point of the war, the battle at which they thought the entire course of history might have been changed forever.[6]

A second element of most Americans' understanding of the Battle of Gettysburg concerned the unquestioned heroism displayed by the soldiers who met in Pennsylvania. In the first three decades after the war, the role of hero was given primarily to Union soldiers. But sometime after the twenty-fifth anniversary of the battle in 1888, many Northerners were willing to recognize the courage and valor shown by their former enemies. The creation of a national park at Gettysburg in 1895 was due partly to the perceived need to place markers on the Confederate side of the field. Significantly, Congressional legislation establishing the park ensured that a Southern perspective would be included in subsequent commemorative activities at the battleground.[7] By the time of the battle's fiftieth anniversary in 1913, most Americans seemed ready to acknowledge that displays of bravery on the battlefield might go a long way toward redeeming one's foes and that fighting honorably in support of one's cause was a noble—and perhaps even a singularly American—trait.

Third, in addition to perceiving Gettysburg as a critically decisive battle in which the soldiers from both armies had struggled heroically, Americans eventually connected Gettysburg with their nation's successful postwar reconciliation. By the early twentieth century, Gettysburg was widely known as the location not only of a famous battle but also as the site where important reunions of

Union and Confederate veterans took place. The Gettysburg battleground thus became associated both with the violence of war and with the beneficence of peace. For the fiftieth anniversary of the battle, the Gettysburg National Military Park hosted a huge Blue and Gray Reunion at which the predominant themes were national forgiveness and veteran camaraderie. During the early twentieth century, the Federal government marked the Confederate lines of battle, and Virginia and North Carolina added enduring memorials to the field honoring their region's soldiers. As part of the seventy-fifth anniversary commemoration of the battle in 1938, two aged veterans—one Union and one Confederate—unveiled a Peace Memorial at Gettysburg dedicated to the lasting spirit of unity and friendship between all Americans. An American Legion Commander went so far as to suggest at the time that only in America could such an example of reconciliation and reunion occur.[8]

The road to that reunion began with recognition of Gettysburg as a crucial contest. The battle's location in the North gave reporters for major Union newspapers ready access to fairly accurate information about the battle, thereby ensuring that many details of the campaign would become widespread knowledge. Press coverage about Gettysburg, however, seemed distinctive almost immediately. One Philadelphia paper, for example, published reports of the fighting under the banner headline "VICTORY! WATERLOO ECLIPSED!!"[9] Over the years, Americans frequently compared Gettysburg to Waterloo and to other world-famous battles, arguing that the Civil War and this battle in particular gave the United States its own history on a grand European scale. Like Waterloo, Gettysburg was seen as decisive. The fact that after 1863 Lee's Confederate forces had failed to invade the North again confirmed for postwar observers that this assessment was correct. Whatever the military importance of this tremendous battle had been, shortly after the war most Americans began to regard it as a turning point.

The conviction that Gettysburg had been a crucial battle contributed to the ferocity of subsequent debates about who would receive credit for the Union victory and blame for the Confederate defeat. As early as 1864, the commander of the Union Third Corps, Gen. Daniel E. Sickles of New York, and his supporters used the forum provided by the Congressional Joint Committee on the Conduct of the War to claim that Sickles had been responsible for saving the Federal army's strong defensive position on July 2, 1863. The ambitious Sickles and his friends disliked and resented Union commander Gen. George G. Meade, and they did everything in their power to call his actions at Gettysburg into question, even going so far as to claim erroneously that Meade had wanted to abandon the field.[10] Partly as a result of the Sickles controversy, Meade failed to win the acclaim one might have expected him to enjoy for having led his army to victory. President Lincoln himself, disappointed that Meade did not completely destroy Lee's army in Pennsylvania, was reportedly dissatisfied with Meade's pursuit of the retreating Southern forces.[11]

Lincoln's own visit to Gettysburg just months after the fighting ended there, and the address he so famously delivered on that hallowed ground, served to elevate both the battle and its site in the public imagination. As the president's postwar reputation grew, Lincoln, rather than Meade, became the Northerner most prominently identified with Gettysburg. His "few appropriate remarks" dedicating Soldiers' National Cemetery represent one of the defining texts of American republicanism. Countless schoolchildren have memorized Lincoln's ringing phrases endorsing the founding fathers' dedication to "the proposition that all men are created equal." Almost independently of popular interest in the military aspects of the Battle of Gettysburg, there developed a deep public interest in Lincoln's Gettysburg associations.

If Lincoln's speech at Gettysburg drew the admiration of Northerners, Southern attention focused on the nobility of Gen. Robert E. Lee during one of his darkest hours. In defending his performance at Gettysburg, Lee's admirers went to great lengths to ensure that he would receive none of the blame for what they came to agree had been a disastrous defeat for the Confederacy. Lee's strategy of taking the offensive at Gettysburg had garnered criticism during the 1860s from a number of observers, and the battle performances of two of Lee's subordinates, Gen. Jubal A. Early and Gen. Richard B. Ewell, were also found wanting.[12] Shortly after Lee's death in 1870, however, Early led a campaign to blame the loss at Gettysburg on Lee's First Corps commander Gen. James Longstreet. In a series of articles published in the *Southern His-*

*torical Society Papers,* Early and several other Virginians argued that damaging and unprofessional delays during Longstreet's assault of July 2, 1863, and the definite lack of enthusiasm with which he oversaw the final Confederate attack on July 3 had combined to cost the Southern army a very real possibility of victory. Longstreet attempted to defend himself against these charges, but his belligerent style and his affiliation after the war with the Republican party served only to harm his reputation even further.[13]

In contrast, Lee's reputation seemed almost unaffected by defeat at Gettysburg. In fact, Lee's standing was enhanced by reports of the humility with which he was said to have borne the loss. The country's embrace of sentimental Lost Cause attitudes about the failed Confederacy also lent poignancy to Lee's post-Gettysburg image. By the end of the nineteenth century, General Lee was admired throughout the country for his gentlemanly manner, for the grace with which he had accepted Confederate defeat in 1865, and, despite the Gettysburg debacle, for his brilliant generalship.

The Lost Cause myth that sustained many Southerners after the Civil War rested in some measure on the belief that Lee might have won the war by winning the Battle of Gettysburg. Such a belief was probably unfounded, for even a victory at Gettysburg would have left the Confederate army battered and bruised and far from its lines of supply. A subsequent battle, fought perhaps in Pennsylvania or in Maryland, might have given Meade his decisive victory and become instead the war's crucial contest. The traditions surrounding Gettysburg would necessarily have been different had the Confederates turned the Union flanks on July 2, for example, but the outcome of the war would (in all likelihood) not ultimately have been changed.

As it happened, the contentious arguments on both sides over what did occur on July 2—the controversy over Sickles's forward line and the debate about Longstreet's supposed tardiness—might have meant that the second day at Gettysburg would receive the lion's share of attention in popular memory. On the whole, however, this did not prove to be the case. Except for a lively interest by the late nineteenth century in the heroic defense of Little Round Top and Gen. Gouverneur K. Warren's role in saving it for the Union, most popular attention eventually converged on the battle's last day, on what came to be known as "Pickett's Charge."[14] In large measure, this perspective had less to do with the actual military significance of the Confederate's final attack on the Union positions along Cemetery Ridge than it did with the dramatic appeal the assault had on the American imagination.

Interpretations of Gettysburg in paintings, for example, centered on the battle's momentous third day. Working shortly after the war to fill a commission from the Pennsylvania legislature to depict the Battle of Gettysburg, artist Peter F. Rothermel chose as his subject the final Confederate assault on Cemetery Ridge. In the middle of Rothermel's canvas a Federal infantryman, standing with one foot on the body of a Southerner, heroically beats back the advancing enemy with his rifle butt. Although General Meade appears as a recognizable figure in the painting, through his central figure Rothermel portrays the battle as an ordinary soldier's fight. On completing his enormous oil painting in 1870, Rothermel said, moreover, that he had conceived of the battle's final moments as the physical and moral triumph of patriotic Union loyalists over an enemy fighting for the right to secede and the right to hold slaves. Rothermel, a Pennsylvania native who was painting under government commission, adopted this moral tone within just a few years of the battle. His attempt to make an overt symbolic statement about the nature of the Civil War's moral conflict was unusual, however, and it distinguishes Rothermel's work from other well-known paintings of the battle.[15]

The most widely known paintings of Gettysburg, a series of cycloramas completed during the 1880s, offered no moral evaluation of the battle or the war. Eleven years after Peter Rothermel's work went on display in Philadelphia, a French panoramist named Paul Philippoteaux began painting his first cyclorama of Pickett's Charge. The final Confederate assault presented the clearest dramatic opportunity for the enormous circular display of a cyclorama painting. Philippoteaux and his assistants created four Gettysburg cycloramas, each measuring about forty feet high and close to four hundred feet in circumference. The public viewed these huge paintings along with their accompanying three-dimensional dioramas at special cyclorama buildings in several large Northern cities. These viewings often included historical lectures, and they represented an inexpensive form of dramatic entertainment not unlike the theater or, later, the cinema.[16]

In his Gettysburg cycloramas, Philippoteaux, who had visited the field and interviewed prominent veterans of the battle, successfully captured the striking beauty of the Pennsylvania landscape. He also won praise for his presumably realistic portrayal of the whirlwind of July third's assault as seen from the center of the Union line. In his attempt to depict the awful turmoil of battle, Philippoteaux crowded his canvas with hundreds of figures, from brigades marching toward Cemetery Ridge to soldiers struggling in hand-to-hand combat. The paintings do not spare the viewer from witnessing the bloody results of nineteenth-century warfare, but neither are they gory or anti-war in tone. In Philippoteaux's hands, the Gettysburg battle is a sweeping spectacle and the deaths of such recognizable figures as Confederate Gen. Lewis Armistead are part of history's stirring drama. Impressed by their audacious scope and disconcerting realism, audiences in the North found these cycloramas entertaining and informative.[17]

A visit to Gettysburg early in this century would have reinforced the notion that Pickett's Charge was both the dramatic and the military climax of the Battle of Gettysburg. Encouraged by the Gettysburg Battlefield Memorial Association, scores of Union regimental organizations erected monuments at Gettysburg during the 1880s and early 1890s. Although many of them marked the fighting that occurred on July 1 and 2, the greatest number seemed to cluster along Cemetery Ridge, particularly at the site of the heaviest fighting on July 3. At the turn of the century, the Gettysburg National Military Park continued to emphasize the third day of the battle when the War Department oversaw the erection of imposing state and federal memorials along the heights defended by the Union army. Gettysburg's monumental excesses reached their apogee with the dedication in 1910 of the enormous Pennsylvania state memorial, a tremendous domed edifice topped by a colossal figure of Victory and including (by 1913) eight heroic-scale bronze statues.

Gen. George Meade, a Pennsylvania native who appears as one of the heroic figures on his state's monument, had already been honored by Pennsylvania with his own equestrian statue. Dedicated in 1896, this powerful image of the Union's commanding general is located near the point on Cemetery Ridge where Meade might have observed the fighting on July 3, 1863. In 1917, Southerners completed the symbolic attention to the battle's final assault with the addition to Seminary Ridge of Virginia's handsome memorial, the first such contribution to the field from a former Confederate state. A bronze equestrian statue of General Lee sits atop the Virginia monument, depicting Lee as he soberly watched his men attempt the impossible on that fateful July 3.[18]

The appeal of paying so much attention to the final day at Gettysburg is evident in the bronze and stone images that populate the field. It is possible to forget while standing on Cemetery Ridge that the battle's brutal and messy second day of fighting probably decided the outcome of the contest. When imagined by a visitor to the scene, the Confederate's last assault, far from being exposed as futile and unwise (as many historians have argued), appears to have been unbelievably heroic and noble, a chance at victory that Lee had to take rather than a desperate measure unlikely ever to have succeeded. Envisaged from the Union perspective, the climactic clash of men and arms seems to have been inevitable. The Federal soldiers could but wait on the crest of Cemetery Ridge and watch the approaching foe with awe and admiration, forced to rain down shot and shell on him and firmly turn the attack aside.

The image of Gettysburg as the "High Water Mark of the Rebellion" was an expression of both the decisive role many people thought the battle had played in the outcome of the war and the public's eventual fascination with Pickett's Charge. The Union army turned back the Southern tide at Gettysburg, Americans learned, and it never again rose beyond the Mason–Dixon line. Some observers acknowledged that the Confederacy might still have won the war by wearing down Northern willingness to continue fighting and dying to preserve the Union, but the belief was widely held that after 1863 and the loss at Gettysburg the South had been incapable of winning the war on the battlefield.

The most visible reminder at Gettysburg of the High Water Mark interpretation of the battle is the High Water Mark of the Rebellion monument, dedicated in 1892 east of the copse of trees on Cemetery Ridge that was said to be the target of the Confederate assault of July 3, 1863. The monument was designed by John B. Bachelder, a self-appointed historian of the battle and acknowledged Gettysburg authority, who through his involvement with the Gettysburg Battlefield Memorial Association had a great deal of influence on the historical interpretations encountered by visitors to the field.[19]

Bachelder's High Water Mark monument features a large bronze book open to two pages that record details of the Confederate army's July 3 attack. On the left page of the book Bachelder listed "Infantry Commands in Longstreet's Charging Column," and on the right page he listed "Infantry Commands Which Met Longstreet's Assault." The fifteen Union states whose forces had repelled the Confederate assault contributed the $6,500 needed to construct this memorial "in recognition of the patriotism and gallantry displayed by their respective troops." It was thus the first national monument erected on the battlefield at Gettysburg rather than within the National Cemetery.[20]

The monument did not praise the "patriotism and gallantry"of the Southerners who tried to take Cemetery Ridge on July 3, but did acknowledge the essential role they played in the climax of the battle. Moreover, this memorial provided an important focal point for visitors to Gettysburg. Bachelder's design, which inscribed a part of the battle's history in bronze, was a powerful statement that the assault on Cemetery Ridge was of lasting national significance. The twin interpretations of the Gettysburg contest as both the turning point of the war and the High Water Mark of the Confederacy received permanent and compelling confirmation. A visitor to the battlefield could stand before this memorial, read its inscriptions, and learn about the nation's history at the place where it occurred. The High Water Mark of the Rebellion monument seemed to locate for Americans the very spot where the outcome of their Civil War had been determined.

At the turn of the century, the emphasis at the park was not only on the image of Gettysburg as a turning point, but also on the heroism displayed there by Federal soldiers. During the 1880s and 1890s, scores of Union veteran associations added regimental monuments to the field. Many of these monuments identified the locations of important events that took place during the battle. But in addition to recording history, these memorials commemorated Northern heroism. Regimental monuments, which usually included only brief historical information about the regiment's fighting at Gettysburg, often served as a way for the survivors of the war to honor their fallen comrades.

While there are many examples on the battlefield of fine statues honoring prominent generals, Gettysburg's large collection of regimental memorials pays tribute, fittingly, to the heroism of the Union's ordinary soldiers. Dedication ceremonies for these regimental monuments provided suitable testaments to the heroism of America's fighting men. In orations given to dedicate Northern memorials in the late 1880s and early 1890s, veterans extolled the virtues and patriotism of Union soldiers and proclaimed the righteousness of the causes for which they fought and died. In September 1889, for example, the 150th New York Volunteer Infantry dedicated its monument on Culp's Hill. Henry A. Gildersleeve's oration read in part:

> We stand to-day on ground made famous by the defenders of the Union. Here was fought more than a quarter of a century ago, the most important battle of our great Civil War. . . . The men who fell upon this field are entitled to no less grateful remembrance than those who fell at Bunker Hill and Valley Forge. . . . [W]e do proudly claim that for no nobler cause did patriots ever fight, that for no grander country did heroes ever die. Yes, and thank God, they died for the whole country, to-day the home of sixty million freemen. The triumph of the Union armies on this field was a victory for the Constitution and the Union, and took no rights away from the South. The blessings flowing from a preserved Union reach all the States, and the fountains it feeds are those of universal liberty and prosperity, at which the Confederate soldier is as welcome to come and drink as the Union Volunteer.[21]

Gildersleeve continued by providing a history of the regiment and describing its part in the Gettysburg battle. The speech included several passages about the horrible deaths suffered by men on the field, but Gildersleeve maintained that "each dying soldier accepted his dreadful fate without a murmur."[22] The oration concluded:

> We dedicate this monument to the memory of the soldiers of the Dutchess County regiment who were killed at the Battle of Gettysburg; men who, when their country called for soldiers, volunteered to fight her battles; brave patriots who willingly gave up their lives to prove to the nations of the earth the success of a republican form of government; men who died to free an enslaved people.[23]

Many battlefield orators spoke explicitly during the thirty years after the battle about the heroic sacrifices Federal soldiers had made in defense of their country and in opposition to slavery. Other speakers offered an olive branch to the South. In 1888, for example, at a reunion of the 142nd Regiment Pennsylvania Volunteers, Col. Horatio N. Warren noted the passage of time since the Union victory:

> We are not here to-day to exult over that victory, for we realize that the quarter of a century that has sped away on the wings of time since then, has to a great extent wiped out the bitter feeling we then entertained towards our southern brothers; and we believe to-day that a large proportion of those men still living, who were against us then, are now lovers of the old Union, and are favorably inclined to rejoice with us that at Gettysburg, Pa., the tide of Lee's invasion was checked.[24]

Northern veterans understandably emphasized the heroism of Union soldiers, but as wartime animosities receded, positive images of Southern soldiers who fought at Gettysburg became more widespread. One popular anecdote about the battle—the story that a temporary truce occurred at Spangler's Spring on the evening of July 2—lends support to the notion that Northerners and Southerners were more alike than different from each other. An impression of the essential sameness of the enemies tended to benefit the Confederates because their secessionist and pro-slavery causes were not especially easy to defend. It is extremely doubtful that men from the opposing forces actually gathered at Spangler's Spring to swap stories and tobacco while they filled their canteens. But the idea that some sort of comradeship had existed between the two armies was so attractive in later years that veterans regularly reenacted the event at battlefield reunions, and a memorial at the Spring recounts the tale.[25]

In such a context, authentic Southern heroes emerged. One of these was Gen. George E. Pickett, commander of a division of Longstreet's First Corps and the putative leader of the Confederate's final attack at Gettysburg, possibly the most famous assault of the entire Civil War. Pickett, a Virginian, was an attractive figure to both Northerners and Southerners for his youth and enthusiasm, his fair-haired good looks, and the gallant adventurism his military career seemed to embody. While the bloodiness and brutality of war held a certain fascination for many Americans, on the whole they preferred the romantic image of battle exemplified by a personality such as Pickett's.[26]

If Pickett was a romantic hero, Gen. Lewis A. Armistead, another Virginian and one of Pickett's brigade commanders, represented the tragic aspects of the Confederate loss at Gettysburg. Armistead and perhaps two hundred of his men breached the Union lines on July 3. The figure of Armistead, hat held aloft on his sword, courageously leading these men to death or capture is one of the enduring images of the war. Well known also was the story of Armistead's prewar friendship with Gen. Winfield S. Hancock, commander of the federal army's Second Corps at Gettysburg. Armistead's words as he fell mortally wounded were said to have been a message of apology to Hancock.

Kindnesses and friendships between enemies formed something of a theme in many of the Gettysburg anecdotes that circulated after the war. In one frequently repeated story, Georgia's Gen. John B. Gordon stops to assist New York's Gen. Francis C. Barlow, gravely wounded on July 1, and orders that Barlow's wife be allowed through Confederate lines to care for him. Gordon, a founder of the United Confederate Veterans who served after Reconstruction in the U.S. Senate and as governor of Georgia, seems in the 1890s to have invented the myth that he aided the wounded Barlow at Gettysburg. Gordon elaborated on the anecdote in his 1903 memoirs, published after Barlow's 1896 death. The Barlow–Gordon incident was only one of many similar stories that appeared in both memoirs and fiction after the war. Gordon's tale appealed to Americans in the same way the Spangler's Spring anecdote had. It confirmed for Americans a belief in the basic decency and goodness of the soldiers from both sides despite the terrible and bloody reality of the conflict.[27]

Perhaps a desire to emphasize the positive results of an awful war also contributed to public enthusiasm for the national veteran reunions held at Gettysburg in 1913 and 1938. A few Southerners had attended the 1888 veteran reunion, but 1913 was the first reunion for which large numbers of Confederates journeyed to Gettysburg. The Military Park's administrators and a reunion commission appointed by the host state of Pennsylvania adopted national reconciliation as a theme for the four-day event. Penn-

sylvania's commission recommended to Congress that the cornerstone for a national Peace Memorial be laid at Gettysburg as part
of the anniversary commemorations. The Grand Army of the Republic and the United Confederate Veterans also helped plan the
event and encouraged their respective members to attend.[28]

Tens of thousands of veterans gathered at Gettysburg for ceremonies held from July 1 through 4, 1913, that received widespread
national press coverage. Approximately 47,000 Union veterans
attended the 1913 reunion, while an estimated 9,000 Confederates made the trip to Gettysburg. Many of the most heartfelt reunions taking place on the field likely were those between former
members of the same regiments, brigades, and divisions. The press
eagerly reported on reunions between former enemies, however,
and on events featuring reconciliationist themes.

Amid scores of speeches and commemorative ceremonies, a
symbolic reenactment of Pickett's Charge stood out. On July 3,
1913, about 150 survivors of the original assault walked across
the fields from Seminary to Cemetery Ridge, preceded by a band
playing "Dixie." Several hundred members of the Philadelphia
Brigade Association met the former Confederates at the crest of
the Ridge, offering handshakes and cheers. The reenactment concluded with the participants singing "My Country 'Tis of Thee."[29]

The following day's events at Gettysburg highlighted reconciliation as well with the laying by President Woodrow Wilson of a
cornerstone for a national Peace Memorial. In his Independence
Day speech, Wilson praised the heroism displayed by all Civil
War soldiers and lauded the fifty years of peace that had followed
the war:

> How wholesome and healing the peace has been! We have found one
> another again as brothers and comrades in arms, enemies no longer,
> generous friends rather, our battles long past, the quarrel forgotten.[30]

A reunion of aged veterans at Gettysburg for the battle's seventy-
fifth anniversary evoked similar reflections on national unity and
reconciliation. Speaking at the unveiling on July 3, 1938, of the
completed Peace Memorial, President Franklin Roosevelt alluded
to Lincoln's Gettysburg Address:

> Lincoln spoke in solace for all who fought upon this field; and the
> years have laid their balm upon its wounds. Men who wore the Blue

and men who wore the Gray are here together, a fragment spared by time. They are brought here by the memories of old divided loyalties, but they meet here in united loyalty to a united cause which the unfolding years have made it easier to see.

All of them we honor, not asking under which flag they fought then—thankful that they stand together under one flag now.

Roosevelt, calling Gettysburg "a shrine of American patriotism," included former Confederates under the mantle of national pride.[31]

The Eternal Light Peace Memorial, whose unveiling Roosevelt witnessed, features an eternal flame symbolizing the existence of everlasting peace between North and South. Located on Oak Hill, the site of the battle's opening shots, the memorial was jointly paid for by two former Confederate states and five former Union states. For the many people present in 1938 who were too young to remember the Civil War in all its horror, the Peace Memorial and the national park surrounding it paid tribute to all the courageous soldiers who had fought at Gettysburg and to the lasting national reconciliation they had later achieved.[32]

In truth, the reunionism of 1913 and 1938 was based on a tacit agreement between Northerners and Southerners to emphasize the bravery and heroism of Civil War soldiers and leave submerged any acknowledgment of the ideological differences that had caused the conflict. President Roosevelt claimed that it did not matter which army the veterans had fought in, that reconciliation and renewed loyalty to the Union earned the former Confederates their share of honor for battlefield sacrifices.

But what of the ideas that Lincoln expressed at Gettysburg on November 19, 1863? On a day that seemed to be light years rather than mere months away from the events of the previous July, Lincoln dedicated a national cemetery that held only the bodies of Federal soldiers. He urged

> that from these honored dead we take increased devotion to that cause for which they gave the last full measure of devotion—that we here highly resolve that these dead shall not have died in vain—that this nation, under God, shall have a new birth of freedom—and that government of the people, by the people, for the people, shall not perish from the earth.[33]

Despite Lincoln's famous words, the great issues of the Civil War period—secession, states' rights, slavery—do not form a significant part of the nation's popular memory of the Battle of Gettysburg. In its role as turning point of the war the battle is seen to contribute to the defeat of the Confederacy and the preservation of the Union, but what that meant for the course of American history remains largely unexplored.

Lincoln's immortal address connected the Gettysburg site to the ideals of equality and republican government, but his words were not fully incorporated into traditions about the battle. Americans in general have chosen to commemorate the valor and gallantry of soldiers and applaud the speed and completeness of national reconciliation rather than closely examine the more troubling aspects of their country's past or present. To be sure, the Gettysburg Address Memorial in the National Cemetery offers a stirring affirmation of equality and union. At the battlefield itself, though, Americans find a beautiful pastoral landscape that seemingly belies the true nature of war. There they can encounter history as a dramatic and heroic episode and experience a romantic illusion of closeness to the past. Messy questions about slavery, emancipation, and the place of blacks in America's postwar society do not, for the most part, intrude on their idealized memories.

In some ways, the images that are left out of the picture most Americans have of the Battle of Gettysburg are as important as those that were included. There were instances where the war's moral and political questions impinged on the emerging popular interpretation of Gettysburg—for example, in Peter Rothermel's painting of Pickett's Charge and in the nineteenth-century commemorative activities of many Union veterans. But overall there was a startling though not uniform lack of attention given to the issues of secession and slavery. Despite efforts during the late nineteenth century by black intellectuals like Frederick Douglass to force the country to face up to the Civil War's legacy of black emancipation, many white Americans preferred to focus on soldier heroism and the shared memories of common wartime experiences that made reconciliation during the postwar period easier.[34]

Under different circumstances the legacy of the Battle of Gettysburg might have emphasized important ideological questions. If, for example, a regiment of black volunteers had fought for the Union at Gettysburg and defended Cemetery Ridge against the Confederates' final assault, a heroic image of the black soldier may have been inescapably linked to a significant Federal victory. Visitors to Gettysburg, rather than thinking of the battlefield as the place where Americans from all regions of the country fought bravely for what they believed in, might then have learned that Gettysburg was the site of a famous Union victory that enabled the United States to find its destiny, end slavery, and commit itself to universal freedom and civil rights.

That, of course, did not happen. The battlefield memorial at Gettysburg and the popular memory of the battle eventually glorified all the dead because they had exemplified what many people believed were distinctly American traits such as self-sacrifice, courage, and a willingness to fight for one's convictions. Americans who could recite Lincoln's Gettysburg Address also stood in awe of Pickett's Charge. Visitors to Gettysburg came away with a nostalgic feeling of connection to a past that they saw as a stirring and dramatic pageant rather than a struggle for the moral and political salvation of their country. They could only wonder that so many men had faced death at Gettysburg and reflect with gratitude on the lasting peace the battle's survivors had helped to secure.

# Notes

## Introduction

1. Richard N. Current, *The Lincoln Nobody Knows* (New York: Hill and Wang, 1963), vi.

2. *Intruder in the Dust* (New York: New American Library, 1949), 125–26.

3. Roy P. Basler, ed., Marion Dolores Pratt and Lloyd A. Dunlap, asst. eds., *The Collected Works of Abraham Lincoln*, 9 vols., 2 suppl. vols. (New Brunswick, N.J.: Rutgers, 1953–55, 1990), 1:112.

## ONE: *The Common Soldier's Gettysburg Campaign*

1. Quoted in Jay Luvaas, "Lee and the Operational Art: The Right Place, the Right Time," *Parameters* 22, No. 3 (Autumn 1992): 2.

2. Lee to Trimble, Mar. 8, 1863; *The War of the Rebellion: A Compilation of the Official Records of the Union and Confederate Armies,* 128 vols. (Washington: GPO, 1880–1901) ser. 1, vol. 25, pt. 2 , p. 658 [hereafter *OR,* with all references in series 1].

3. Hotchkiss diary, Feb. 23, 1863. Archie P. McDonald, ed., *Make Me a Map of the Valley* (Dallas: SMU Press, 1973), 116.

4. Lee to Davis, Apr. 16, 1863. *OR,* vol. 25, pt. 2, p. 725.

5. [George Patterson] to Friend, May 19, 1863. Josiah Collins Papers, North Carolina Division of Archives and History [hereafter NCDAH]; Horace Smith diary, May 3, 1863. Horace Smith Papers, State Historical Society of Wisconsin [hereafter SHSW]; Daniel Brown to Wife, May 10, 1863. Isaac Brown Papers, NCDAH; Ned [Bridgman] to Sidney, May 9, 1863. Edward Bridgman, SHSW.

6. J. Thomas Petty diary, May 5, 1863. J. Thomas Petty Papers, Museum of the Confederacy [MC]; John B. Colding to Sister, May 29, 1863. 60th Regiment Georgia Volunteer Infantry, Co. G Papers, Georgia Department of Archives and History [hereafter GADAH].

7. Horace Smith diary, May 6, 1863

8. Robert Goldthwaite Carter, *Four Brothers in Blue or Sunshine and Shadows of the War of the Rebellion* (Austin: University of Texas Press, 1978), 283.

9. Gary Gallagher, ed., *Fighting for the Confederacy: The Personal Recollec-*

*tions of General Edward Porter Alexander* (Chapel Hill: University of North Carolina Press, 1989), 222.

10. W. J. Seymour journal, June 15, 1863. Schoff Collection, Clements Library, University of Michigan.

11. W. James Kincheloe diary, June 12, 1863. 49th Virginia Infantry, Company C Papers, GADAH.

12. Seymour journal, June 23, 1863.

13. General Orders, No. 45. HQ, 2nd Army Corps. June 15, 1863. 45th North Carolina Infantry. Log Book of General and Special Orders, 1862–1863, NCDAH; C.C. Blacknall to Bro George, June 18 [1863]. Oscar W. Blacknall Papers, NCDAH; Watkins Kearns diary, June 21, 1863. Watkins Kearns Papers, Virginia Historical Society [hereafter VAHS].

14. Wm. H. Routt to Bettie, June 23, 1863. Routt Papers, MC.

15. Bud to Sister, July 18, 1863. Ralph G. Poriss Papers, U.S. Army Military History Institute [hereafter USMHI]; Arthur J. L. Fremantle diary, June 27, 1863. Walter Lord, ed., *The Fremantle Diary: Being the Journal of Lieutenant Colonel Arthur James Lyon Fremantle* (Boston: Little, Brown, 1954), 191.

16. See General Orders, No. 72. HQ.ANV. June 21, 1863. *OR*, vol. 27, pt. 3, pp. 912–13.

17. L. M. Blackford to Father, June 28, 1863. Launcelot Minor Blackford Papers, University of Virginia [hereafter UVA]; K to Sue, July 17, 1863. Alice V. D. Pierrepont, *Reuben Vaughn Kidd: Soldier of the Confederacy* (Petersburg: Published by the Author, [1947]), 329. Also see Campbell Brown journal for late June and early July. Copy in Brake Collection, USMHI.

18. George P. Collins to Miss Mary, Aug. 18, 1863. Pettigrew Family Papers, NCDAH.

19. Elias Davis to Georgia, June 27, 1863. Elias Davis Papers, Southern Historical Collection, University of North Carolina [hereafter SHC, UNC]; K to Sue, July 17, 1863. Pierrepont, *Reuben Vaughn Kidd,* 329.

20. B. L. Farinholt to Lelia, July 1, 1863. Benjamin Lyons Farinholt Papers, VAHS; A member of Cutshaw's Battery to Father, July 7, 1863, in *Richmond Enquirer,* July 17, 1863.

21. Turner Vaughn diary, June 28, 1863. "Diary of Turner Vaughn," *Alabama Historical Quarterly* 18, No. 4, 588.

22. Jerome Farnsworth to Mother, May 14, 1863. Farnsworth Papers, Minnesota Historical Society [hereafter MNHS].

23. Elon Francis Brown diary, June 15, 1863. Elon Francis Brown Papers, SHSW.

24. John [Ames] to Mother, June 28, 1863. John Ames Papers, USMHI.

25. Charles E. Belknap diary, June 29, 1863. Copy in Brake Collection, USMHI. Also see Charles C. Perkins dairy, June 30, 1863. Civil War Times Illustrated Collection, USMHI. See also Circular, HQ, Army of the Potomac, June 30, 1863; Meade to [Reynolds], June 30, 1863. *OR*, vol. 27, pt. 3, pp. 417, 420.

26. Brown diary, June 26, 1863. Also see entry for June 21, 1863.

27. Edwin D. Benedict diary, July 1, 1863; John W. Plummer to Brother, undated. Published in the Minneapolis *State Atlas,* 26 August 1863. Copy in Brake Collection, USMHI.

28. Horatio Dana Chapman diary, June 30, 1863. Copy in Brake Collection, USMHI.

29. Flavius J. Bellamy diary, July 1, 1863. Copy in Brake Collection, USMHI.

30. Quoted in Edwin B. Coddington, *The Gettysburg Campaign: A Study in Command* (New York: Scribners, 1968), 271; quoted in Alan T. Nolan, *The Iron Brigade: A Military History* (Bloomington: Indiana University Press, 1994), 239; Rufus R. Dawes, *Service with the Sixth Wisconsin Volunteers* (Madison: State Historical Society of Wisconsin, 1962), 169.

31. Henry Berkeley diary, July 2, 1863. William H. Runge, ed., *Four Years in the Confederate Artillery: The Diary of Private Henry Robinson Berkeley* (Chapel Hill: University of North Carolina Press, 1961), 50.

32. Jas. H. Wilkes to [Mary], July 16, 1863. Ward Family Papers, Library of Congress [hereafter LC].

33. Brown journal, May 6, 1863; John D. Vautier diary, July 1, 1863. John D. Vautier Papers, USMHI.

34. Wilkes to [Mary], July 16, 1863.; Thomas J. Webb to Brother, July 18, 1863. Brake Collection, USMHI; John W. Daniel on Gettysburg, Nov. 20, 1863. John Warwick Daniel Papers, VAHS.

35. Oates, William C., *The War Between the Union and the Confederacy* (Dayton: Morningside, 1974 [reprint of 1905 ed.]), 212.

36. The author would like to thank D. Scott Hartwig and Thomas Desjardin for providing copies of letters, diaries, and journals from men in the 20th Maine. Nathan S. Clark's diary claims Chamberlain gave the order, but his is clearly not a diary but a journal, written some time after the battle and most likely after Chamberlain's report became public. Many of the "diaries" are actually journals, prepared after the event, and influenced by Chamberlain's report.

37. Circular. HQ, Army of the Potomac. June 30, 1863. *OR*, vol. 27, pt. 3, p. 415; Plummer to Brother, undated. See Harry W. Pfanz, *Gettysburg: The Second Day* (Chapel Hill: University of North Carolina Press, 1987), 284.

38. W. P. Heflin, *Blind Man "On the Warpath"* (n.p., [190?]), 24.

39. Chapman diary, July 3, 1863. Plummer to brother, undated. Also see Allan Nevins, ed., *A Diary of Battle: The Personal Journals of Colonel Charles S. Wainwright, 1861–1865* (New York: Harcourt, 1962), 249.

40. J. B. Crawford to wife, July 8, 1863. J. B. Crawford Papers, Mississippi Department of Archives and History [hereafter MSDAH].

41. Franklin Sawyer, *A Military History of the 8th Regiment Ohio Vol. Inf'y* (Cleveland: Fairbanks, 1881), 132.

42. Belknap diary, July 3, 1863.

43. Smith [Brown] to Parents, July 4, 1863. Morris Brown Papers, Hamilton College. Officially, three soldiers in the regiment received Medals of Honor for capturing flags. *OR*, vol. 27, pt. 2, p. 282.

44. A to   , in *Richmond Enquirer*, July 24, 1863; Taylor [Scott] to Fan, Aug. 5, 1863. Keith Family Papers, VAHS.

45. See Gorgas to Mallet, June 4, 1863. Personal Papers, J. W. Mallet. Records and Pension Office, Document File #568,231. Record Group 94, National Archives; Mallet to Gorgas, July 14, Aug. 3, 1863. Letters Sent, Superintendent of Laboratories, Macon, Georgia, Apr. 1863–Apr. 1864. W. N. Smith to Mallet, July 25, 1863.

Letters Received, Superintendent of Laboratories, Macon, Georgia. Record Group 109, National Archives; Special Order, No. 175. Headquarters, Department of South Carolina, Ga. & Fla. Sept. 6, 1863. E. P. Alexander to Gorgas, Nov. 7, 1863. Experiments on rate of burning of fuzes, Dec. 1863, Jan. 1864. MC3, M600. J. W. Mallet Papers, MC.

46. Chapman diary, July 3, 1863.

47. John Henry [Burrill] to Parents, July 13, 1863. Joseph [Twitchell] to Sis, July 5, 1863. Copies in Brake Collection, USMHI.

48. Campbell Brown journal, July 4, 1863.

49. [Ames] to Mother, July 9, 1863.

50. Ibid., July 8, 1863.

51. Quoted in James I. Robertson, Jr., *Soldiers Blue and Gray* (Columbia: University of South Carolina Press, 1988), 226.

52 Seymour journal, July 5, 1863.

53. A. N. Buck to Brother & Sister, July 9, 1863. Copy in Brake Collection, USMHI.

54. Chapman diary, July 7, 1863; Felix Brannigan to Father, (n.d. [July 1863]). Copy in Brake Collection, USMHI; Eseck G. Wilbur to [Parents], July 15, 1863. Eseck G. Wilbur Papers, Rice University.

55. See C. H. Salter to Friend, July 12, 1863. Brake Collection, USMHI.

56. ? to Absent Friend, Aug. 4, 1863. Bowles-Jordan Papers, UVA; T.T. Fogle to Sister, July 16, 1863. Theodore T. Fogle Papers, Emory University.

57. Robert [Stiles] to Mother, July 29, [1863]. Robert A. Stiles Papers, VAHS; Caspar C. to Cousin, July 12, 1863. Caspar C. Hinkel Papers, MC.

58. Dod [Ramseur] to Darling, July 8, 1863. Stephen Dodson Ramseur Papers, SHC, UNC; After Action Report of Capt. J. J. Young, July 4, 1863. *OR*, vol. 27, pt. 2, p. 645; Eugene [Blackford] to Mother, July 8, 1863. Lewis Leigh Collection, USMHI; James E. Phillips memoirs, 26. James Eldred Phillips Papers, VAHS.

59. S. W. N. Feamster to Mother, July 27, 1863. Feamster Family Papers, LC; J. Thomas Petty diary, Aug. 11, 1863. J. Thomas Petty Papers, MC; Caspar C. to Cousin, July 12, 1863. Hinkel Papers; AAR of R. E. Lee, July 31, 1863. *OR*, vol. 27, pt. 2, p. 309. W. B. Sturtevant to Jimmie, July 27, 1863.

60. W. B. Sturtevant to Jimmie, July 27, 1863. W. B. Sturtevant Papers, MC; Dick [Manson] to Mother, July 30, [1863]. Civil War Miscellany, USMHI; Walter to [Dick], July 17, 1863. R. Lockwood Tower, ed., *Lee's Adjutant: The Wartime Letters of Colonel Walter Herron Taylor, 1862–1865* (Columbia: University of South Carolina Press, 1995), 62. Thanks to friend Gary Gallagher for mentioning the Taylor letter.

**TWO:** *Joshua Chamberlain and the American Dream*

1. "The Battle of Gettysburg," Nov. 1868, newspaper clipping, Scrapbook, Chamberlain Papers, Library of Congress, Washington, D. C.; "Gen. Chamberlain's Lecture—The Battle of Gettysburg," Nov. 1868, newspaper clipping, ibid.; "The Bay State Lecture," ibid.

2. Joshua L. Chamberlain, "Do It! That's How," *Bowdoin*, 64 (Spring–Summer 1991), 12. The article is an excerpt from Chamberlain's unfinished and previously

unpublished autobiography located in the Chamberlain Collection, Bowdoin College Library, Brunswick, Maine.

3. Chamberlain to Frances (Fannie) Chamberlain, Oct. 10, 26, Nov. 3, 1862, Chamberlain Papers, Library of Congress, Washington, D.C.; Chamberlain, "My Story of Fredericksburg," in *"Bayonet! Forward": My Civil War Reminiscences*, ed. Stan Clark, Jr. (Gettysburg: Stan Clark Military Books, 1994), 7. The article was originally published in *Cosmopolitan Magazine*, 54 (December 1912): 148–59.

4. Chamberlain, *The Passing of the Armies* (New York: Putnam, 1915), 19–20, 76, 331, 385–86.

5. Ibid., 260–61. See also John B. Gordon, *Reminiscences of the Civil War* (New York: Scribners, 1903), 444–45.

6. Chamberlain, *Passing of the Armies*, 386.

7. Chamberlain, "Address of Gen. Chamberlain at the Springfield City Hall," *Springfield (Mass.) Republican*, June 4, 1897; Chamberlain, "Oration on the One-Hundredth Anniversary of the Birth of Abraham Lincoln" (1909), in Clark, ed., *"Bayonet! Forward,"* 244.

8. Chamberlain Association of America, *Joshua Lawrence Chamberlain: A Sketch* (n.p., [1906]), 15–16. On Grant's field promotion of Chamberlain see Ulysses S. Grant, *Memoirs and Selected Letters* (New York: Library of America, 1990), 601–602.

9. G. W. Carleton to A. B. Farwell, January 6, 1866, Frost Family Papers, Yale University Library, New Haven, Conn.; Gordon, *Reminiscences*, 444; Theodore Gerrish, *Army Life: A Private's Reminiscences of the Civil War* (Portland, Me.: Hoyt, Fogg, & Donham, 1882), 347.

10. Chamberlain, "Address . . . at Springfield City Hall." Chamberlain wrote during the war: "I belive in destiny—one, I mean, divinely appointed." Chamberlain to Sarah D. B. Chamberlain, [Autumn 1864], Chamberlain Collection, Bowdoin College.

11. Chamberlain, "Joshua as a Military Commander," *The Sunday School Times* (Philadelphia), December 1, 1883.

12. Report of Colonel Joshua L. Chamberlain, July 6, 1863, U.S. War Department, *The War of the Rebellion: A Compilation of the Official Records of the Union and Confederate Armies*, 128 vols., index, and atlas (Washington, D. C.: GPO, 1880–1901), ser. 1,vol. 27, pt. 1, 622–26 (hereafter *OR*, with all references in series 1). Actually this report, although dated just after the battle, was written by Chamberlain in 1884, after the editors of the *OR* informed him that his original report was missing from the War Records files and asked him to supply a replacement. He did so by trying to reconstruct his original report from memory. See Joshua L. Chamberlain to George B. Herenden, July 6, 1863 [ca. Mar. 15, 1884], Records of the War Records Office, Entry 729, "Union Battle Reports," RG 94 (Records of the Adjutant General's Office), National Archives, Washington, D.C. One can only guess how much of this report can be attributed to Chamberlain's hazy memory or wishful thinking. Another battle report by Chamberlain does exist, also dated July 6, 1863, and this one seems to be a copy of the original lost report. See Chamberlain to Herenden, July 6, 1863, Maine State Archives, Augusta, Maine. My thanks to Thomas A. Desjardin for graciously sharing with me his discovery of when Chamberlain actually wrote his published official report.

13. Chamberlain to Frances Chamberlain, July 4, 1863, July 17, 1863, Chamberlain Papers, LC; Chamberlain to Governor Abner Coburn, July 21, 1863, Maine State Archives.

It is not true that the 20th Maine actually defeated an entire Confederate brigade, as Chamberlain had claimed. For an examination of the numbers of troops involved in the Little Round Top fight, see Thomas A. Desjardin, *Stand Firm Ye Boys from Maine: The 20th Maine and the Gettysburg Campaign* (Gettysburg: Thomas Publications, 1995), Appendix 1.

14. Chamberlain to Frances Chamberlain, July 17, 1863, Chamberlain Papers, LC; Report of Colonel James C. Rice, July 31, 1863, *OR,* vol. 27, pt. 1, pp. 618, 620; Report of General James Barnes, Aug. 24, 1863, ibid., 603–604; Chamberlain to Frances Chamberlain, July 4, 1863, Chamberlain Papers, LC.

15. Chamberlain to Frances Chamberlain, Nov. 3, 1862, Chamberlain Papers, LC; *Bridgton (Maine) News,* April 29, 1898; James Barnes to Chamberlain, Sept. 1, 1863, Maine State Archives; Chamberlain to Barnes, Sept. 3, 1863, Barnes Papers, New-York Historical Society, New York; James Rice to William Pitt Fessenden, Sept. 8, 1863, Maine State Archives.

16. Charles H. Howard to Chamberlain, Sept. 14, 1863, Joshua L. Chamberlain Military Personnel File, Letters Received by the Commission Branch of the Adjutant General's Office, 1863–1870, RG94, NA; Adelbert Ames to Edwin S. Stanton, Sept. 21, 1863, ibid.; John H. Rice to Abraham Lincoln, Sept. 26, 1863, ibid.; Israel Washburn to Stanton, Sept. 27, 1863, ibid.; Charles Griffin to Seth Williams, Oct. 7, 1863, Maine State Archives; Charles Gilmore to Abner Coburn, Oct. 8, 1863, ibid.; Hannibal Hamlin to Lincoln, Oct. 16, 1863, ibid.; E. B. French to Stanton, Oct. 29, 1863, Chamberlain Military Personnel File, NA.

17. Joseph B. Mitchell, *The Badge of Gallantry: Recollections of Civil War Congressional Medal of Honor Winners* (New York: Macmillan, 1968), 130; Chamberlain, *Passing of the Armies,* xiv, 255.

18. Chamberlain Association, *Sketch,* 12–14; Willard M. Wallace, *Soul of the Lion: A Biography of Joshua L. Chamberlain* (New York: Nelson, 1960), 128–36; Alice Rains Trulock, *In the Hands of Providence: Joshua L. Chamberlain and the American Civil War* (Chapel Hill and London: University of North Carolina Press, 1992), 198–218, 229–86, 301–11; "Gov. Chamberlain's Lecture" [at G.A.R. Post, No. 9], n.d., newspaper clipping, Scrapbook, Chamberlain Papers, LC; "A Lecture from Gen. Chamberlain," c. 1866, newspaper clipping, ibid.; "The Military Career of General Chamberlain," c. 1866, newspaper clipping, ibid.; "Four Years Ago— And Now," c. 1867, newspaper clipping, ibid.; "General Chamberlain at Lake Forest," c. 1868, newspaper clipping, ibid.

19. "General Chamberlain at Lake Forest," c. 1868, newspaper clipping, ibid.; [Political Meeting at Calais], c. Oct. 1868, newspaper clipping, ibid.' "The Battle of Gettysburg," Nov. 1868, newspaper clipping, ibid.; "Gen. Chamberlain's Lecture— The Battle of Gettysburg," Nov. 1868, newspaper clipping, ibid.; "The Left at Gettysburg," c. 1869, newspaper clipping, ibid.; "Gen. Joshua L. Chamberlain in the Battle of Gettysburg," c. 1884, newspaper clipping, ibid.

20. Trulock, *In the Hands of Providence,* 176; John B. Bachelder to Chamberlain, Nov. 16, 1865, Aug. 1869, Aug. 14, 1869, Chamberlain Papers, LC; Report of

the Reunion of Officers of the Army of the Potomac, Aug. 22–28, 1869, John P. Nicholson Papers, Huntington Library, San Marino, Cal.

21. Chamberlain, "General Chamberlain's Address," in *Dedication of the Twentieth Maine Monuments at Gettysburg, Oct. 3, 1889* (Waldoboro, Me.: News Steam Job Print, 1891), 26–31; Chamberlain, "General Chamberlain's Address," in Charles Hamlin et al., eds., *Maine at Gettysburg: Report of the Commissioners* (Portland, Me.: Lakeside Press, 1898), 546–59.

22. See, for example, Amos M. Judson, *History of the Eighty-Third Regiment Pennsylvania Volunteers,* ed. John J. Pullen (Dayton, Oh.: Morningside Press, 1986 [orig. publ. 1865]), 123–41; William C. Oates, "Gettysburg—The Battle on the Right," *Southern Historical Society Papers,* 6 (1878): 172–182; An Old Private [Theodore Gerrish], "The Twentieth Maine at Gettysburg," *Portland Advertiser,* Mar. 13, 1882; James H. Nichols,"Letter of Theodore Gerrish," *Lincoln County News,* April 1882; Gerrish, *Army Life,* 100–19; Holman S. Melcher, "The 20th Maine at Gettysburg," *Lincoln County News,* Mar. 13, 1885; Spear, "Memorial Day Speech Given at Warren, Maine," May 30, 1888, in the possession of the late Abbott Spear, Warren, Maine.

23. Chamberlain, "Gen. Chamberlain's Address," in *Dedication,* 27–29; Carswell McClelland to Chamberlain, May 12, 22, 1891, Chamberlain Papers, LC.

24. Thomas Hubbard to the Secretary of War, Feb. 15, 1893, Chamberlain Military Personnel File, NA; Fitz John Porter to the Secretary of War, May 19, 1893, ibid.; Alexander S. Webb to the Secretary of War, May 23, 1893, ibid.; Henry B. Cleaves to the Secretary of War, June 7, 1893, ibid. On the Twentieth Maine Regimental Association, which had been founded in 1876, see William B. Styple, ed., *With a Flash of His Sword: The Writings of Major Holman S. Melcher, 20th Maine Infantry* (Kearny, N.J.: Belle Grove, 1994), 245–91.

25. Memorandum, Aug. 11, 1893, Chamberlain Military Personnel File, NA; F. C. Ainsworth to Chamberlain, Aug. 17, 1893, William C. Oates Correspondence, Gettysburg National Military Park, Gettysburg, Penn. (hereafter GNMP); Chamberlain to Ainsworth, Sept. 16, 1893, Chamberlain Military Personnel File, NA; Memorandum, Mar. 21, 1897, ibid.; Chamberlain to Ainsworth, Sept. 24, 1907, ibid.; Ainsworth to Chamberlain, Sept. 30, Oct. 19, 1907, ibid.; Chamberlain to Ainsworth, Oct. 21, 1907, ibid.; Chamberlain, *Passing of the Armies,* 390. The official citation reads: "Daring heroism and great tenacity in holding his position on the Little Round Top against repeated assaults, and carrying the advance position on the Great Round Top." U. S. Army, *The Medal of Honor of the United States Army* (Washington, D.C.: GPO, 1948), 139.

26. For example, see William E. S. Whitman and Charles H. True, *Maine in the War for the Union: A History* (Lewiston, Me.: Nelson Dingley, 1865), 493–94; William Swinton, *Campaigns of the Army of the Potomac* (New York: Scribners, 1882 [orig. publ. 1866]), 346–47; Samuel P. Bates, *The Battle of Gettysburg* (Philadelphia: Davis, 1875), 117–20; Louis Philippe Albert d'Orleans, Comte de Paris, *The Battle of Gettysburg* (Philadelphia: Porter & Coates, 1886), 167, 171, 177–78, 182; Jacob Hoke, *The Great Invasion of 1863, or, General Lee in Pennsylvania* (Dayton: Shuey,1887), 332–33; James H. Stine, *History of the Army of the Potomac* (Philadelphia: Rodgers, 1892), 511–12; William H. Powell, *The Fifth*

*Army Corps (Army of the Potomac)* (New York: Putnam, 1896), 525–31; John M. Vanderslice, *Gettysburg: Then and Now* (New York: Dillingham, 1899), 155.

27. Bachelder to Chamberlain, Dec. 21, 1892, Chamberlain Papers, LC; Hubbard to the Secretary of War, Feb. 15, 1893, Chamberlain Military Personnel File, NA; Chamberlain Association, *Sketch,* 30. Chamberlain Avenue no longer exists on Little Round Top; it was torn up and removed many years ago, although the old roadbed is still plainly visible.

28. Holman S. Melcher to Chamberlain, Mar. 4, May 15, 1895, Chamberlain Papers, LC; Samuel L. Miller to Chamberlain, May 21, 1895, ibid.; Spear to Chamberlain, May 22, 1895, ibid.; Charles Hamlin to Chamberlain, May 23, 1895, ibid.; George W. Verrill to Chamberlain, June 11, 1896, ibid.; Hamlin to Chamberlain, July 3, 6, 7, 1896, ibid. For the articles, see "Twentieth Maine Regiment, Third Brigade, First Division, Fifth Army Corps, at the Battle of Gettysburg," in Hamlin et al., eds., *Maine at Gettysburg,* 252–62; "Historical Sketch By an Officer of the Regiment," in ibid., 273–85.

29. Chamberlain to William C. Oates (incomplete draft), Feb. 27, 1897, Chamberlin Collection, Bowdoin College; Oates to Chamberlain, Mar. 8, 1897, William Clements Library, University of Michigan, Ann Arbor, Michigan.

30. Oates to William M. Robbins, Apr. 1, 1902, Oates Correspondence, GNMP; Oates to Root, June 2, 1903, ibid.; Nicholson to Chamberlain, Aug. 6, 1903, ibid.; Chamberlain to Nicholson, Aug. 14, 1903, ibid.; Nicholson to Chamberlain, Aug. 21,1903, ibid.; Nicholson to Chamberlain, Aug. 24, 1903, ibid.; Oates to Robbins, July 18, 1904, ibid.

31. Oates to Nicholson, Mar. 1, 1905, Oates Correspondence, GNMP; Oates to Chamberlain, Apr. 14, 1905, ibid.; Chamberlain to Oates, May 18, 1905, ibid.; Nicholson to Chamberlain, May 22, 1905, ibid. Oates's Civil War recollections, which contain a full account of the attack on Little Round Top, were published in 1905. See Oates, *The War Between the Union and the Confederacy and Its Lost Opportunities* (New York and Washington, D.C.: Neale, 1905), 206–209.

32. Ellis Spear, "The 20th Maine at Gettysburg," n.d., newspaper clipping, pasted in Diary of John Chamberlain, Pejepscot Historical Society, Brunswick, Maine; Spear to Chamberlain, July 2, 1882, Chamberlain Papers, LC; Spear, "Memorial Day Speech"; Spear to Bachelder, Nov. 15, 1892, Bachelder Papers, New Hampshire Historical Society, Concord, New Hampshire; Spear to Chamberlain, May 22, 1895, Chamberlain Papers, LC.

33. Styple, ed., *With a Flash of His Sword,* 294; W. F. Beyer and O. F. Keydel, eds., *Deeds of Valor: How America's Heroes Won the Medal of Honor,* 2 vols. (Detroit, Mich.: Perrien-Keydel, 1905), 1:246–48.

34. Chamberlain, "My Story of Fredericksburg," in Clark, ed., *"Bayonet! Forward,"* 1–15; Chamberlain, "Through Blood and Fire at Gettysburg," *Hearst's Magazine,* 23 (June 1913), 894–909; Trulock, *In the Hands of Providence,* 528n; Spear, "The Hoe Cake of Appomattox," in *War Papers, No. 93, Read Before the Military Order of the Loyal Legion of the United States, Washington, D.C., Commandery,* May 7, 1913; Abbott Spear, *The 20th Maine at Fredericksburg: The 1913 Accounts of Generals Chamberlain and Spear* (Warren, Me.,1987); Spear, "Left at Gettysburg"; Spear,"Recollections" (typescript), n.d., 20th Maine Infantry folder, GNMP. Chamberlain expressed displeasure with the way his article in *Hearst's*

*Magazine* had been "mutilated" and "corrected" by its editors. See Chamberlain to Mrs. Eckstrom, May 28, 1913, Fogler Library Special Collections, University of Maine, Orono, Me. My thanks to Thomas A. Desjardin for bringing this letter to my attention.

35. Norton to Spear, Jan. 12, 1916, in the possession of the late Abbott Spear; Spear to Norton, Jan. 18, 1916, in Styple, ed., *With a Flash of His Sword,* 297–98; Spear to Norton, Feb. 1, 1916, ibid., 298–99; Oliver Willcox Norton, *The Attack and Defense of Little Round Top: Gettysburg, July 2, 1863* (New York: Neale, 1913).

36. See, for example, Henry Sweetser Burrage, *Gettysburg and Lincoln: The Battle, the Cemetery, and the National Park* (New York and London: Putnam, 1906), 42–43; E. A. Nash, *History of the Forty-Fourth Regiment New York Volunteer Infantry in the Civil War, 1861–1865* (Chicago: Donnelley, 1911), 143–48; Jesse Bowman Young, *The Battle of Gettysburg: A Comprehensive Narrative* (New York and London, Harper, 1913), 237–38.

37. Trulock, *In the Hands of Providence,* 374–76; Wallace, *Soul of the Lion,* 310; Bruce Catton, "Survivor," *American Heritage,* 30 (Dec. 1978): 111.

38. Kenneth Roberts, *Trending into Maine* (Boston: Little, Brown, 1938), 42–51; Earl Schenk Miers and Richard A. Brown, eds., *Gettysburg* (New Brunswick, N.J.: Rutgers University Press, 1948), 145–51; Bruce Catton, *Glory Road* (Garden City, N.Y.: Doubleday, 1952), 292–93; John J. Pullen, *The Twentieth Maine: A Volunteer Regiment in the Civil War* (Philadelphia: Lippincott, 1957), 3; Wallace, *Soul of the Lion.*

39. Michael Shaara, *The Killer Angels* (New York: McKay, 1974), 250.

40. Ibid., 126, 229, 239.

41. [Boyd M. Harris], *Field Manual 22-100: Military Leadership (October 1983)* (Washington: U. S. Department of the Army, 1983), 4–17, 56–62, 71–72, 82,90–91, 121–27, 138–39, 148–49, 168–70, 174–75, 190–91, 265–66. Army personnel who attend "staff rides" on the Gettysburg battlefield usually hear about Chamberlain as well. See Jay Luvaas and Harold W. Nelson, eds., *The U. S. Army War College Guide to the Battle of Gettysburg* (Carlisle, Pa.: South Mountain Press, 1986), 84–88.

42. See, for instance, Richard Pindell, "Fighting for Little Round Top: The 20th Maine," *Civil War Times Illustrated,* 21 (Feb. 1983), 12–20; Champ Clark et al., eds., *Gettysburg: The Confederate High Tide* (Alexandria, Va.: Time-Life Books, 1985), 83–84; Harry W. Pfanz, *Gettysburg: The Second Day* (Chapel Hill and London: University of North Carolina Press, 1987), 232–36, 402–403; Richard Wheeler, *Witness to Gettysburg* (New York: Harper, 1987), 190–97; David F. Cross, "Mantled in Fire and Smoke," *America's Civil War,* 4 (Jan. 1992): 39–44; Eric J. Wittenberg, "The Fighting Professor: Joshua Lawrence Chamberlain," *Civil War,* 10 (July–Aug. 1992): 8–14; James M. McPherson, *Gettysburg* (Atlanta: Turner, 1993), 56–63. Kent Gramm, *Gettysburg: A Meditation of War and Values* (Bloomington: Indiana University Press, 1994), 135–41.

43. "A 'Civil War' for the Masses," *Los Angeles Times,* July 22, 1990; "'Civil War': A Triumph on All Fronts," *Washington Post,* Oct. 2, 1990; Geoffrey C. Ward, with Ric Burns and Ken Burns, *The Civil War: An Illustrated History* (New York: Knopf, 1990).

44. "When War Was All Glory and Bands and Death," *New York Times,* Oct. 8, 1993. See also C. Peter Jorgensen, "Gettysburg: How a Prize-Winning Novel Became a Motion Picture," *Civil War Times Illustrated,* 32 (Nov.–Dec. 1993): 40–49, 92. The film has since been shown in several foreign countries, broadcast on cable television, and released on video cassette.

45. Geoffrey C. Ward, "Hero of the 20th," *American Heritage,* 43 (Nov. 1992): 14; Trulock, *In the Hands of Providence.*

46. Michael Golay, *To Gettysburg and Beyond: The Parallel Lives of Joshua Lawrence Chamberlain and Edward Porter Alexander* (New York: Crown, 1994); Desjardin, *Stand Firm Ye Boys from Maine.*

47. Oates to F. A. Dearborn, Mar. 28, 1898, Oates Family Papers in the possession of Mrs. Robert H. Charles, Washington, D.C.; Gary W. Gallagher, ed., *Fighting for the Confederacy: The Personal Recollections of General Edward Porter Alexander* (Chapel Hill and London: University of North Carolina Press, 1989), 241–42; Spear to Norton, Feb. 1, 1916, in Styple, ed., *With a Flash of His Sword,* 299.

## THREE: *"Old Jack" Is Not Here*

1. Edward M. Daniel, ed., *Speeches and Orations of John Warwick Daniel* (Lynchburg: J. P. Bell, 1911), 80–81; John W. Daniel, "Commentary on John B. Gordon's *Reminiscences of the Civil War,*" John W. Daniel Papers, University of Virginia; John W. Daniel, "Account of Gettysburg," p. 3, John Warwick Daniel Papers, Virginia Historical Society; Harry W. Pfanz, *Gettysburg: Culp's Hill and Cemetery Hill* (Chapel Hill: University of North Carolina Press, 1993), 57.

2. Louise W. Hitz, *The Letters of Frederick C. Winkler* (n.p., 1911), 71; Daniel, "Commentary on John B. Gordon's *Reminiscences of the Civil War;*" John W. Daniel Papers, University of Virginia; Pfanz, *Culp's Hill,* 39, 45.

3. Pfanz, *Culp's Hill,* 1–4.

4. Jedediah Hotchkiss, "Draft Review of 'From Manassas to Appomattox,'" Jedediah Hotchkiss Papers, Library of Congress; Douglas Southall Freeman, *Lee's Lieutenants,* 3 vols. (New York: Scribner, 1949-51), 2: 713.

5. U.S. War Department, *The War of the Rebellion: A Compilation of the Official Records of the Union and Confederate Armies* (hereafter *OR,* with all references in series 1), 128 vols. (Washington: GPO, 1880–1901), ser. 1, vol. 27, pt. 2, pp. 305, 313.

6. Ibid., pp. 440–43.

7. Ibid., pp. 307, 316, 443–44, 468, 503, 552; Pfanz, *Culp's Hill,* 33.

8. *OR,* vol. 27, pt. 2, p. 444; Trimble to Bachelder, 8 Feb. 1883, David L. Ladd and Audrey J. Ladd, eds., *The Bachelder Papers,* 2 vols. (Dayton: Morningside House, 1994) 2:927.

9. Pfanz, *Culp's Hill,* 22–26. For a full account, see Warren W. Hassler, Jr., *Crises at the Crossroads: The First Day at Gettysburg* (Gaithersburg, Md.: Butternut Press, 1986), 26–74.

10. *OR,* vol. 27, pt. 2, p. 444; Pfanz, *Culp's Hill,* 33.

11. *OR,* vol. 27, pt. 2, p. 444, 552; Hassler, *Crises,* 88; Pfanz, *Culp's Hill,* 30–34.

12. *OR,* vol. 27, pt. 2, 444; Hassler, *Crises,* 88; Pfanz, *Culp's Hill,* 35, 38, 40.

13. *OR*, vol. 27, pt. 2, 444; Hassler, *Crises,* 88; Pfanz, *Culp's Hill,* 30.

14. *OR*, vol. 27, pt. 2, 444-45; Pfanz, *Culp's Hill,* 38–39.

15. Ibid., 71.

16. Ibid., 71–72; Henry K. Douglas, *I Rode with Stonewall* (Atlanta: Mockingbird Books, 1976), 238–39; John B. Gordon, *Reminiscences of the Civil War* (Dayton: Morningside, 1985), 153-55.

17. Pfanz, *Culp's Hill,* 72; Douglas, *I Rode,* 239.

18. James P. Smith, "General Lee at Gettysburg," *Southern Historical Society Papers* (hereafter *SHSP),* 47 vols. (Richmond, 1876–1930), 33:144–45; James P. Smith, "With Stonewall Jackson," *SHSP,* 43:56; Walter H. Taylor, *Four Years with General Lee* (Bloomington: Indiana University Press, 1962), 95–96; *OR* vol. 27, pt. 2, p. 445; Pfanz, *Culp's Hill,* 72–78.

19. *OR*, vol. 27, pt. 2, p. 445, 469; Pfanz, *Culp's Hill,* 78.

20. *OR*, vol. 27, pt. 2, p. 445, 504; Pfanz, *Culp's Hill,* 78–79.

21. *OR*, vol. 27, pt. 2, p. 446; Jubal A. Early, "Causes of Lee's Defeat at Gettysburg," *SHSP* vol. 4, pp. 271–75; Pfanz, *Culp's Hill,* 81–85.

22. *OR*, vol. 27, pt. 2, p. 446; Pfanz, *Culp's Hill,* 85–87, 422.

23. *OR*, vol. 27, pt. 2, p. 448; Pfanz, *Culp's Hill,* 365–66.

24. John W. Daniel, "Memoirs of Gettysburg," 17, Virginia Historical Society; Early, "Causes," *SHSP,* 4:257–58; Pfanz, *Culp's Hill,* 366–67.

25. *The Times* (London), Aug. 18, 1863; *Richmond Enquirer,* July 21, 1863.

26. H. S. Turner to Jubal A. Early, Mar. 29, 1878, Jubal A. Early Papers, Virginia Historical Society; William Allen to Jubal Early, Mar. 26, 1872, Jubal A. Early Papers, Library of Congress; William Allan, "The Strategy of the Gettysburg Campaign," Ken Bandy and Florence Freeland, *The Gettysburg Papers,* I (Dayton: Morningside, 1978), 62.

27. Comte de Paris, *The Battle of Gettysburg* (Philadelphia: John C. Winston Co., 1907), 125; Jesse Bowman Young, *The Battle of Gettysburg* (New York: Harper, 1913), 202–203; Henry J. Hunt, "The First Day at Gettysburg," Robert U. Johnson and Clarence C. Buel, *Battles and Leaders of the Civil War,* 4 vols. (New York: Thomas Yoseloff, 1956), 2:284; Cecil Battine, *The Crises of the Confederacy* (London: Longmans, Green, 1905), 200.

28. Gordon, *Reminiscences,* 153–54; *OR,* vol. 27, pt. 2, p. 469.

29. Smith, "General Lee," *SHSP,* 33:144; Smith, "With Stonewall Jackson," *SHSP,* 43:56; Randolph H. McKim,"The Gettysburg Campaign," *SHSP,* 43:272–73; Taylor, *Four Years,* 95; Freeman, *R.E. Lee,* 3:77; Early, "Causes," *SHSP,* 4:271–73.

30. Trimble, "The Battle and Campaign of Gettysburg," *SHSP,* 26:120-24; Freeman, *Lee's Lieutenants,* 2:700–701, 3:94–95; McKim, "The Gettysburg Campaign," *SHSP,* 40:273; Pfanz, *Culp's Hill,* 31–32.

31. Freeman, *R.E. Lee,* 3:72, 77–80; Smith, "General Lee," *SHSP,* 33:144.

32. Freeman, *Lee's Lieutenants,* 3:92–93.

33. Ibid., 94–96.

34. Edwin B. Coddington, *The Gettysburg Campaign,* (Dayton: Morningside, 1979), 317–18, 710.

35. *OR*, vol. 27, pt. 2, pp. 445, 555; Early, "Causes," *SHSP,* 4:66–67.

36. Coddington, *The Gettysburg Campaign,* 319–22; Pfanz, *Culp's Hill,* 76–77.

**FOUR:** *The Chances of War: Lee, Longstreet, Sickles, and the First Minnesota Volunteers*

I am grateful to the Aldeen Fund and the Wisconsin Arts Board for funding several visits to Chancellorsville and Gettysburg to examine the terrain.

1. Richard Moe, *The Last Full Measure: The Life and Death of the First Minnesota Volunteers* (New York: Holt, 1993), 268.

2. Ibid. The exact wording of Hancock's order remains obscure.

3. Ibid.

4. Glenn Tucker, *Hancock the Superb* (Dayton: Morningside, 1980), 144–45.

5. Moe, *Full Measure*, 269.

6. Ibid.; Robert W. Meinhard, "The First Minnesota at Gettysburg," *Gettysburg Magazine 5* (July 1991), 82; Moe, *Full Measure*, 270.

7. Ibid.; Meinhard, *Gettysburg Magazine*, 82.

8. Edwin B. Coddington, *The Gettysburg Campaign* (Dayton: Morningside, 1979), 422, 425; Harry W. Pfanz, *Gettysburg: The Second Day* (Chapel Hill: University of North Carolina Press, 1987), 389, 417.

9. John Day Smith, *The History of the Nineteenth Regiment of Maine Volunteer Infantry 1862–1865* (Minneapolis: Great Western, 1909), 70; Pfanz, *Second Day*, 375; Coddington, *Campaign*, 426.

10. John W. Busey and David G. Martin, *Regimental Strengths and Losses at Gettysburg* (Hightstown, N.J.: Longstreet House, 1986), 242; Meinhard, *Gettysburg Magazine*, 87. The erroneous figure of 82 percent inscribed on the First Minnesota monument at Gettysburg is stubborn, appearing even in Pfanz, Catton, Foote, and McPherson.

11. Glenn Tucker, *Lee and Longstreet at Gettysburg* (Indianapolis: Bobbs-Merrill, 1968), 83.

12. Ibid., 53.

13. "It's all my fault; I thought my men were invincible," Lee said shortly after the battle, Douglas Southall Freeman, *Lee's Lieutenants*, 3 vols. (New York: Scribner, 1944), 3:136, a statement that sounds to me like a way of saying, "It's all their fault."

14. Douglas Southall Freeman, *R. E. Lee: A Biography*, 4 vols. (New York: Scribner, 1935), 2:347.

15. Tucker, *Lee and Longstreet*, 72.

16. Gary W. Gallagher, ed., *The Second Day at Gettysburg* (Kent, Oh.: Kent State University Press, 1993), 15.

17. Alan T. Nolan, *Lee Considered: General Robert E. Lee and Civil War History* (Chapel Hill: University of North Carolina Press, 1991), 95–96; Gary Gallagher, ed., *Fighting for the Confederacy: The Personal Recollections of Edward Porter Alexander* (Chapel Hill: University of North Carolina Press, 1989), 233–34.

18. Ibid.; Gallagher, ed., *Second Day*, 29–30, 32.

19. Jubal A. Early, *War Memoirs: Autobiographical Sketch and Narrative of the War Between the States,* Frank E. Vandiver, ed. (Bloomington: Indiana University Press, 1960), 271–72, 278.

20. Freeman, *Lee's Lieutenants*, 3:114–15; Freeman, *R. E. Lee*, 3:149; Tucker, *Lee and Longstreet*, 261–62.

21. Ibid., 30–31, 41, 59.

22. Ibid., 59.

23. For a recent example of this accusation, see Robert K. Krick, "If Longstreet . . . Says So, It Is Most Likely Not True," in Gallagher, ed., *Second Day.*

24. Tucker, *Lee and Longstreet,* 57.

25. Longstreet is erroneously described not only as phlegmatic but "burly" time and again. The quotations are from ibid., 57–58.

26. Ibid., 62–64, 262 note 14. One might also wonder how a defense of Lee can afford to claim that Lee was not paying attention to his attacking force.

27. Ibid., 58.

28. Gallagher, ed., *Second Day,* 77.

29. Coddington, *Gettysburg Campaign,* 445.

30. W. A. Swanberg, *Sickles the Incredible* (New York: Ace Books, 1956), 376, 387.

31. Ibid., 385.

32. Ibid., 340.

33. Ibid., 67.

34. Ibid., 63.

35. Ibid., 58.

36. Ibid., 373, 378.

37. Ibid., 389.

38. Clarence C. Buel and Robert U. Johnson, eds., *Battles and Leaders of the Civil War,* 4 vols. (New York: Yoseloff, 1956 reprint), 3:409.

39. Swanberg, *Incredible,* 174.

40. Ibid., 250.

41. Ibid., 249–50; David. B. Downs, "His Left Was Worth a Glance," *Gettysburg Magazine* 7 (July 1992): 36; Buel and Johnson, eds., *Battles and Leaders,* 3:409; Swanberg, *Incredible,* 205, 236, 257.

42. Ibid., 234.

43. See Downs, *Gettysburg Magazine,* 29–30, for a review of recent literature, and the rest of his article for a refutation.

44. Swanberg, *Incredible,* 373.

45. In looking for the right word, I have temporarily settled on "contingency," which in general usage refers to something being dependent on either chance or conditions about which we are uncertain. James M. McPherson uses this word in relation to the possibility at several chancy points of the Confederacy's not having had to lose the war. See "American Victory, American Defeat," in Gabor Boritt, ed., *Why the Confederacy Lost* (New York: Oxford University Press, 1992), 40. Unfortunately, the word in Philosophy means *free* as opposed to *determined.* Nevertheless, the etymology of "contingent" means *touching together,* which seems appropriate for its usage here.

46. James Gleick, *Chaos: Making a New Science* (New York: Viking, 1987), 8, 15, 19, 21, 22, 85.

## FIVE: *Eggs, Aldie, Shepherdstown, and J. E. B. Stuart*

1. H. B. McClellan, *The Life and Campaigns of Major-General J. E. B. Stuart* (Secaucus, N. J.: Blue and Grey Press edition, 1993), 364–66; Robert J. Trout, *They*

*Followed the Plume: The Story of J. E. B. Stuart and His Staff* (Mechanicsburg, Pa., 1993), 197–204.

2. Douglas Southall Freeman, *Lee's Lieutenants: A Study in Command,* 3 vols. (New York, 1942), 3:51–72; Emory M. Thomas, *Bold Dragoon: The Life of J. E. B. Stuart* (New York, 1986), 214–31; Stephen Z. Starr, *The Union Cavalry in the Civil War,* 3 vols. (Baton Rouge, 1979–1985), 1:391–95; John W. Thomason, Jr., *Jeb Stuart* (New York, 1930), 410; *War of the Rebellion: A Compilation of the Official Records of the Union and Confederate Armies,* 70 vols. in 127 (Washington, D. C., 1880–1901), ser. 1, vol. 27, pt. 2, pp. 679–85. Hereafter *OR* with all references to series 1.

3. Biographies of Stuart include Thomas, *Bold Dragoon;* McClellan, *J. E. B. Stuart;* and Thomason, *Stuart.*

4. McClellan, *J. E. B. Stuart,* 296-314; *OR,* vol. 27, pt. 3, pp. 913–15.

5. *OR,* vol. 27, pt. 3, pp. 924–25, 930–33; Emory M. Thomas, "Ambivalent Visions of Victory: Jefferson Davis, Robert E. Lee, and Confederate Grand Strategy," *Douglas Southall Freeman Historical Review* (Spring 1994), 19–27.

6. *OR,* vol. 27, pt. 3, pp. 913, 915, 923; McClellan, *J. E. B. Stuart,* 316.

7. *OR,* vol. 27, pt. 2, pp. 692–94; McClellan, *J. E. B. Stuart,* 318–24; W. W. Blackford, *War Years with Jeb Stuart* (New York, 1945), 223.

8. McClellan, *J. E. B. Stuart,* 324–32; Blackford, *War Years,* 223–28; John Esten Cooke, *Wearing of the Gray* (Bloomington, Ind., 1959) 236–46; *OR,* vol. 27, pt. 2, pp. 693–97; Thomas, *Bold Dragoon,* 241-46.

9. Freeman, *Lee's Lieutenants,* 3:139; Mark Nesbitt, *Saber and Scapegoat: J. E. B. Stuart and the Gettysburg Controversy* (Mechanicsburg, Pa., 1994), xv–xvi, 89–91.

10. *OR,* vol. 27, pt. 2, p. 321; Nesbitt, *Saber and Scapegoat,* xv; Thomas L. Connelly, *The Marble Man: Robert E. Lee and His Image in American Society* (New York, 1977), 88–90.

11. Freeman, *Lee's Lieutenants,* 3:170–71, 189; Edwin B. Coddington, *The Gettysburg Campaign: A Study in Command* (New York, 1968), 207.

12. Michael Shaara, *The Killer Angels* (New York, 1974), 252, 271; film *Gettysburg* produced by Ron Maxwell.

13. McClellan, *J. E. B. Stuart,* 332–37; John S. Mosby, "The Confederate Cavalry in the Gettysburg Campaign," in Robert Underwood Johnson and Clarence Clough Buel, eds., *Battles and Leaders of the Civil War,* 4 vols. (New York, 1887), 3:251–52; Nesbitt, *Saber and Scapegoat,* xvii.

14. Thomas, *Bold Dragoon,* 254–56.

15. *Southern Historical Society Papers,* 4:269–70.

16. Lee to Davis, June 10, 1863, in Clifford Dowdey and Louis H. Manarin, eds., *The Wartime Papers of R. E. Lee* (New York, 1961), 508.

17. *Southern Historical Society Papers,* 26:121.

18. Freeman, *Lee's Lieutenants,* 3:48–49 and n.

19. *OR,* vol. 26, pt. 2, pp. 307–308; Douglas Southall Freeman, *R. E. Lee: A Biography,* 4 vols. (New York, 1934-35), 3:64–75.

20. Coddington, *Gettysburg Campaign,* 523–25.

21. See, for example, Vincent J. Esposito, ed., *West Point Atlas of American Wars,* 2 vols. (New York, 1959).

22. *OR,* vol. 27, pt. 2, pp. 697–98; McClellan, *J. E. B. Stuart,* 337–39.

23. McClellan, *J. E. B. Stuart,* 339–41.

24. William E. Miller, "The Cavalry Battle Near Gettysburg," in Johnson and Buel, eds., *Battles and Leaders,* 3:402–405; *OR,* vol. 27, pt. 1, pp. 956–57, 998; pt. 2, pp. 697–99; Robert J. Driver, Jr., *14th Virginia Cavalry* (Lynchburg, Va., 1988), 23.

25. McClellan, *J. E. B. Stuart,* 346; Starr, *Union Cavalry,* 1:437–38.

26. Stuart to Flora Stuart, June 23, 1863, J. E. B. Stuart Papers, Virginia Historical Society, Richmond, Virginia; McClellan, *J. E. B. Stuart,* 314.

27. McClellan, *J. E. B. Stuart,* 323–24.

28. Coddington, *Gettysburg Campaign,* 202.

29. *OR,* vol. 27, pt. 2, pp. 695–97.

30. Cooke, *Wearing of the Gray,* 245–46.

31. Quoted in Robert Krick, *9th Virginia Cavalry* (Lynchburg, Va., 1982), 24.

32. Thomas P. Nanzig, *3rd Virginia Cavalry* (Lynchburg, Va., 1989), 39; Kenneth Stiles, *4th Virginia Cavalry* (Lynchburg, Va., 1985), 33; Krick, *9th Virginia,* 24.

33. Miles and rates of march must be approximate. A convenient map is in Thomas, *Bold Dragoon,* 243.

34. Information about Stuart's earlier escapades comes from ibid., 111–29, 145–50, 173–81, and 195–200.

35. Krick, *9th Virginia,* 26, 22; Daniel T. Balfour, *13th Virginia Cavalry* (Lynchburg, Va., 1986), 22, 24–25; U. R. Brooks, *Butler and His Cavalry in the War of Secession, 1861–1865* (Columbia, S. C., 1909), 171.

36. The classic statement of the "fog of war" is in Freeman, *Lee,* 2:581–82 and *Lee's Lieutenants,* 2:659 and n.

37. Blackford, *War Years,* 225.

38. James Longstreet, "Our March Against Pope," in Johnson and Buel, eds, *Battles and Leaders,* 2:525.

## SIX: *"I Think the Union Army Had Something to Do with It": The Pickett's Charge Nobody Knows*

1. Oration of Maj. J. W. Slagle, Sept. 11, 1889, in *Pennsylvania at Gettysburg, Ceremonies at the Dedication of the Monuments Erected by the Commonwealth of Pennsylvania to Mark the Portion of the Pennsylvania Commands Engaged in the Battle* . . . John Page Nicholson, 2 vols. (Harrisburg: Meyers, 1893), 2:742–43.

2. This oft-repeated story can be found in many sources, but see LaSalle Corbell Pickett, "My Soldier," *McClure's Magazine* (1908), 569.

3. Edwin B. Coddington, *The Gettysburg Campaign: A Study in Command* (New York: Scribner, 1968), 451–52.

4. John Gibbon, *Personal Recollections of the Civil War* (Dayton: Morningside, 1988 reprint), 145.

5. Even Edwin B. Coddington, the closest student of the battle in the twentieth century, ignores many of Meade's actions before noon on July 3, is critical of his command arrangements, or gives excessive credit to Hancock, John Newton, or some other subordinate. The author seems to work on the assumption that

Cemetery Ridge was the only potential hot spot on July 3; therefore, he does not appreciate Meade's need to keep a certain amount of flexibility in his deployments. See Coddington, *The Gettysburg Campaign,* 481–82, 484.

6. The preceding four recollections appear in George Stewart, *Pickett's Charge: A Microhistory of the Final Attack at Gettysburg, July 3, 1863* (New York: Fawcett, [1959] 1963 reprint), 120–121.

7. William Haines, *History of the Men of Co. F, with Description of the Marches and Battles of the 12th New Jersey Vols.* (Mickelton, N. J.: n.p., 1897), 40–41.

8. Major A. R. Small, *The Sixteenth Maine Regiment in the War of the Rebellion* (Portland, Me.: Thurston, 1886), 122.

9. Joseph R. C. Ward, *History of the One Hundred and Sixth Regiment Pennsylvania Volunteers, 2d Brigade, 2d Division, 2d Corps, 1861–1865* (Philadelphia: McManus, 1906), 197.

10. D. G. Crotty, *Four Years Campaigning in the Army of the Potomac* (Grand Rapids: Dygert, 1874), 92.

11. Letter of Captain Phillips, July 6, 1863, quoted in *History of the Fifth Massachusetts Battery* (Boston: Cowles, 1902), 652.

12. Nineteenth Maine Association, *Reunions of the Nineteenth Maine Regiment Association . . .* (Augusta, Me.: Sprague, Owen & Nash, 1878), 12.

13. Return I. Holcombe, *History of the First Regiment Minnesota Volunteer Infantry 1861–1864* (Stillwater, Minn.: Easton & Masterman, 1916), 366.

14. Henry N. Blake, *Three Years in the Army of the Potomac [11th Massachusetts],* (Boston: Lee and Shepard, 1865), 216.

15. Mark Nickerson, *Recollections of the Civil War by a High Private in the Front Ranks* (n.p., privately published, 1991), 69.

16. Close students of the battle have explained this. The notion does not seem to have captured the popular imagination, however. See Coddington, *The Gettysburg Campaign,* 503; Stewart, *Pickett's Charge,* 164, 168.

17. Coddington, *The Gettysburg Campaign,* 503.

18. George Grenville Benedict, *Army Life in Virginia: Letters from the Twelfth Vermont Regiment and Personal Experiences of Volunteer Service in the War for the Union, 1862–63* (Burlington: Free Press, 1895), 177.

19. Russell C. White, ed., *The Civil War Diary of Wyman S. White, First Sergeant, Company F, 2nd United States Sharpshooters* (Baltimore: Butternut and Blue, 1993), 170.

20. James Longstreet, "Lee in Pennsylvania," in *The Annals of the War Written by Leading Participants North and South* (Dayton: Morningside, [1878] 1988 reprint), 427.

21. See George Stewart, *Pickett's Charge,* 159; Kathy Georg Harrison and John W. Busey, *Nothing but Glory: Pickett's Division at Gettysburg* (Hightstown, N. J.: Longstreet House, 1987), 9–13.

22. J. C. Williams, *Life in Camp* (Claremont, N. H.: Claremont Manufacturing, 1864), 145.

23. J. Howard Wert, *A Complete Hand-book of the Monuments and Indications and Guide to the Positions on the Gettysburg Battle-field* (Harrisburg: Sturgeon, 1886), 34.

24. Nineteenth Maine Association, *Reunions of the Nineteenth Maine Association*, 13.

25. "Hancock at Gettysburg," *National Tribune*, Oct. 28, 1886.

26. See a cursory estimate in Coddington, *The Gettysburg Campaign*, 509–12; a more comprehensive study appears in John W. Busey and David G. Martin, *Regimental Strengths and Losses at Gettysburg* (Hightstown, N. J.: Longstreet House, 1986), 27, 39–41, 43–44.

27. Robert Garth Scott, ed., *Fallen Leaves: the Civil War Letters of Major Henry Livermore Abbott* (Kent, Oh.: Kent State University Press, 1991), 188.

28. *New York Times*, July 6, 1863.

29. Meade to his wife, July 6, 1863, copy in box 7, Robert L. Brake Collection, U. S. Army Military History Institute, Carlisle Barracks, PA [hereafter USMHI].

30. Charles W. Belknap diary, entry for July 3, 1863, copy in 125th New York folder, box 10, Brake Collection, USMHI.

31. Tully McCrae memoir, March 30, 1904, copy in box 12, Brake Collection, USMHI.

32. Joseph Bishop, "Revisiting Gettysburg," *National Tribune*, Nov. 28, 1889.

33. Charles D. Page, *History of the Fourteenth Regiment, Connecticut Volunteer Infantry* (Meriden, Conn.: Horton, 1906), 151.

34. "What Mean These Stones?" by Chaplain Ezra D. Simons, Oct. 3, 1888, *New York at Gettysburg*, 2: 889.

35. Edwin B. Houghton, *The Campaigns of the Seventeenth Maine* (Portland, Me.: Short & Loring, 1866), 95–96.

36. "Story of a Cannoneer," *National Tribune*, Nov. 14, 1889.

37. Franklin Sawyer, *A Military History of the 8th Regiment Ohio Volunteer Infantry; Its Battles, Marches and Army Movements* (Cleveland: Fairbanks, 1881), 130–31.

38. G. G. Benedict to John Bachelder, Dec. 24, 1863, in John B. Bachelder Papers, New Hampshire Historical Society.

39. "Co. I, 13th VT., Three Days' Fighting," *National Tribune*, Aug. 30, 1894.

40. Sergeant James A. Wright memoir, 1st Minnesota Infantry, in Minnesota Historical Society; copy in box 10, Brake Collection, USMHI.

41. For the development of this image, see Carol Reardon, "Pickett's Charge: The Convergence of Myth and History in the Southern Past," in Gary W. Gallagher, ed., *The Third Day at Gettysburg and Beyond* (Chapel Hill: University of North Carolina Press, 1994), 56–92.

42. Ralph Orson Sturtevant, *Pictorial History, Thirteenth Vermont Volunteers, War of 1861–1865* (n.p., n.d. [after 1908]), 301.

43. John L. Brady to John Bachelder, May 24, 1886, Bachelder Papers.

44. Oration of Col. Clinton MacDougall, June 26, 1891, in *New York at Gettysburg*, 2: 802.

45. Frank A. Haskell, *The Battle of Gettysburg* (Madison: Wisconsin History Commission, 1910), 182.

46. Sawyer, *History of the 8th Ohio*, 131.

47. See Ezra D. Simons, *A Regimental History. The One Hundred and Twenty-fifth New York State Volunteers* (New York: Ezra D. Simons, 1888), 137–38.

48. William M. Harmon, "Co. C at Gettysburg," *Minneapolis Journal,* June 30, 1897, copy in box 10, Brake Collection, USMHI.

49. One good source for this fight is the full explanation in Theodore B. Gates to John Bachelder, Jan. 30, 1864, Bachelder Papers. Coddington only alludes to it briefly in *The Gettysburg Campaign,* 512.

50. Lt. Hamilton to John Bachelder, April 22, 1864, Bachelder Papers.

51. Col. George N. Macy to John Bachelder, May 12, 1866, Bachelder Papers.

52. A. C. Plaisted to John Bachelder, June 11, 1870, Bachelder Papers.

53. Page, *History of the Fourteenth Connecticut,* 153.

54. "Fighting Them Over," *National Tribune,* May 3, 1894.

55. See, for instance, Henry J. Hunt, "The Third Day at Gettysburg," in *Battles and Leaders of the Civil War* (New York: Century, 1888), 3:369–84; Francis A. Walker, "General Hancock and the Artillery at Gettysburg," ibid., 385; and Hunt's rejoinder, ibid., 386.

56. Coddington, *The Gettysburg Campaign,* 515.

57. See summary in Stewart, *Pickett's Charge,* 253–54.

58. *An Address Delivered at Gettysburg, August 27, 1883, by Gen. Alexander S. Webb, at the Dedication of the 72d Pa. Vols. Monument . . .* (Philadelphia: Porter & Coates, 1883), 12.

59. "Reply of the Philadelphia Brigade Association to the Foolish and Absurd Narrative of Lieutenant Frank A. Haskell, which appears to be Endorsed by the *MOLLUS* Commandery of Massachusetts and the Wisconsin History Commission," 9, undated manuscript, no. 41, box 2, *MOLLUS* Papers, USMHI.

60. "At Gettysburg," *National Tribune,* Sept. 15, 1892.

61. Alexander Webb to Mrs. Webb, Aug. 8, 1863, Alexander S. Webb Papers, Yale University; copy in box 4, Brake Collection, USMHI. Apparently Hays's death in battle redeemed him in Webb's eyes. When he spoke at the dedication of the 72nd Pennsylvania's monument in 1883, Webb praised Hays as "a glorious fighter" who "tells of his front without an attempt to take from any one their laurels fairly won." See *Address Delivered at Gettysburg, August 27, 1883 by General Alexander S. Webb,* 12.

62. Oration of Col. Clinton D. MacDougall, June 26, 1891, *New York at Gettysburg,* 2:802.

63. This oft-repeated story can be found in many places, but see Gilbert Adams Hays, *Under the Red Patch: Story of the Sixty-third Regiment Pennsylvania Volunteers 1861–1864* (Pittsburgh: Market Review, 1908), 199. Hays had commanded the 63rd Pennsylvania earlier in the war and the men never lost their affection for him.

64. Albert Lawson, *War Anecdotes and Incidents of Army Life* (Cincinnati: Beasley, 1888), 125–26.

65. Sturdevant, *Thirteenth Vermont,* 307.

66. Frederick Fuger, "Battle of Gettysburg and Personal Recollections of that Battle by Colonel Fred. Fuger (retired)," copy in box 12, Brake Collection, USMHI.

67. Boston *Journal,* July 6, 1863.

68. Williams, *Life in Camp,* 143.

69. Oration of Brig. Gen. Henry H. Bingham, Sept. 11, 1889, in *Pennsylvania at Gettysburg,* 1:51.

70. Oration of Chaplain Stevens, July 3, 1883, quoted in Page, *History of the Fourteenth Connecticut,* 336.

71. "On to Gettysburg," *National Tribune,* June 10, 1886.

72. "3d Corps Reunion—Monuments Dedicated," *Grand Army Scout and Soldiers' Mail,* July 10, 1886, 5.

73. "25 Years After," *National Tribune,* July 12, 1888. The fact that Berdan had met Wilcox (III Corps) and not Longstreet apparently did not matter to anyone in 1888.

74. Col. Thomas Rafferty, "Gettysburg," *National Tribune,* Feb. 9, 1888.

75. Oration of Private Thomas V. Cooper, Sept. 11, 1889, in *Pennsylvania at Gettysburg,* 1:184.

76. "Cui Bono," 107th Oshkosh Volunteers, "Podunksburg," *National Tribune,* April 21, 1887.

77. John L. Parker and Robert G. Carter, *History of the Twenty-second Massachusetts Infantry, the Second Company Sharpshooters, and the Third Light Battery, in the War of the Rebellion* (Boston: Avery, 1887), p. 342; Captain Robert Goldthwaite Carter, *Four Brothers in Blue or Sunshine and Shadows of the War of the Rebellion, a Story of the Great Civil War from Bull Run to Appomattox,* (Austin: University of Texas Press, 1978), 319–21.

78. Address of Capt. W. C. Dunton, in G. G. Benedict, *A Short History of the 14th Vermont Regiment* (Bennington: Parese, 1887), 30.

79. Theodore B. Gates, *The Ulster Guard [20th New York State Militia] and the War of the Rebellion* (New York: Tyrrel, 1879), 473–74.

80. P. DeLacy, *143d Regiment Pennsylvania Volunteers, Second Brigade, Third Division, First Army Corps* (n.p.: n.p., c. 1889), 9.

81. Oration of Lt. Col. George E. Wagner, Sept. 11, 1889, in *Pennsylvania at Gettysburg,* 1:474.

82. Address of Captain J. V. Pierce, July 1, 1888, in *New York at Gettysburg,* 3:993.

83. Edmund Randolph Brown, *The Twenty-seventh Indiana Volunteer Infantry in the War of the Rebellion . . .* (n.p., n. pub., 1899), 391.

84. Address of Gen. L.S. Trowbridge, in *Michigan at Gettysburg, July 1st, 2nd and 3rd, 1863, June 12th, 1889* (Detroit: Winn & Hammond, 1889), 38. Meade blamed Slocum—with justice—for the lack of attention given to the XII Corps but the men did not know that. *OR,* vol. 27, pt. 1, p. 769.

85. Oration by Chaplain J. Hervey Beale, Sept. 2, 1890, in *Pennsylvania at Gettysburg,* 2:789.

86. Oration of General James Wood, Oct. 16, 1888, in *New York at Gettysburg,* 2:923.

87. "A Boy Spy in Dixie," *National Tribune,* May 31, 1888.

88. Adin B. Underwood, *The Three Years' Service of the Thirty-third Mass. Infantry Regiment 1862-1865* (Boston: Williams, 1881), 138.

89. See Carol Reardon, "Pickett's Charge: The Convergence of Myth and History in the Southern Past," esp. 64–88.

90. A. W. Bartlett, *History of the Twelfth Regiment, New Hampshire Volunteers in the War of the Rebellion* (Concord: Evans, 1897), 134.

91. Address of Col. John A. Danks, Sept. 11, 1889, *Pennsylvania at Gettysburg*, 1:359.

92. Philadelphia *North American*, May 4, 1904, copy in box 11, Brake Collection, USMHI.

93. "The Movies," *National Tribune*, June 12, 1913.

94. Haskell, *The Battle of Gettysburg*, 184.

## SEVEN: *Gettysburg's Gettysburg: What the Battle Did to the Borough*

1. Sarah Broadhead, *The Diary of a Lady of Gettysburg, Pennsylvania,* July 4, 1863. Typescript in the Adams County Historical Society [hereafter ACHS].

2. *Gettysburg Compiler,* Oct. 9, 1865.

3. Albertus McCreary, "Gettysburg: A Boy's Experience of the Battle." Typescript at ACHS. Also published in *McClure's Magazine* (July 1909).

4. Maris Vinovskis, "Have Social Historians Lost the Civil War? Some Preliminary Demographic Speculations," in Vinovskis, ed., *Toward a Social History of the American Civil War: Exploratory Essays* (New York: Cambridge University Press, 1990), 3–7. Of course America's losses during the Civil War include men who fell on both sides.

5. United States Census of 1860, Gettysburg, Pennsylvania. (All calculations in this chapter are from computer databases created at the Civil War Institute, Gettysburg, Pa.) Despite the borough's clear Northern sympathies, William Frassanito has unearthed evidence of several antebellum residents or Gettysburg College alumni who went on to serve with the Confederacy. See William A. Frassanito, *Early Photography at Gettysburg* (Gettysburg: Thomas, 1995), 124–28, 368–83.

6. Peter C. Vermilyea, "'We Did Not Know Where Our Colored Friends Had Gone': The Effect of the Confederate Invasion of Pennsylvania on Gettysburg's African-American Community." (Unpublished independent study, Gettysburg College. Gettysburg, 1994); Census of 1860.

7. *Adams Sentinel,* Oct. 3, 1860.

8. *Compiler,* Apr. 22, 1861 and *passim; Sentinel,* Apr. 24, 1861.

9. *Sentinel,* Apr. 24, 1861 and *passim; Compiler,* Apr. 29, May 6, 13, 27, June 17, 1861.

10. *Compiler,* May 6, 13, 20, June 3, 17, 1861; *Sentinel,* June 12, 1861; Bloom, 185–86. On May 20, for instance, the *Compiler* reported that the Ladies' Union Relief Society was preparing goods to send to York, Pennsylvania.

11. *Sentinel,* July 31, 1861; *Compiler* Aug. 5, 1861.

12. *Compiler,* Sept. 9, 1861.

13. The Town Council ended up paying the Relief Committee $204.58 of the appropriated $500; the remainder of the Committee's 1861 expenses were covered by the County Commissioners. "Excerpts of the Minute Book of the Gettysburg Town Council," Apr. 20, Sept. 30, 1861, GNMPL; *Compiler,* July 1, 1861. The County Commissioners reinstated the tax at a reduced level the following April. *Compiler,* Apr. 28, 1862.

14. *Compiler,* Aug. 26, 1861; *Sentinel,* Aug. 28, 1861.

15. *Compiler,* Dec. 30, 1861; *Sentinel,* Jan. 1, 1862.

16. *Compiler,* Jan. 6, Feb. 10, Mar. 3, 10, 1862; *Sentinel,* Jan. 29, Feb. 12, 1862.

17. Salome Myers Stewart Diary, 1862, ACHS. Quotation from Mar. 14, 1862.

18. *Sentinel,* Mar. 12, 1861.

19. Ibid., Oct. 23, 1861. The United States Sanitary Commission and the United States Christian Commission were two national bodies with local auxiliaries in communities across the North. Both raised tremendous funds to send supplies to soldiers at the front. The two bodies were different in several ways, the most obvious being the Christian Commission's delivery of bibles and religious tracts along with other necessities. See J. Matthew Gallman, *The North Fights the Civil War: The Home Front* (Chicago: Ivan Dee, 1994).

20. *Compiler,* Jan. 6, 1862; *Sentinel,* Jan. 8, 1862.

21. *Compiler,* July 8, 1861.

22. Ibid., July 21, 28, Aug. 4, 11, 1862; *Sentinel,* Aug. 12, 1862.

23. *Sentinel,* Aug. 28, 1861.

24. *Compiler,* Apr. 21, 1862.

25. *Sentinel,* Aug. 12, 1862.

26. *Compiler,* Mar. 2, 1863.

27. Ibid., May 18, June 1, 1863; *Sentinel,* May 19, 26, 1863.

28. Broadhead, *Diary,* July 3–4, 1863.

29. Tillie Pierce Alleman, *At Gettysburg: Or What a Young Girl Saw and Heard of the Battle* (New York: Borland, 1889), 16, 90.

30. Fannie Buehler, *Recollections of the Great Rebel Invasion and One Woman's Experiences During the Battle of Gettysburg* (ACHS, 1896), 11; McCreary, "A Boy's Experience"; Stewart, "Recollections of the Battle of Gettysburg," Diary entry for June 21, 1863, ACHS; Jacob Taughenbaugh, "In Occupied Pennsylvania," edited by T. W. Herbert, *Georgia Review* (Summer 1950): 104–105.

31. Alleman, *At Gettysburg,* 26; *Compiler,* July 13, 20, 27, Aug. 17, 1863, Oct. 9, 1865; *Sentinel,* July 14, 28, 1863.

32. Buehler, *Recollections,* 17; *Compiler,* July 20, 1863.

33. Buehler, *Recollections,* 5; Harriet Bayly, "Story of the Battle," ACHS, 1; William Bayly, "Memoir of a Thirteen-year-old Boy Relating to the Battle of Gettysburg" (typescript 1903), 2–3, ACHS.

34. Broadhead, *Diary,* June 27, July 11, 1863.

35. Ibid., July 9, 13, 1863.

36. *Sentinel,* Nov. 24, 1863.

37. *Compiler,* Aug. 24, 1863. Men selected on draft day still had several routes to avoid service. They could demonstrate one of a long list of personal or medical exemptions or, failing that, they could furnish a substitute. Thus, the number drawn does not reflect the actual number of men who ended up serving in uniform. The draft and recruiting appeared regularly in both newspapers from June through August.

38. *Compiler,* July 13, 1863, Mar. 21, 28, 1864.

39. *Sentinel,* Oct. 25, Nov. 8, 15, 1864; *Compiler,* Oct. 31, Nov. 7, 14, 1864, Mar. 20, 1865. In 1864 Adams County backed McClellan 2,886 to 2,362.

40. *Sentinel,* Dec. 13, 1864, Jan. 24, Apr. 25, 1865; *Compiler,* Dec. 12, 1864. Neither newspaper offered any comment at the seemingly light sentence.

41. The Poor-House Accounts were published several times each year in the local newspapers, generally beginning in the first week of March.

42. Three women were on the local branch of the USCC; three served on the Sanitary Fair committee; and two were on the Ladies' Relief Society. Several women served on more than two of these organizations.

43. *Sentinel,* Apr. 4, 11, 1865.

### EIGHT: *The Pennsylvania Gambit and the Gettysburg Splash*

1. Thomas Lawrence Connelly and Archer Jones, *The Politics of Command: Factions and Ideas in Confederate Strategy* (Baton Rouge: Louisiana State University Press, 1974), 44.

2. Pemberton's force was sometimes called the "Army of the Department of Mississippi and East Louisiana" and "the Army of Mississippi" after the territorial department it defended. On occasion, however, it was also known as the "Army of Vicksburg" and that name is used herein for clarity and convenience. United States War Department (com), *The War of the Rebellion: Official Records of the Union and Confederate Armies* (Washington: GPO, 1880–1902), ser. 1, vol. 17, pt. 2, pp. 787, 792; vol. 24, pt. 2, p. 326 [Hereinafter cited as *OR,* with all references to volumes in series 1].

3. Historians bicker over the numerical strength of Civil War armies and doubtless will continue to do so until Clio's last roll call at the Great Archive in the sky. In truth, Civil War strength returns, like all numerical data, can be manipulated in dozens of ways to "prove" almost anything. Rebel returns included such categories as "present for duty," "effective present," "aggregate present," "present and absent," and so on. Totals for these categories were determined by different criteria and often varied by as much as 20 percent. On March 31, 1863, for example, Bragg's army reported 54,305 "present for duty"; 49,915 "effective total"; 65,583 "aggregate present"; and 96,290 "aggregate present and absent." Then, just to confuse matters, the army reported its effective strength on the following day as 45,551.

I believe the "present for duty strength" to be the most valid measure of a commander's available force. It has the additional advantage of having been a category used by both Federal and Confederate armies and is, therefore, a better number for comparison than any other strength category. In all cases cited above and in the text, the totals include garrison troops and other support units under the command of the general named.

For the reports from which the above data are drawn, see *OR,* vol. 24, pt. 3, pp. 163, 702; vol. 15, pt. 2, pp. 180, 696, and vol. 23, pt. 2, pp. 197, 733. For an example of historians squabbling over such numbers, see Thomas L. Connelly, "Robert E. Lee and the Western Confederacy: A Criticism of Lee's Strategic Ability," *Civil War History,* 15 (1969), 120; and Albert Castel, "The Historian and the General: Thomas L. Connelly versus Robert E. Lee," ibid., 16 (1970), 54–55.

4. In the winter of 1863–64 the Confederates attempted to develop a plan by which they would take the offensive to drive the Yankees from Tennessee. Owing to their lack of an overall command structure and the great distrust among the leading

Rebels, they were unable to do so. Such an effort to regain their own territory is not the same as an offensive on the enemy's land. Even if such an effort had taken place, it would not negate the statement in the text which would still be accurate for the period prior to 1864.

5. For details of the basic differences between the Eastern and Western theaters and how those differences favored the Confederates in the East and hampered them in the West (the reverse was true for the Federals), see Richard M. McMurry, *Two Great Rebel Armies: An Essay in Confederate Military History* (Chapel Hill, 1989), Chapters 2–4 and 8. One of the best examples of how well Davis's system worked in the East came in the late spring of 1864. Rebel forces from all over western Virginia converged to pounce on an invading Union force at New Market, defeated it, and then immediately dispersed to operate in other areas. At about the same time, Confederates brought to Virginia from the Atlantic coastal areas reached the Old Dominion in time to hold Petersburg. On the stalemate in Virginia, see also Richard E. Beringer; Herman Hattaway; Archer Jones; and William N. Still, Jr., *Why the South Lost the Civil War* (Athens: University of Georgia Press, 1986), 160–163.

6. *OR,* vol. 14, p. 933; vol. 15, p. 1042; vol. 18, pp. 1027–30; pt. 2, pp. 751, 752, 778, 780, 791, 798, 799, 800, 814, 820, 822. More often than not, the simultaneity of such myriad Yankee activities was the product of happy coincidence. To the Rebels, however, such threats appeared as parts of a planned offensive.

7. Ibid., vol. 23, pt. 2, pp. 795, 798; vol. 24, pt. 3, pp. 730, 733, 734, 735, 738, 739, 741, 745, 751.

8. Joseph E. Johnston is an excellent example of localities. In the fall of 1863, when he was commanding in Mississippi, he sent two brigades to North Georgia, being careful to specify that they were "to serve in battle only and then return." In March 1864, when he commanded in North Georgia, he was anxious to have troops sent from Mississippi to Georgia. A "temporary transfer," he called it—which meant he could keep them for awhile and was not committed to their immediate use in a battle. Ibid., vol. 31, pt. 3, p. 739; vol. 32, pt. 3, p. 649.

9. Ibid., vol. 23, pt. 2, pp. 726, 833; Craig L. Symonds, *Joseph E. Johnston: A Civil War Biography* (New York: Norton, 1992), 199–200, 205–211; William Davis, *Jefferson Davis: The Man and His Hour: A Biography* (New York: Harper-Collins, 1991), 501–504; Michael Ballard, *Pemberton: A Biography* (Jackson, Miss., 1991), 143, 155, 166.

10. *OR,* vol. 15, pp. 879, 902, 903, 922; vol. 17, pt. 2, pp. 753, 757, 768, 777, 782–84, 787–88, 793. William Cooper has pointed out that, in the case cited in the text, Davis's decision to allow Holmes discretion in the matter of reinforcements for Vicksburg was at least partially political. The president was unwilling to sacrifice Arkansas. ("Jefferson Davis and the Political Dimensions of Confederate Strategy," paper presented May 5, 1990, at a Fredericksburg, Va., Civil War seminar sponsored by the Association for the Preservation of Civil War Sites.) Steven Woodworth notes that neither Davis nor Holmes saw that the loss of Vicksburg and the Mississippi meant, for all practical purposes, the loss of Arkansas. Woodworth calls Davis's unwillingness or inability to give clear orders to his generals "almost certainly his most serious fault" as commander-in-chief. *Jefferson Davis and His Generals: The Failure of Confederate Command in the West* (Lawrence, Ks., 1990), 182, 315–16.

11. *OR,* vol. 13, pt. 2, p. 745.

12. Ibid., vol. 14, pp. 923–26, 933, 938.

13. *OR,* vol. 24, pt. 3, pp. 745, 747, 751–53, 769, 800; vol. 25, pt. 1, pp. 795–96.

14. James Longstreet, *From Manassas to Appomatox* (Indianapolis: Indiana University Press, 1960), 327.

15. *OR,* vol. 24, pt. 3, pp. 967, 970.

16. On the Western concentration bloc see Connelly and Jones, *Politics of Command,* 49–86; Herman Hattaway and Archer Jones, *How the North Won: A Military History of the Civil War* (Urbana, 1983), 278–83. Beauregard's letters are in *OR,* vol. 14, p. 955; vol. 15, pp. 744–45; vol. 17, pt. 2, p. 591; vol. 18, p. 825; vol. 23, pt. 2, pp. 836–39. See also Thomas Lawrence Connelly, *Autumn of Glory: The Army of Tennessee, 1862–1865* (Baton Rouge, 1971), 100–101; T. Harry Williams, *G. T. Beauregard: Napolean in Gray* (Baton Rouge: Louisiana State University Press, 1955), 181–82; and Jones, *Confederate Strategy,* 209–10.

17. Longstreet, *Manassas to Appomattox,* 327–28. See also *OR,* vol. 18, pp. 959–60, 962; Archer Jones, *Confederate Strategy From Shiloh to Vicksburg* (Baton Rouge, 1961), 206–209; Douglas Southall Freeman, *Lee's Lieutenants: A Study in Command,* 3 vols. (New York: Scribners, 1942–1944), 3:40–44; and H. J. Eckenrode and Bryan Conrad, *James Longstreet: Lee's War Horse* (Chapel Hill: University of North Carolina Press, 1986), 151, 160, 172. The most recent discussions of Longstreet's role are in William Garrett Piston, *Lee's Tarnished Lieutenant: James Longstreet and His Place in Southern History* (Athens: University of Georgia Press, 1987), 41–45; and Jeffry D. Wert, *General James Longstreet: The Confederacy's Most Controversial Soldier: A Biography* (New York: Simon and Schuster, 1993), 239–47.

Longstreet's position regarding the proper response for the Confederates to make to the crisis of April–May 1863 has been shrouded in controversy that stems more from the postwar squabbles in which he became embroiled than the ideas he expressed in 1863. Most of the squabbles concerned matters of tactical minutiae at Gettysburg, not the grand strategy that led to the battle.

It is clear that Longstreet's May 6 suggestion was based on the belief that the Rebels in Virginia were to remain quiescent and abandon Vicksburg to her fate. He thus originally saw the choice as being between having the Army of Northern Virginia do nothing in the summer of 1863 or using it to reinforce the secessionist forces in the West.

Once he conferred with Lee (May 11–13) and realized that Lee proposed to launch an offensive into the North, Longstreet concluded that "the prospect for an advance [by Lee's army] changes the aspect of affairs entirely." Such a campaign, if successful, would demoralize the Northerners and might, he wrote, "shake off Grant from Vicksburg." In addition to the works by Piston and Wert cited above, see Glenn Tucker, *Lee and Longstreet at Gettysburg* (Indianapolis: Bobbs-Merrill, 1968), 228–33.

18. *OR,* vol. 23, pt. 2, pp. 712, 727, 741, 745; Clifford Dowdey and Louis H. Manarin, eds., *The Wartime Papers of R. E. Lee* (Boston: Little, Brown, 1961), 430.

19. For examples of Lee's fear of the Western climate, see *Lee Papers,* 430, 482, 503, 505. Lee's concern about the deleterious effect of the Deep South climate has

provoked ridicule. See Connelly, "Robert E. Lee," 125; Connelly and Jones, *Politics of Command,* 40. Richard M. McMurry, "Marse Robert and the Fevers: A Note on the General as Strategist and on Medical Ideas as a Factor in Civil War Decision Making," *Civil War History,* 35 (1989), 197–207, demonstrates that Lee's ideas about the Deep South climate were widely shared and that there was much validity to them. For Lee's worry about how his troops might be used in the West, see *OR*, vol. 25, pt. 2, p. 790; *Lee Papers,* 482.

20. Ibid.,430, 435, 483–84. Connelly and Jones, "Robert E. Lee,"128–29; *Politics of Command,* 43–44, read the evidence differently and accuse Lee of practicing a "double standard" by consistently refusing to send any of his men to reinforce other areas while constantly requesting that troops be transferred from other Rebel armies to strengthen his. Lee made these suggestions, they maintain, despite his assertions (expressed when the proposal was to transfer troops from his army to other areas) that it was not practicable for the Rebels to move troops about to meet Federal advances.

Several points should be noted. First, almost all of Lee's suggestions were to the effect that troops from other areas be sent to Virginia *if* they were to be idle or that they be moved north to get them away from the dangerous summer climate of the Deep South (see note 19 above). See *Lee Papers,* 293, for an example. Second, the tenor of Lee's writings suggests (although to my knowledge he never made the point) that he would have drawn a distinction between rushing Rebel troops about to meet a specific enemy campaign once it had gotten underway (impracticable—at least over great distances) and shifting reinforcements in anticipation of an enemy threat or to support a Confederate offensive (practicable). Third, Lee seems to have developed the idea of having local Rebel commanders attempt to disrupt the Yankees by offensive actions in the spring of 1863. The instances of "inconsistency" that Connelly and Jones cite from late 1862 would, therefore, not be valid examples of inconsistencies in Lee's arguments. Fourth, the later examples that Connelly and Jones cite of Lee's requests to have reinforcements sent to Virginia from the Atlantic Coast are not relevant. The Confederates could and did shift troops along their eastern coast. The problem was the great difficulty of transporting troops to, from, and within the Confederate West. Finally, in calling for reinforcements, Lee simply did what almost every commander does.

I believe that the real fallacy in Lee's proposal was the assumption that Confederate commanders were capable of conducting "judicious operations." With a very few notable exceptions, Rebel generals usually proved spectacularly inept at carrying out any military operations.

21. Alexander, *Fighting for the Confederacy: The Personal Recollections of General Edward Porter Alexander,* ed. by Gary W. Gallagher (Chapel Hill: University of North Carolina Press, 1988), 276.

22. Longstreet once objected to the idea of an offensive in the East because, he maintained, there was not enough time to get organized for it. Yet he thought that there was sufficient time to move masses of troops to Central Tennessee, organize them into an army, and launch an offensive there. See Wert, *Longstreet,* 244.

23. *OR*, vol. 23, pt. 2, pp. 757–58, 779; Connelly, "Robert E. Lee," 126.

24. *OR*, vol. 23, pt. 2, pp. 379, 846.

25. Ibid., 799, 826; vol. 52, pt. 2, p. 499; Connelly, *Autumn of Glory,* 71;

Connelly and Jones, *Politics of Command,* 63. Woodworth, *Davis and His Generals,* 206, raises the question of Davis's own health in 1863 and its effect on his performance—a question to which he returns in his study of the war in Virginia *Davis & Lee at War* (Lawrence: University Press of Kansas, 1995), 220–21 and *passim.* Lee was also unwell that summer, but not to the extent that Davis, Bragg, and Johnston were.

26. Alexander, *Fighting for the Confederacy,* 242.

27. *Lee Papers,* 482; *OR,* vol. 20, pt. 2, pp. 487–88; vol. 52, pt. 2, pp. 493–94.

28. Woodworth, *Davis and His Generals,* 200–21, takes the oxymoronic position that Davis's decision to send Lee north was wrong but that sending even two-thirds of Lee's infantry to Mississippi "would probably" have done no good.

29. See the discussion of Gettysburg and the other summer 1863 operations in Beringer, et al., *Why the South Lost,* 263–67; and Hattaway and Jones, *How the North Won,* 419–23 n. 91. Confederates at the time had a better insight into the overall meaning of Gettysburg than have most later historians. They realized that the loss of Vicksburg was a far more serious defeat than the battle in Pennsylvania. See Gary W. Gallagher, "Lee's Army Has Not Lost Any of Its Prestige: The Impact of Gettysburg on the Army of Northern Virginia and the Confederate Home Front," in Gallagher, ed., *The Third Day at Gettysburg and Beyond* (Chapel Hill: University of North Carolina Press, 1993), 1–30.

## NINE: *From Turning Point to Peace Memorial: A Cultural Legacy*

1. Robert Hunt Rhodes, ed., *All for the Union: The Civil War Diary and Letters of Elisha Hunt Rhodes* (New York: Orion Books, 1985), 115–16.

2. Ibid., 117.

3. J. Paxton Lloyd to "Mother, Brother . . . ," July 31, 1863, Huntington Library, MC 106, San Marino, Cal.

4. Ibid. For Imboden's account of the retreat from Gettysburg, see John D. Imboden, "The Confederate Retreat from Gettysburg," *Battles and Leaders of the Civil War,* Robert Underwood Johnson and Clarence Clough Buell, eds., 4 vols. (New York: Century, 1888), 3: 420–29.

5. U.S. Department of War, *Annual Report of the Gettysburg National Military Park Commission to the Secretary of War, 1905* (Washington, D.C.: GPO, 1905), 5–6; Emmor B. Cope, "Gettysburg National Military Park," [1925], Gettysburg National Military Park Archives [hereafter cited as GNMP] , Gettysburg, Pa. For additional information on battlefield preservation, commemorative activities, and tourism at Gettysburg, see Amy J. Kinsel, " 'From These Honored Dead': Gettysburg in American Culture, 1863–1938" (Ph.D. dissertation, Cornell University, 1992); and Kinsel, *Gettysburg in American Culture, 1863–1938* (Chapel Hill: University of North Carolina Press, forthcoming).

6. Gettysburg continues to be seen as the Civil War's turning point. Ken Burns's 1990 documentary, *The Civil War,* treated Gettysburg as the war's most important battle. See Gabor S. Boritt, "Lincoln and Gettysburg: The Hero and the Heroic Place," Robert Brent Toplin, ed., *Ken Burns's The Civil War: Historians Respond* (New York: Oxford University Press, 1996), 81–100.

7. For the congressional legislation on Gettysburg, see An Act to Establish a National Military Park at Gettysburg, Pennsylvania, ch. 80, 28 Stat. 651 (1895). See also *U.S. v. Gettysburg Electric Railway Co.*, 160 U.S. 576 (1896).

8. *New York Times*, July 3, 1938.

9. *Philadelphia Inquirer*, July 6, 1863.

10. U.S. Congress, Senate, *Reports of the Committees of the Senate of the United States*, 38th Cong., 2d sess., 1864–65, vol. 1, pp. lv–lxxvii, and 296–524; U.S., Department of War, *The War of the Rebellion: A Compilation of the Official Records of the Union and Confederate Armies* (Washington, D.C.: GPO, 1880–1901), 128 volumes (hereafter *OR*) ser. 1, vol. 27, pt. 1, pp. 128–36 and 700; W. A. Swanberg, *Sickles the Incredible* (New York: Scribner, 1956), 236–38; Richard A. Sauers, "Gettysburg: The Meade–Sickles Controversy" *Civil War History* 26 (1980): 197–217.

11. See Gabor S. Boritt, "'Unfinished Work': Lincoln, Meade, and Gettysburg," in Boritt, ed., *Lincoln's Generals* (New York: Oxford University Press, 1994).

12. For a discussion of the initial assessments of Lee at Gettysburg, see Thomas L. Connelly, *The Marble Man: Robert E. Lee and His Image in American Society* (New York, 1977), 56–59. See also William Garrett Piston, *Lee's Tarnished Lieutenant, James Longstreet and His Place in Southern History* (Athens: University of Georgia Press, 1987), 96–99; Gaines Foster, *Ghosts of the Confederacy*, 57–58; and Alan T. Nolan, *Lee Considered: General Robert E. Lee and Civil War History* (Chapel Hill: University of North Carolina Press, 1991), 169–70.

13. James Longstreet, "Lee in Pennsylvania," from [A. K. McClure, ed.], *The Annals of the War Written by Leading Participants North and South* (Philadelphia: The Times, 1879), and Jubal A. Early, "Reply to General Longstreet," *Southern Historical Society Papers* 4, no. 6 (Dec. 1877) reprinted in Gary W. Gallagher, ed., *Lee the Soldier* (Lincoln, Neb., 1996), 381–433.

14. Col. Joshua L. Chamberlain of the Twentieth Maine Regiment has become a prominent Gettysburg hero in the twentieth century. Michael Shaara's 1974 novel *The Killer Angels* (New York: Random House) featured Chamberlain, his regiment, and the leadership he displayed on July 2, 1863. *Gettysburg*, Ron Maxwell's 1994 movie based on Shaara's novel, reinforced Chamberlain's heroic reputation and made him the star of the film.

15. Edwin B. Coddington, "Rothermel's Paintings of the Battle of Gettysburg," *Pennsylvania History* XXVII (January 1960): 1–27. The large central canvas was accompanied by five smaller paintings that depicted additional scenes from the Battle of Gettysburg. Rothermel's "The Battle of Gettysburg" is currently located at the Pennsylvania State Museum Building in Harrisburg, Pa.

16. For more on cycloramas, see Robert Wernick, "Getting a Glimpse of History from a Grandstand Seat," *Smithsonian* (August 1985), 68–86.

17. Kinsel, " 'From These Honored Dead'," 468–77. Most of the 1884 version of Philippoteaux's cyclorama survives; it is located at the Gettysburg National Military Park in Gettysburg, Pa.

18. Wayne Craven, *The Sculptures of Gettysburg* (n.p.: Eastern Acorn Press, 1982); and "Monuments, Markers, and Memorials" file, GNMP, Gettysburg, Pa.

19. Bachelder served as the Memorial Association's Superintendent of Tablets and Legends from 1883 to 1894, and exercised control over the location and

inscriptions of all the markers and monuments placed on land owned by the Association.

20. The dedication to Union troops is inscribed on the monument. See also "Monuments, Markers, and Memorials" file, GNMP, Gettysburg, Pa.; and Bachelder correspondence, reel 5, GNMP.

21. Early in his address, Gildersleeve compared Gettysburg's significance to that of Austerlitz and Waterloo. Henry A. Gildersleeve, *Oration by Henry A. Gildersleeve, Delivered on the Battlefield of Gettysburg, September 17th, 1889* (n.p.: n.d.), 4 and 5. A copy of this pamphlet is located at the Cornell University Library.

22. Gildersleeve, *Oration,* 14.

23. Gildersleeve, *Oration,* 18.

24. Horatio N. Warren, *Two Reunions of the 142d Regiment, Pa. Vols. Including A History of the Regiment, Dedication of the Monument, a Description of The Battle of Gettysburg, Also A Complete Roster of the Regiment* (Buffalo, N.Y.: Courier Company, 1890), 8.

25. Herbert L. Grimm and Paul L. Roy, *Human Interest Stories of the Three Days Battles at Gettysburg* (Gettysburg, 1927), 41; and W.C. Storrick, *The Battle of Gettysburg* (Harrisburg, 1931), 32–33.

26. See Gary W. Gallagher, "A Widow and Her Soldier: LaSalle Corbell Pickett as Author of the George E. Pickett Letters" *Virginia Magazine of History and Biography* 94 (1986): 329–44.

27. John B. Gordon, *Reminiscences of the Civil War* (New York, 1903), 150–53; Benjamin A. Botkin, ed., *A Civil War Treasury of Tales, Legends, and Folklore* (New York, 1960), 263–65; Storrick, *Battle of Gettysburg,* 20–21; Gilbert, *Blue and Gray,* 52–53; Grimm and Roy, *Human Interest Stories,* 26. For an article debunking the tale, see William F. Hanna, "A Gettysburg Myth Exploded: The Barlow–Gordon Incident?—The Yankee Never Met the Reb" *Civil War Times Illustrated* (May 1985): 43–47.

28. Commonwealth of Pennsylvania, Fiftieth Anniversary of the Battle of Gettysburg Commission, "Report to the Joint Committee of the Congress of the United States," 1912, GNMP, Gettysburg, Pa. Pennsylvania appropriated $25,000 toward the reunion in 1911. The War Department also contributed to the cost of the event by housing the veterans in tents on the battlefield, and many states allocated funds to pay travel expenses for veterans. The reunion was open to all Civil War veterans, not just to those who had fought at Gettysburg.

29. "Pickett's Charge Fifty Years After," *New York Times,* July 4, 1913; Herbert Francis Sherwood, "Gettysburg Fifty Years Afterward," *The Outlook* 104 (July 19, 1913): 612; Echoes From Gettysburg," *Confederate Veteran* 21 (1913): 429. For a photograph see "Gettysburg Fifty Years After," *American Review of Reviews* 48 (August 1913): 179. See also Kinsel, "'From These Honored Dead'," 273–90.

30. "The President's Address," *New York Times,* July 5, 1913; "President Wilson's Address at Gettysburg," *Confederate Veteran* 21 (1913): 378.

31. *New York Times,* July 4, 1938.

32. Veterans from the Spanish-American War and the First World War participated in a two-hour parade at Gettysburg on July 2, 1938. See *Chicago Sunday Tribune,* July 3, 1938; and *New York Times,* July 3, 1938.

33. Garry Wills, *Lincoln at Gettysburg: The Words That Remade America* (New York: Simon & Schuster, 1992), 263. See page 261 for "Spoken Text."

34. On Frederick Douglass, see David W. Blight, "'For Something beyond the Battlefield': Frederick Douglass and the Struggle for the Memory of the Civil War" *Journal of American History* 75 (March 1989): 1156–78. See also, Kinsel, "'From These Honored Dead,'" 547–56.

The emphasis on soldier experience and national reconciliation continues into the late twentieth century. Ken Burns's epic documentary *The Civil War* concludes with footage of veteran reunions at Gettysburg. See Eric Foner, "Ken Burns and the Romance of Reunion," in Toplin, ed., *Ken Burns's The Civil War*, 101–18.

# For Further Reading:
# A Bibliography

ONE: *The Common Soldier's Gettysburg Campaign*
JOSEPH T. GLATTHAAR

This chapter is based largely on manuscript sources in repositories all around the country. Among published sources, the first place to start on the Gettysburg Campaign is Harry Pfanz's two books, *Gettysburg: The Second Day (1987) and Gettysburg: Culp's Hill and Cemetery Hill* (1993). These are detailed analyses of the battle, integrating the experience of high command with the battle from the ground level. Selected essays in Gary Gallagher, ed., three volume collection—*The First Day at Gettysburg (1992); The Second Day at Gettysburg* (1993); and *The Third Day at Gettysburg and Beyond* (1993)—provide some keen insights into the campaign from various perspectives. The best unit history is Alan T. Nolan's *The Iron Brigade* (1961), an outfit that was in the thick of the fight. George R. Stewart's *Pickett's Charge: A Microhistory of the Final Attack at Gettysburg* (1959) has stood the test of time well.

Among the huge number of published primary sources on the two major armies of the Eastern Theater, Robert Goldthwaite Carter's *Four Brothers in Blue or Sun-shine and Shadows of the War of the Rebellion* (1978) provides a very thoughtful depiction of life in the Union army. A gripping, controversial tale, written shortly after the battle, is Franklin A. Haskell's *The Battle of Gettysburg* (1908). For the Confederate side, see William H. Runge, ed., *Four Years in the Confederate Artillery: The Diary of Private Henry Robinson Berkeley* (1961) for an enlisted man's view of the raid into Pennsylvania. General Edward Porter Alexander's memoirs, *Fighting for the Confederacy* (1989), edited by Gary Gallagher, offers some interesting commentary on the high command, as does R. Lockwood Tower, ed., *Lee's Adjutant: The Wartime Letters of Colonel Walter Herron Taylor,*

*1862–1865* (1995). Walter Lord, ed., *The Fremantle Diary* (1954), written by a British military observer with Lee's army, is indispensable.

More general volumes on the common soldier for the Union and Confederacy have become plentiful in recent years. Bell Irvin Wiley's *Life of Johnny Reb* (1943) and *Life of Billy Yank* (1952) established the guideposts by which all subsequent volumes are measured. Wiley's book on the Union volunteers benefits from his World War II experiences and is clearly the superior of the two. More recently, Reid Mitchell has written *Civil War Soldiers* (1988) and *The Vacant Chair* (1994), which meld social and cultural history. More in line with Wiley is the work of his acclaimed student, James I. Robertson, Jr., in *Soldiers Blue and Gray* (1988), which is based more on published primary sources.

Two other books of interest are Grady McWhiney and Perry Jamieson's controversial *Attack and Die* (1982) and Gerald Linderman's *Embattled Courage* (1987). McWhiney and Jamieson argue that Southern character manifested itself in assault tactics, and the authors view Gettysburg as a prime example. Linderman sees courage as the glue that kept Civil War units intact. According to Linderman, volunteers had a warped perception of leadership. Enlisted men expected officers to lead in the front, and officers had to demonstrate their courage in battle after battle, long after the realities of war indicated its futility.

For students of the Civil War who wish to examine manuscripts, the best repositories for this campaign from the Confederate perspective are the Virginia Historical Society, the Museum of the Confederacy, Duke University, and the Southern Historical Collection at the University of North Carolina, Chapel Hill. All Southern state archives hold a wealth of information. For the Union, State Historical Society of Wisconsin, Pennsylvania Historical Society, New-York Historical Society, Massachusetts Historical Society, and Ohio Historical Society are the strongest, but all Northern states have rich holdings. Overall, the best repository is the U.S. Army Military History Institute in Carlisle Barracks, Pennsylvania.

**TWO:** *Joshua Chamberlain and the American Dream*
GLENN LAFANTASIE

A small, but very solid, shelf of books on Joshua Lawrence Chamberlain reveals various facets of his life, public and private. An early work, issued several years before his death, gives a contemporary perspective on his life and achievements: Chamberlain Association of America, *Joshua Lawrence Chamberlain: A Sketch* (n.p., [1906]). It is possible that Chamberlain wrote the *Sketch* himself. After he died in 1914, the Military Order of the Loyal Legion of the United States, Commandery of the State of Maine, an organization in which Chamberlain was very active, published *In*

*Memoriam: Joshua Lawrence Chamberlain,* Circular No. 5, Whole Number 328 (Portland, Me., 1914), which offers some tidbits of information not available elsewhere. A book by Willard Wallace, *Soul of the Lion: A Biography of Joshua L. Chamberlain* (New York, 1960), is a modern study of the man and his worlds that does not slight Chamberlain's private side or his foibles. More detailed and thorough, and showing the bounty of painstaking research, is Alice Rains Trulock's *In the Hands of Providence: Joshua L. Chamberlain and the American Civil War* (Chapel Hill, 1992). Trulock, who spent many years working on the book, reveals endless facts about Chamberlain's life and times. Unfortunately, she does so from the perspective of a hagiographer. More satisfying is Michael Golay's briefer portrait, *To Gettysburg and Beyond: The Parallel Lives of Joshua Lawrence Chamberlain and Edward Porter Alexander* (New York, 1994), which brings Chamberlain to life by employing superb anecdotes and effective quotes.

On Chamberlain and the 20th Maine, the best account is John J. Pullen's *The Twentieth Maine: A Volunteer Regiment in the Civil War* (Philadelphia, 1957), one of the best Civil War regimental histories ever written. Pullen's chapters on the 20th at Gettysburg are informative and entertaining, but nothing surpasses Chamberlain's own telling of the story in "Through Blood and Fire at Gettysburg," *Hearst's Magazine,* 23 (June 1913), 894–909, which has been conveniently reprinted in Chamberlain, *"Bayonet! Forward": My Civil War Reminiscences,* ed. Stan Clark, Jr. (Gettysburg, 1994). In *The Passing of the Armies* (New York, 1915), which is available in several modern reprints, Chamberlain says practically nothing about Gettysburg, but does reveal a great deal about himself.

For alternative accounts of the fight for Little Round Top, see William C. Oates, *The War Between the Union and the Confederacy and Its Lost Opportunities* (New York, 1905) and William B. Styple, ed., *With a Flash of His Sword: The Writings of Major Holman Melcher, 20th Maine Infantry* (Kearny, N.J., 1994). A most judicious secondary account of the struggle for Little Round Top is Harry W. Pfanz, *Gettysburg: The Second Day* (Chapel Hill, 1987). An older account, which contains generous excerpts from official reports and other important sources, is Oliver Willcox Norton, *The Attack and Defense of Little Round Top: Gettysburg, July 2, 1863* (New York, 1913), also available in reprinted editions. But by far the very best secondary account of the 20th Maine's defense of Little Round Top is Thomas A. Desjardin's *Stand Firm Ye Boys from Maine: The 20th Maine and the Gettysburg Campaign* (Gettysburg, 1995), a well-written scholarly narrative that digs deeply into the extant sources and, surprisingly, finds new things to say about the fight and its many legacies.

Lastly, Michael Shaara's novel, *The Killer Angels* (New York, 1974), is a legend in its own right. More than anything, Shaara's book is responsible for bringing Chamberlain to life for modern readers, making him a sympathetic character, and advancing the Chamberlain legend into the millennium. The success of the novel has been phenomenal. Winning the Pulitzer Prize for fiction in 1975 did not hurt. Some critics complain that the novel is flawed by errors of fact. But its fans admire the way Shaara makes the battle of Gettysburg seem so real, so human, so tragic.

### THREE: *"Old Jack" Is Not Here*
HARRY W. PFANZ

The best overall history of the Gettysburg campaign and battle at present is Edwin B. Coddington's, *The Gettysburg Campaign: A Study in Command* (New York, 1968; Dayton, 1979). Coddington was thoroughly familiar with the campaign area and the battlefield and made judicious use of essentially all available sources on the subject. It seems unlikely that Coddington's work will be rivaled in the foreseeable future and his conclusions seriously challenged.

Coddington's coverage of the battle of July 1 has been supplemented by more detailed studies of that day itself. One of these is Warren Hassler's *Crises at the Crossroads: The First Day at Gettysburg* (Montgomery, 1970 and Gaithersburg, 1986), which seems all too short. My own book, *Gettysburg: Culp's Hill and Cemetery Hill* (Chapel Hill, 1993), deals rather intensively with Ewell's direction of his portion of the battle particularly with his decision not to press the attack against Cemetery Hill. Not to be overlooked are the essays on the battle of July 1 edited by Gary Gallagher and published under the title *The First Day at Gettysburg* (Kent, Oh., 1992) and various articles in *The Gettysburg Magazine* published by Morningside House of Dayton, Ohio.

Douglas Southall Freeman's *R. E. Lee: A Biography* (New York, 1934-1935) and *Lee's Lieutenants: A Study in Command* (New York, 1942-1944) continue to be the standard works on Lee and the Army of Northern Virginia, and they are joined by Emory M. Thomas's *Robert E. Lee: A Biography* (New York, 1995). All are well worth reading. Unfortunately, Freeman based his work on some rather biased sources, and he fails to give due consideration to what was happening on the Union side of the field. Sad to say, there are yet no comparable studies relating to the Army of the Potomac.

Serious students of the battle will want to delve deeper into the subject. Their starting point will be the principle works cited in the volumes above. These will include, of course, reports presented in "Official Records" or *The War of the Rebellion: Official Records of the Union and Confederate Armies.* The three parts of Volume 27 (Washington, 1888 and Dayton,

1981) deal with Gettysburg. These should be supplemented by personal accounts of participants that were published initially in the *Southern Historical Society Papers,* the Philadelphia *Times,* and several other organs. Not to be overlooked are book length accounts by key participants including: Jubal A. Early's *War Memoirs* (Bloomington, 1960), Oliver O. Howard's, *Autobiography of Oliver Otis Howard,* vol. 1 (New York, 1907); Carl Schurz's, *Reminiscences of Carl Schurz,* vol. 3 (New York, 1908), and those of soldiers of less rank. All personal accounts must be examined critically for accuracy and objectivity, particularly those written long after the battle.

## FOUR: *The Chances of War: Lee, Longstreet, Sickles, and the First Minnesota Volunteers*
KENT GRAMM

It is sobering, if not humbling, to view the succession of historical and biographical works that deal with a great event in human history. New information becomes available, conclusions that once seemed obvious are shown to be faulty, whole new emphases and considerations come to light, making any person's thoughts and arguments very fragile. But humbling, even disturbing, in a more important way is the apparent fact that new information, arguments, and emphases are continually *developed.* That is, what we seem to have are not changing perspectives on the "actual" battle of Gettysburg, but rather a succession of literary creations, paintings rather than photographs—made not by eyewitnesses but by imaginative persons with the same wishes and fears that normally affect any human being's imagination: the desire to say something new; to defend oneself; to attack someone else; to make or preserve a reputation—military, academic, or otherwise; a sentimental attachment to certain "historical" persons or movements. Trying to "get it right" is an uncertain task indeed, with such a maze supplying the main body of sources; and if someone actually "got it right," who would know? Is such "knowledge" possible at all?

Having delivered myself of that cheery preface, I will enumerate my chief sources for this essay (a word that means no more than "attempt"). In dealing with Robert E. Lee, the great work of Douglas Southall Freeman must be consulted: *R. E. Lee* (1935) and *Lee's Lieutenants* (1944). These seven volumes convey a massively researched, admiring portrait of Robert E. Lee in a dignified manner appropriate to their great subject. However, recent writers have found some of Freeman's conclusions, particularly regarding the Longstreet–Gettysburg question, to be based on previous writers, such as Jubal Early, *War Memoirs* (1912, 1960), who wanted to blame someone else, such as Longstreet, instead of Lee or themselves for the failures in Pennsylvania. Porter Alexander's recently published *Fighting for the Confederacy* (1989), Gary Gallagher, ed., is a memoir that seems, by contrast, to be clear-headed, perceptive, and unprejudiced. Accordingly, recent writers, beginning with Thomas L. Connelly in *The Marble Man: Robert E. Lee and His Image in American Society* (1977), have begun to doubt and reexamine the claims traditionally made for Lee's military excellence. Alan Nolan's *Lee Considered* (1991) is a particularly sharp, forcefully argued book that is not afraid to examine the legend for error or hypocrisy. As to the controversy pertaining to Longstreet at Gettysburg, Glenn Tucker's *Lee and Longstreet at Gettysburg* (1968) thoroughly analyzes the question and comes out clearly in Longstreet's favor. The last word, of course, has not been pronounced. A couple of recent books, *The Second Day at Gettysburg* (1993), edited by Gary Gallagher, and *Why the Confederacy Lost* (1992), edited by Gabor Boritt, provide specific and general considerations, respectively, for thinking about what happened on July 2 and why. See also Jeffrey D. Wert's *General James Longstreet: The Confederacy's Most Controversial Soldier—A Biography.* The new study of Lee by Emory Thomas, *Robert E. Lee: A Biography* (1995) quickly accepts the anti-Longstreet point of view regarding Gettysburg.

In that connection, Edwin B. Coddington's standard *The Gettysburg Campaign* (1968) and the now-standard *Gettysburg: The Second Day* (1987) by Harry Pfanz provide careful considerations of command decisions. My *Gettysburg: A Meditation on War and Values* (1994) contains material pertaining to the Sickles controversy. Francis A. Walker's "Meade at Gettysburg" in *Battles and Leaders of the Civil War* (reissued 1956) and David B. Downs's "His Left Was Worth a Glance" in *The Gettysburg Magazine* (July 1992) defend Meade and roundly condemn Sickles. The flamboyant New Yorker has received excellent biographical treatment in W. A. Swanberg's *Sickles the Incredible* (1956). The most comprehensive examination of the issue is Richard A. Sauers's *A Caspian Sea of Ink: The Meade-Sickles Controversy* (1989).

In evaluating Hancock's military abilities, one might consult Glenn Tucker's *Hancock the Superb* (1960). I relied on two excellent treatments of the First Minnesota, the first being Robert W. Meinhard's article in *The Gettysburg Magazine* (July 1991), "The First Minnesota at Gettysburg." (Every Civil War scholar, perhaps every person, should admire and appropriate Meinhard's statement, "I am not an authority on the Civil War, but a student of the war.") Richard Moe's *The Last Full Measure: The Life and Death of the First Minnesota Volunteers* (1993) is an outstanding regimental history, thorough and affecting.

**FIVE:** *Eggs, Aldie, Shepherdstown, and J. E. B. Stuart*
EMORY M. THOMAS

Principle sources for an understanding of J. E. B. Stuart and Gettysburg include his manuscript correspondence, the best collections of which are at
the Virginia Historical Society in Richmond, Virginia. Fundamental, too,
is *War of the Rebellion: A Compilation of the Official Records of the
Union and Confederate Armies* (Washington, D. C., 1880–1901). Memoirs of Stuart's staff include H. B. McClellan, *The Life and Campaigns of
Major-General J. E. B. Stuart* (Blue and Grey Press edition, Secaucus,
1993), W. W. Blackford, *War Years with Jeb Stuart* (New York, 1945),
and John Esten Cooke, *Wearing of the Gray* (Bloomington, 1959).

About the campaign, Edwin B. Coddington, *The Gettysburg Campaign:
A Study in Command* (New York, 1968) is still standard. Douglas Southall
Freeman, *Lee's Lieutenants* (New York, 1942) is the best study of the
Army of Northern Virginia. Stephen Z. Starr, *The Union Cavalry in the
Civil War* (Baton Rouge, 1979–1985) is a sound summary of Stuart's ene-
mies.

Biographies of Stuart include McClellan's cited above, John W. Thomason, Jr., *Jeb Stuart* (New York, 1930), and Emory M. Thomas, *Bold Dragoon: The Life of J. E. B. Stuart* (New York, 1986). More specialized studies are Robert J. Trout, *They Followed the Plume: The Story of J. E. B.
Stuart and His Staff* (Mechanicsburg, Pa., 1993), Mark Nesbitt, *Saber
and Scapegoat: J. E. B. Stuart and the Gettysburg Controversy* (Mechanicsburg, 1994), and Edward G. Longacre, *The Cavalry at Gettysburg*
(Rutherford, N. J., 1986). Unit histories are important and one of the best
of these is Robert Krick, *9th Virginia Cavalry* (Lynchburg, 1982). Helpful
is Craig L. Symonds, *Gettysburg: A Battlefield Atlas* (Baltimore, 1992).

Three recent novels deserve mention—Michael Shaara, *The Killer Angels*
(New York, 1974), Douglas Savage, *The Court Martial of Robert E. Lee,*
and M. A. Harper, *For the Love of Robert E. Lee* (New York, 1992). The
latter work is the best portrait of Robert E. Lee in American fiction.

The notes for this chapter offer more bibliography on significant subjects.


**SIX:** *"I Think the Union Army Had Something to Do with It":
The Pickett's Charge Nobody Knows*
CAROL REARDON

Pickett's Charge has inspired a sizeable literature over the years. An important caveat must be stated at the start, however: as the name "Pickett's
Charge" suggests, much of the extant literature is highly partisan in tone,
most often promoting Virginia troops, criticizing Pettigrew's and Trimble's

commands, and downplaying, if not ignoring, the Union soldiers who repulsed the attack.

Interesting early works that perpetuate the Virginia version of Pickett's Charge include Old Dominion journalist Edward A. Pollard's several volumes on the Confederate war effort, William Swinton's works on the great campaigns of the Army of the Potomac, and Walter Harrison's *Pickett's Men* (1870), one of the first published unit histories for any command, North or South; all are available in modern reprint editions. The Virginia version of July 3 also played a key role in the "Lee cult's" efforts to blame James Longstreet for the Confederacy's defeat at Gettysburg, played out on the pages of *The Southern Historical Society Papers*.

Attacking the Virginia version of Pickett's Charge to restore to the historical record the efforts of Trimble's and Pettigrew's survivors became a postwar obsession among many North Carolinians, Tennesseans, Mississippians, and Alabamians. William R. Bond's *Pickett or Pettigrew?* (1880) attacked the Virginia version of the events of July 3 so virulently and to such an enthusiastic audience that it was reprinted several times by 1900. Walter Clark, editor for the North Carolina Historical Commission's five-volume *Histories of the Several Regiments and Battalions . . . from North Carolina* (1901), included several individual essays that attacked the Virginia version of events in addition to giving close attention to the charge in every appropriate regimental narrative. All these works have been reissued as modern reprints.

A number of key figures left memoirs or have received biographical treatments of wildly varying quality. James Longstreet's *From Manassas to Appomattox* (1896), E. Porter Alexander's *The Military Memoirs of a Confederate* (1907), and Gary W. Gallagher's edited version of Alexander's *Fighting for the Confederacy* (1989) provide important insights by Confederate commanders. John Gibbon's *Personal Recollections of the Civil War* (1928) provides a view from the Union lines. Pickett left no memoirs and has not yet received his just due from a biographer. His widow, LaSalle Corbell Pickett, tried to secure her husband's memory with *Pickett and His Men* (1899) and then with a collection of fabricated personal letters entitled *Heart of a Soldier* (1913). Her Victorian prose in praise of the man she called "My Soldier" requires considerable patience and toleration from the reader, however. The often ignored J. Johnston Pettigrew has been rescued from obscurity in Clyde N. Wilson's *Carolina Cavalier* (1990). Frank A. Haskell's *The Battle of Gettysburg* (1910), despite its author's self-indulgence on occasion, deserves its accolade as a classic in American war literature.

The controversies of July 3 constitute an important part of any credible study of the battle of Gettysburg. Douglas Southall Freeman's four-volume masterpiece *R. E. Lee* (1935) and three-volume companion study *Lee's*

*Lieutenants* (1942), both of which excoriate Longstreet, require some balance that can be found in Glenn Tucker's *High Tide at Gettysburg* (1958) and *Lee and Longstreet at Gettysburg* (1968). E. B. Coddington's *The Gettysburg Campaign: A Study in Command* (1968) is certainly more objective than either Freeman or Tucker and remains the best single-volume study of the battle. Michael Shaara's Pulitzer Prize–winning novel *The Killer Angels* (1975) leans to Longstreet's side of the controversies of the day and provides the interpretation of the charge used in the 1993 movie *Gettysburg*.

A few more specific studies can enlighten as well. George Stewart's *Pickett's Charge: A Microhistory of the Final Attack at Gettysburg, July 3, 1863* (1959) remains the best modern treatment of the day's events; it is the only currently published work on those events to accord the Union troops anything like equal treatment. Kathy Georg Harrison and John W. Busey's *Nothing but Glory: Pickett's Division at Gettysburg* (1987) examines in detail the muster rolls and maneuvers of the Virginia division, but it pays scant attention to the rest of the Confederate attackers or to the Union defenders. Richard Rollins's *Pickett's Charge: Eyewitness Accounts* (1993) offers an interesting assortment of Northern and Southern descriptions, reports, and memoirs. Carol Reardon's "Pickett's Charge: The Convergence of Myth and History in the Southern Past," in *The Third Day at Gettysburg and Beyond* (1994) makes clear the partisan nature of most writing about the historical phenomenon called "Pickett's Charge."

## SEVEN: *Gettysburg's Gettysburg: What the Battle Did to the Borough*
J. Matthew Gallman

The experiences of Gettysburg's civilians during the battle are extremely well documented. The Adams County Historical Society has collected roughly eighty civilian accounts of the battle, many of which are quoted in this chapter. Among the most interesting personal accounts are Sarah Broadhead's privately printed "Diary" and Tillie Pierce Alleman, *At Gettysburg: Or What a Young Girl Saw and Heard of the Battle* (New York, 1988). These two narratives, and many others, are cited in the chapter. Two recent histories make heavy use of the personal accounts. See Robert L. Bloom, "'We Never Expected a Battle': The Civilians at Gettysburg, 1863," *Pennsylvania History* 55 (October 1988) and Gerald R. Bennett, *Days of "Uncertainty and Dread": The Ordeal Endured by the Citizens at Gettysburg* (Camp Hill, Penn., 1994). For contemporary photographs of the borough and various civilians, as well as detailed reconstructions of some of their lives, see William A. Frassanito, *Early Photography at Gettysburg* (Gettysburg, 1995). On the experiences of Gettysburg's African

Americans see Peter C. Vermilyea, "'We Did Not Know Where Our Colored Friends Had Gone': The Effect of the Confederate Invasion of Pennsylvania on Gettysburg's African-American Community," (unpublished independent study, Gettysburg College, Gettysburg, 1994). The best single-volume history of the Gettysburg campaign, including some attention to the impact on civilians, is Edwin B. Coddington, *The Gettysburg Campaign: A Study in Command* (New York, 1968).

Gettysburg's wartime history is best told through the pages of two competing local newspapers, the Democratic *Gettysburg Compiler* and the Republican *Adams County Sentinel*. These newspapers, cited only where quoted directly, provide much of this chapter's narrative structure. Salome Myers Stewart's (unpublished) diary spanning most of the war is available in the Adams County Historical Society. The Gettysburg National Military Park Library has small but valuable archives. Among the printed materials stored there are "Excerpts of the Minute Book of the Gettysburg Town Council," typescripts on "Shoes at Gettysburg," and "Description of the 1863 Gettysburg Environment" (the latter written in 1976 by Kathy Georg). The population data from 1860 and 1870 are from the United States Census of Population, as compiled on computer at the Civil War Institute in Gettysburg. For county and state politics, see Robert L. Bloom, *A History of Adams County, Pennsylvania, 1700–1990* (Gettysburg, 1992) and Erwin Stanley Bradley, *The Triumph of Militant Republicanism: A Study of Pennsylvania and Presidential Politics 1860–1872* (Philadelphia, 1964).

For general histories of the North during the Civil War see J. Matthew Gallman, *The North Fights the Civil War: The Home Front* (Chicago, 1994) and Phillip Shaw Paludan, *"A People's Contest": The Union and the Civil War, 1861–1865* (New York, 1988). Both volumes include extensive bibliographic essays. On the Confederate home front see Emory M. Thomas, *The Confederate Nation: 1861–1865* (New York, 1979) and George C. Rable, *Civil Wars: Women and the Crisis of Southern Nationalism* (Urbana, 1991). For the economic impact of the war, see Stanley Engerman and J. Matthew Gallman, "The Civil War Economy: A Modern View," in Stig Forster and Jorg Nagler, eds., *On the Road to Total War: The American Civil War and the German Wars of Unification, 1861–1871* (New York, 1997). The best history of Union recruiting and conscription is James W. Geary, *We Need Men: The Union Draft in the Civil War* (DeKalb, Ill., 1991).

The literature on "gender spheres" in nineteenth-century America is vast. For the crucial early study see Nancy Cott, *The Bonds of Womanhood: "Women's Sphere" in New England, 1780–1835* (New Haven, 1977). For an excellent analysis of the public roles of women in three mid-nineteenth-century cities—with particular attention to the Civil War see

Mary Ryan, *Women in Public: Between Banners and Ballots, 1825–1880* (Baltimore, 1990). The women of Gettysburg received special treatment in the numerous postwar discussions of patriotic women. See, for instance, Frank Moore, *Women of the War* (Hartford, 1866) and Linus P. Brockett and Mary C. Vaughan, *Woman's Work in the Civil War* (Philadelphia, 1867). For a recent account of one Gettysburg heroine see Cindy L. Small, *The Jennie Wade Story* (Gettysburg, 1991).

Several collections of essays provide a sampling of recent scholarship on the home front. See Maris Vinovskis, ed., *Toward a Social History of the American Civil War: Exploratory Essays* (New York, 1990) and Catherine Clinton and Nina Silber, eds., *Divided Houses: Gender and the Civil War* (New York, 1992). Drew Gilpin Faust's essay, "Altars of Sacrifice: Confederate Women and the Narratives of War," *Journal of American History* (March 1990), reprinted in the Clinton and Silber collection, is a particularly interesting reading of the South's "war stories."

**EIGHT:** *The Pennsylvania Gambit and the Gettysburg Splash*
RICHARD M. McMURRY

Most of the writing that deals with the July 1863 military events at Gettysburg focuses on the tactical details of the great battle. Over the years, authors have produced massive volumes in which they have traced the movements of this or that brigade, regiment, or even company across the battlefield on an almost minute-by-minute level. Other students of the battle have devoted hundreds of pages to evaluations of the performance of some general in the battle. Why did he do this? Why didn't he do that? Those who wish to do so can explore almost any military aspect of Gettysburg, no matter how minute, in seemingly inexhaustible detail. Readers who desire to delve into the larger aspects of the battle—Why did it come about? What was its impact on the war?—are not so lucky. They will find slim pickings.

The Gettysburg Campaign cannot be understood independently of the military situation that existed in the spring and early summer of 1863. The maneuvers in the Mississippi Valley that brought on the crisis of April–May 1863 and precipitated the debate that led the Rebels to Pennsylvania are recounted in Gettysburg-like detail in Edwin C. Bearss's three-volume *Campaign For Vicksburg* (Dayton, Oh., 1985–1986). Those who desire a less comprehensive, yet perfectly adequate account may consult *The Final Fortress: The Campaign for Vicksburg, 1862–1863* by Samuel Carter III (New York, 1980). The sorry state of the Rebels' western command (and commanders) is described in Thomas Lawrence Connelly's two-volume history of the secessionists' main western force: *Army of the Heartland: The Army of Tennessee, 1861–1862* and *Autumn of Glory:*

*The Army of Tennessee, 1862–1865* (Baton Rouge, 1967, 1971). Steven E. Woodworth's *Jefferson Davis and His Generals: The Failure of Confederate Command in the West* (Lawrence, Kan., 1990) is a more wide-sweeping and in many ways a better written and more usable study.

The best way to understand Confederate response to the crisis is to read the correspondence of the leading Rebels—especially that of Jefferson Davis and Robert E. Lee—in March, April, May, and June 1863. It should be noted, however, that many of their earlier writings also contain clues as to their ideas about the Confederacy's military situation and about the proper grand strategy that each thought the South should adopt. Most of these letters are to be found in the United States War Department's great compilation *The War of the Rebellion: The Official Records of the Union and Confederate Armies* (Washington, 1880–1902). Volumes 24, 25, and 27 of the OR cover specifically the spring and summer of 1863, but other important communications can be found scattered throughout volumes 17, 20, 21, 23, 51, and 52.

Other relevant, and often unofficial, letters are to be found in *Jefferson Davis: Constitutionalist: His Letters, Papers, and Speeches*, 10 vols., edited by Dunbar Rowland (Jackson, Miss., 1923). Haskell Monroe, et al., eds., *The Papers of Jefferson Davis* (Baton Rouge, 1971–) will eventually supersede the 1923 collection. Volumes one through eight, published as of this writing, cover the Rebel chieftain's life through 1862. Volume nine will deal with the Gettysburg year.

Additional Lee documents can be found in *The Wartime Papers of R. E. Lee,* edited by Clifford Dowdey and Louis H. Manarin (Boston, 1961); and in *Lee's Dispatches: Unpublished Letters of General Robert E. Lee, C. S. A., to Jefferson Davis and the War Department of the Confederate States of America, 1862–65,* edited by Douglas Southall Freeman, published originally in 1914, but reissued with some new material and a new foreword by Grady McWhiney in 1994 (Baton Rouge).

Once readers have mastered this material, they should be in position to understand how the Southerners got themselves into the crisis of April–May 1863 and what the Rebels proposed to do about their plight. They can then turn to biographies of the leading Confederate policy makers. None of these, however, treats the Gettysburg Decision in any great detail. For the Southern president, see William C. Davis, *Jefferson Davis: The Man and His Hour: A Biography* (New York, 1991). This work is by far the best biography of Davis, but it is seriously flawed by the author's decision not to make use of the vast body of secondary literature on the Confederacy. Lee is best approached thorough Douglas Southall Freeman's classic *R. E. Lee: A Biography* (New York, 1934–1935). Volume 3 covers the Gettysburg Campaign. Clifford Dowdey's *Lee* (Boston, 1965) treats Lee in much the same manner but in less detail. Emory M. Thomas's

*Robert E. Lee: A Biography* (New York, 1995) slights the general's military career and covers the period from mid-May through mid-July 1863 in only twenty pages. (Freeman, by contrast, devotes 160 pages to the same events.) *Lee: The Soldier,* edited by Gary W. Gallagher (Lincoln, 1996), is a collection of writings on the Confederate commander. Several of these essays shed light on Lee's role in the Gettysburg decision.

The roles of some of the lesser participants involved in the Rebel debate over grand strategy can be followed in *T. Harry Williams, P. G. T. Beauregard: Napoleon in Gray* (Baton Rouge, 1955); Ben H. Proctor, *Not Without Honor: The Life of John H. Reagan* (Austin, 1962); Alvy L. King, *Louis T. Wigfall: Southern Fire-Eater* (Baton Rouge, 1970); and Jeffry Wert, *James Longstreet: The Confederacy's Most Controversial Soldier: A Biography* (New York, 1993).

General works on Civil War military history offer some insight into the Rebel grand strategy and the men and factors that shaped it. Thomas Lawrence Connelly and Archer Jones, *The Politics of Command: Factions and Ideas in Confederate Strategy* (Baton Rouge, 1973); and Jones's *Civil War Command and Strategy: The Process of Victory and Defeat* (New York, 1992) are provocative works that offer many fresh insights into the shady corners of Confederate military politics and policies. Steven E. Woodworth's *Davis and Lee at War* (Lawrence, Kan., 1995) is even more valuable for the study of the two leading Rebels and how they perceived their nation's situation and needs. Woodworth, in my opinion, overstates what he believes was a fundamental difference between the two men on how to carry on the war.

Two other useful general works that cover the subject matter dealt with in this chapter (and much more) are Herman Hattaway and Archer Jones, *How the North Won: A Military History of the Civil War* (Urbana, 1983); and Hattaway, Jones, Richard E. Beringer, and William N. Still, Jr, *Why the South Lost the Civil War* (Athens, Ga., 1986). My own *Two Great Rebel Armies: An Essay in Confederate Military History* (Chapel Hill, 1989) explores the factors, some unknown to the participants, that played a major role in shaping the secessionists' war effort in both East and West. These factors meant that the Southerners were most unlikely to win any great success in the West and that the Federals could not gain victory in the East.

James A. Kegel's *North With Lee and Jackson: The Lost Story of Gettysburg* (Mechanicsburg, Pa., 1996) appeared after this chapter was written. Kegel argues that the 1863 Rebel march into Pennsylvania was the outgrowth of a plan proposed by Thomas J. ("Stonewall") Jackson in 1861, adopted by Confederate authorities in 1862, and implemented in 1863. Kegel's thesis is overstated and has many weak links. Even if he is correct, however, one must still answer the question why didn't the Rebels in 1863 postpone their long-planned invasion in order to send reinforcements from Lee's army to drive Grant away from Vicksburg or to attack Rosecrans in Tennessee? After all, as Kegel himself argues, they chose to postpone the invasion in 1862 in order to use Jackson's own army to drive the Yankees away from Richmond. (See especially Chapter 9, "Jackson's Plan Accepted—Invasion Postponed.")

Efforts to assess Gettysburg's impact on the war have pretty much been confined to spouting the old clichés about the engagement being the "turning point," the "high watermark," the "decisive battle," and/or the "pivotal battle." In keeping with American custom, no effort has been made to define these terms. So far as I am aware, no one has made any serious effort to explain how the course of the war after Gettysburg was any different from what the course of the war had been before the Confederates marched into southern Pennsylvania.

## NINE: *From Turning Point to Peace Memorial: A Cultural Legacy*
AMY J. KINSEL

The Battle of Gettysburg is an overwhelming topic for any historian, not least for the historian of American culture. As a complete bibliography, Richard Allen Sauers's book-length list of material on Gettysburg is now dated but still very useful: Sauers, *The Gettysburg Campaign, June 3–August 1, 1863: a Comprehensive, Selectively Annotated Bibliography* (Westport, Conn., 1982). Anyone interested particularly in Gettysburg's cultural legacy will need to consult broadly in the general literature while focusing on several specific areas of interpretation.

Three volumes of essays edited by Gary W. Gallagher offer a good introduction to historical questions about the battle: *The First Day at Gettysburg: Essays on Confederate and Union Leadership* (Kent, Ohio, 1992); *The Second Day at Gettysburg: Essays on Confederate and Union Leadership* (Kent, 1993); and *The Third Day at Gettysburg and Beyond* (Chapel Hill, 1994). For a recent treatment of one of the most contentious of the historical debates, see Richard A. Sauers, *A Caspian Sea of Ink: The Meade–Sickles Controversy* (Baltimore, 1989). And a new collection of essays on Robert E. Lee, also edited by Gary Gallagher, includes many selections related to Gettysburg: *Lee the Soldier* (Lincoln, Neb., 1996).

The views of participants in the battle are well documented in the U. S. War Department's history of the Civil War, *The War of the Rebellion: A Compilation of the Official Records of the Union and Confederate Armies* (Washington, 1880–1901). The material on Gettysburg appears in series 1, volume 27. Published memoirs are another source of participants' opinions. E. Porter Alexander's *Fighting for the Confederacy: The Personal Recollections of General Edward Porter Alexander,* edited by Gary W. Gallagher (Chapel Hill, 1989), is an especially rewarding example of the genre.

States and regimental associations published extensive histories of their participation both in the battle and in commemorative activities at the battlefield See, for example, Indiana, Gettysburg Anniversary Commission, *Indiana at the Fiftieth Anniversary of the Battle of Gettysburg* (Indianapolis, 1913). The commemorative and fraternal activities of Union veterans have recently been examined by Stuart McConnell in his *Glorious Contentment: The Grand Army of the Republic, 1865–1900* (Chapel Hill, 1992). Periodicals aimed at Civil War veterans printed many articles on Gettysburg, especially around the time of reunions. See *Confederate Veteran* (July 1913), for example. Extensive coverage of veteran reunions and monument dedications may also be found in national newspapers such as the *New York Times.*

There are two major archival sources of material related to Gettysburg's cultural significance. The Gettysburg National Military Park houses at the battlefield extensive administrative records dating from the 1890s. These include files on diverse topics from monument design and dedications to tourism and the licensing of battlefield guides. Private memorabilia collected by John P. Nicholson, a longtime chairman of the War Department's Gettysburg park commission, are located at the Huntington Library in San Marino, California. Nicholson's collection is particularly rich in such things as obscure battlefield guide books and programs from events held at Gettysburg. In addition, the papers of noted Gettysburg historian, John B. Bachelder, have recently been published: David L. and Audrey L. Ladd, eds., *The Bachelder Papers: Gettysburg in Their Own Words* (Dayton, Ohio, 1994).

On the subject of the preservation of America's battlefields, an important essay by Ronald F. Lee, *The Origin and Evolution of the National Military Park Idea* (Washington, 1973), has recently been supplemented by analysis of what battlefields have meant to Americans. See Edward Tabor Linenthal, *Sacred Ground: Americans and Their Battlefields* (Urbana, 1991); and John S. Patterson, "From Battle Ground to Pleasure Ground: Gettysburg as a Historic Site," in *History Museums in the United States: A Critical Assessment,* ed. Warren Leon and Roy Rosenzweig (Urbana, 1989). See also Patterson, "A Patriotic Landscape: Gettysburg, 1863–1913" *Prospects* (1982): 315–33.

Photographs played a large part in the impressions Americans had about the Gettysburg campaign. See especially a collection of famous photographs published by Alexander Gardner in 1866, *Gardner's Pho-*

*tographic Sketch Book of the Civil War* (Washington, 1866; reprint ed., New York, 1959). For a modern scholar's analysis of many Gettysburg photographs, consult two books by William A. Frassanito, *Gettysburg: A Journey in Time* (New York, 1975) and *Early Photography at Gettysburg* (Gettysburg, 1995).

The Battle of Gettysburg was not particularly well represented in art or fiction. For a general history of Civil War art, see a fine recent volume, Harold Holzer and Mark E. Neely, Jr., *Mine Eyes Have Seen the Glory: The Civil War in Art* (1993). On fictional accounts of the Battle of Gettysburg, see Robert L. Bloom, "The Battle of Gettysburg in Fiction," *Pennsylvania History* 18 (October 1976): 309–27. An interesting collection of short stories from a Northern author is Elsie Singmaster's *Gettysburg, Stories of the Red Harvest and the Aftermath* (Boston, 1913). One of the better novels inspired by the Battle of Gettysburg is MacKinlay Kantor's *Long Remember* (New York, 1934).

The memory of the Civil War and the process of national reconciliation have been the subject of several good books. On the memory of the war in the South, see especially Gaines M. Foster, *Ghosts of the Confederacy: Defeat, the Lost Cause, and the Emergence of the New South* (New York, 1987). On reunionism in the North, see Nina Silber, *The Romance of Reunion* (Chapel Hill, 1993).

# Contributors

GABOR S. BORITT is Robert C. Fluhrer Professor of Civil War Studies and Director of the Civil War Institute at Gettysburg College. He recently edited and co-authored *Why the Confederacy Lost* (Oxford, 1992) and *Why the Civil War Came* (Oxford, 1996). He is writing a book now titled *Storm of Heaven, Storm of Battle: Gettysburg.*

J. MATTHEW GALLMAN is Professor of History, Loyola College, Baltimore. His books include *Mastering Wartime: A Social History of Philadelphia During the Civil War* (Cambridge University Press, 1990) and *The North Fights the Civil War: The Home Front* (Ivan Dee, 1994). Susan Baker, his student and research associate, graduated from Loyola in 1995.

JOSEPH T. GLATTHAAR is Professor of History at the University of Houston. His books include, *Forged in Battle: The Civil War Alliance of Black Soldiers and White Officers* (The Free Press, 1990), and *Partners in Command: Relationships Between Leaders in the Civil War* (The Free Press, 1994).

KENT GRAMM, professor at Wheaton College in Illinois, is the author of *Gettysburg: A Meditation on War and Values* (Indiana University Press, 1994). He is currently J. Omar Good Distinguished Visiting Professor at Juniata College.

AMY J. KINSEL, winner of the 1993 Allan Nevins Prize for best written doctoral dissertation in American history, is the author of the forthcoming *Gettysburg in American Culture, 1863–1938.*

GLENN LAFANTASIE, whose writings cover a broad range of topics from Puritan New England to the Eisenhower presidency, is the editor of

269

*Gettysburg: Colonel William C. Oates, C.S.A., and Lieutenant Frank A. Haskell, U.S.A.,* Eyewitness of the Civil War Series (New York: Bantam Books, 1992). He is working on a book about the encounter between Chamberlain and Oates on Little Round Top and its aftermath.

RICHARD M. McMURRY's most recent book is *Two Great Rebel Armies: An Essay in Confederate Military History* (University of North Carolina Press, 1989).

HARRY W. PFANZ, the dean of Gettysburg scholars, former Chief Historian of the National Park Service, is author of *Gettysburg: The Second Day* (University of North Carolina Press, 1987), *Gettysburg: Culp's Hill and Cemetery Hill* (University of North Carolina Press, 1993).

CAROL REARDON, Associate Professor of History, Pennsylvania State University, is the author of *Soldiers and Scholars: The U.S. Army and the Uses of Military History, 1865–1920* (University of Kansas, 1990), and the forthcoming *Pickett's Charge in History and Memory* (University of North Carolina , 1997).

EMORY M. THOMAS, Regents Professor, University of Georgia, is the author of *Bold Dragoon: The Life of J. E. B. Stuart* (Harper & Row, 1986), and *Robert E. Lee: A Biography* (W. W. Norton & Company, 1995).